I0824962

Six Seasons
of Pasta

Six Seasons of Pasta

A New Way with Everyone's Favorite Food

Joshua McFadden
WITH MARTHA HOLMBERG

Library of Congress Cataloging-in-Publication Data is on file.

ISBN 978-1-64829-192-0

Design by Toni Tajima

Published by Artisan,
an imprint of Workman Publishing,
a division of Hachette Book Group, Inc.
1290 Avenue of the Americas
New York, NY 10104
artisanbooks.com

Printed in China (APO) on responsibly sourced paper

10 9 8 7 6 5 4 3 2

Contents

Introduction

Pasta Is Perfect

I grew up in Wisconsin in a family that was not Italian, but pasta was my favorite meal. My German grandmother was the cook, and the mealtime ritual was always the same: We'd start by passing around a big bowl of spaghetti (a bit watery from not being drained well) followed by the sauce, made from freshly milled tomatoes from the garden, and then the cheese, which was in a tall green cylinder labeled Kraft Parmesan. We always had a salad made from a ton of garden vegetables dressed in bottled Italian dressing, and the table was set with plenty of bread and butter.

To ten-year-old me, the meal was outrageously delicious, and the scene—everyone joyfully helping themselves to a simple meal centered around noodles—transformed me from the kid who loved his grandma's spaghetti to the kid who loved food and cooking so much that he ended up working in professional kitchens with a desire to learn everything possible about the actual Italian table, including pasta, of course.

I still love pasta, and I can't think of another food that has as many positive attributes. Some of them are easily describable: The noodle itself is made from just two or three ingredients and is not expensive, and dried noodles (the focus of this book) last for ages in your cupboard. And a vast array of noodle shapes can be found in an ordinary grocery store, so you always have something new to explore, a new noodle adventure.

And oh, the things that pair with pasta: olive oil; aromatics like garlic, chiles, and fresh herbs; umami-rich Parmigiano-Reggiano and tender mozzarella cheeses; meats, seafood, and poultry; and, of course, the ingredients most dear to this cook's heart—seasonal vegetables. Your pasta dish can be a showcase for the best of the season, from delicate fava beans in spring to meaty tomatoes in late summer to deeply roasted butternut squash in winter, and so much in between.

WHAT YOU'LL FIND IN THIS BOOK

Most people think cooking pasta is simple: Boil some noodles, make a sauce, sprinkle on some cheese. But cooking pasta is simple in the way writing haiku is simple. Sure, a haiku has only three lines and seventeen syllables, but for the poem to resonate, each element must be just so, in the right position, able to carry nuance and meaning. Same with pasta.

My goal in this book is to identify all the steps involved in making a poetic plate of pasta, going deep into each one to examine the ways to best control it. None of the steps are difficult, but all ask the cook to pay attention, have patience, and make many nuanced decisions during the cooking and serving processes.

The main method I teach in this book is what I call "building in the skillet." This is how we make pasta in restaurants, and the techniques involved are what make a pasta dish served at a good Italian restaurant so sublime. I'll also teach you to make ragus, those big pots of rich sauce that make your kitchen smell wonderful. When it comes time to pair a ragu with noodles, you'll still use the skillet method, based on one simple but magical ingredient—pasta water.

In this chapter (and in the recipes themselves), I'll walk you through making a pasta dish in detailed fashion, beginning with how to boil water. Literally. I'll take you from boiling the water to adding the noodles to making the sauce and—most critically—managing the marriage of noodles and sauce.

And because one of the principles of my cooking is to "dial in" the final flavors and textures of a dish, I'll walk you through options for finishing touches: fresh herbs, butter, olive oil, dollops of creamy ricotta, showers of crisp breadcrumbs, and, of course, Parmigiano, always and forever.

Some of my explanations may seem simplistic—you know how to boil water!—but one thing that I've learned in my years of cooking is that simple is never simple. Every time you cook pasta, little variables are different and unexpected situations arise, and the better you've absorbed the details, the better you can adapt to the moment.

All this explaining takes a lot of words, so some of the recipes look long. But long doesn't equal complicated or time-consuming, and in fact, I sincerely hope that the more details I share in the recipes, the fewer questions you'll have and the quicker you'll get a bowl of pasta on the table.

Once you grasp the overall structure of my pasta dishes, the process will become second nature. You won't need to measure out the water for the pasta—you'll just know how far up 1 gallon (4 L) of water fills your favorite pasta pot. You'll learn that one brand of pasta cooks a bit faster than the package says it will, and that pancetta makes a dish saltier so you don't need to use so much already-salted pasta water in the finish. You'll develop an instinct for how loose the sauce should be in the skillet in order for it to thicken to a perfect cloaking consistency by the time it reaches the table. Focusing—even obsessing—on the details at the beginning of your pasta journey will lead to freedom for the rest of your cooking life.

In addition to my thoughts on noodles, sauce, and how the two should get married and live happily ever after, please read my recommendations for equipment, products to have in your cupboard and fridge, types and shapes of dried pasta, and nifty components—whipped ricottas, flavored butters, a variety of crunchy toppings—to make and deploy either as enhancements to your sauce or as the sauce itself, instantly elevating your pasta game.

SO, WHICH SEASON IS PASTA SEASON?

Pasta is the perfect showcase for seasonal bounty. Tender noodles welcome seasonal vegetables and can take on whatever character the weather requires, from the delicate flavors of a springtime Artichokes, Peas, Favas, and Asparagus (page 157) to the woodsy, autumnal flavors of Mushrooms with Onion, Pancetta, and Cream (page 347). So why is the book organized into six seasons instead of four? As you may have read in my first book, *Six Seasons: A New Way with Vegetables*, I believe a more accurate way of dividing the year is by six seasons—spring, early summer, midsummer, late summer, fall, and winter—because the bounty of the summer months seems to come in three different waves; the crisp carrots and celery of early summer have a different character than the fleshier, more intense tomatoes and peppers of late summer, for example.

Of course, many of the vegetables I use in the recipes in this book are available across a few seasons, depending on your location, or even year-round. You can make whatever you want, whenever you want. But a good way to trigger inspiration is to first look through the recipes in the present season.

The book also has a section called Any Season, which includes classic pasta dishes that don't use seasonal vegetables per se, and should be made year-round, often, such as Cacio e Pepe (page 106), Carbonara (page 110), and "Penne" alla Vodka (page 116). These Any Season recipes also offer important technique lessons that you'll use when making other recipes throughout the book—cooking garlic, blending in cheese, toasting tomato paste for the richest flavor, and so on. I'm calling these "Pasta Knowledge."

And, of course, always read through any recipe you plan to make before you start cooking, ideally before you start shopping (which is really the first step in the cooking process). Gather all your ingredients and prep them as instructed in the ingredients list (this is called doing your mise en place) so that once you turn on the heat under your pots and pans, you are ready to go and won't need to interrupt the action in order to frantically toast nuts or grate cheese.

AN IMPORTANT NOTE ON SERVING SIZES

Most of the recipes in the book call for 8 ounces (225 g) of dried pasta, which I find to be the ideal amount to manage easily, in terms of a few things.

For the build-in-the-skillet recipes, the ingredients fit nicely into the type of pan I like to use, which is a 10-inch (25 cm) stainless-steel pan (mine is from All-Clad), either a straight-sided sauté pan or a slope-sided skillet type. This size gives me plenty of room to stir and toss the ingredients, even after adding the noodles. If my recipe seems to use a lot of ingredients, I'll sometimes opt for a 12-inch skillet. And note that some short shapes, like rigatoni, grow a lot in volume after they're cooked, so a larger pan could be in order. This is critical—do not use a pan that's too small!

So how many people will 8 ounces (225 g) of dried noodles serve? Two. Or three. Or wait, maybe four? So much depends on the people, the richness of the recipe, and when the dish is served in the meal. Aglio e Olio (page 100), for example, is about as minimal a pasta as you can get, and 8 ounces (225 g) of dried noodles prepared this way will produce a good amount for dinner for two not-starving adults, perhaps with a Caesar salad (page 46) on the side.

The recipes beyond just noodles and a simple sauce will yield more generous portions. One recipe of Cacio e Pepe (page 106) will produce smaller portions than one recipe of Mushrooms with Sausage, Spicy Chiles, and Burrata (page 344). Both are delicious; one is more filling and could serve more than two diners.

In each recipe, I'll indicate how filling I think the recipe is by listing a range of main-course servings (e.g., *Serves 2 or 3*), but you should also use your judgment, knowing the appetites of you and your diners.

To cook more than 8 ounces (225 g) of dried pasta, just scale up the recipe, use a larger pan, and for sure allow a bit more time for the sauce ingredients, such as pasta water, wine, tomatoes, or cream, to reduce in the skillet.

A good move when serving a larger group is to make a baked pasta (see How to Invent Your Own Baked Pasta, page 358), which will happily serve six. And with the ragu recipes (beginning on page 56), which make quantities of sauce from 3 cups to 2 quarts (750 g to 1 kg), you could serve a greater number of people as long as you have capacious pots and pans and you respect the noodle-to-sauce ratio (see page 64).

FLOUR + WATER
Organic Campanelle
from North American durum semolina.
NET WT. 1LB (453g)
The Source for Great Pasta.
FLOUR + WATER
Organic Campanelle
Bronze die pasta.

The Noodle

Picking a high-quality noodle and choosing from among the hundreds of available shapes are the first two steps toward a good bowl of pasta.

WHY ONLY DRIED?

All the recipes in this book use dried pasta, as opposed to fresh. I like fresh pasta, I might even love fresh pasta, but for daily life, I—and millions of Italians—prefer using dried pasta, for a number of reasons.

First, the texture. Tender but still resilient, dried pasta gives you something to actually chew on. Paired with a luscious sauce, the springy bite of dried pasta cooked al dente is addictive.

Next, the availability. Even a middle-of-the-road grocery store will have several brands to choose from, each brand offering multiple shapes. Better grocery stores, specialty markets, and Italian markets will have a vast array, playgrounds of pasta. And, of course, you can find any pasta you like online.

And then there's the affordability. While some people think of pasta as a "cheap eat" (certainly the case for countless broke college kids), I think of it as an affordable luxury. While mass-market brands such as Barilla spaghetti, for example, can be had for under $2 per pound (450 g), making it truly inexpensive, the price for the very best imported artisanal pasta noodles hovers around $10 per pound; my favorite go-to brand, Rustichella d'Abruzzo, costs about $8 per pound. I recommend 4 ounces (115 g) per portion, so a serving of artisanal pasta for one person would cost $2, plus the sauce ingredients—a reasonable price for so much deliciousness.

Finally, convenience. Dried pastas are extremely low in moisture, which means they can maintain good quality for at least two years in the cupboard. Pasta looks good stored in decorative jars, but I prefer to keep mine in the original packaging so I can be reminded of the brand and, most important, the producer's recommended cooking time.

WHAT MAKES A GOOD DRIED PASTA?

As with any food product, the better the raw ingredients, the better the final product. The best pastas are made from durum wheat, a hard wheat with a high protein content, around 13 percent. Protein equates to gluten, which equates to the noodle being able to hold its shape and deliver the wonderful springy-chewy texture we love in pasta, and well-grown durum wheat has a rich flavor that makes good pasta noodles more than just a neutral vehicle for sauce.

The best pastas are extruded (shaped by being forced through a mold) or cut using bronze dies. These metal dies produce a slightly rough surface on the noodle, which allows the cooked noodle to better hold on to sauce and gives it a more pleasing overall texture. Cheaper pastas are cut with Teflon-coated dies, creating a smooth and therefore slippery surface.

Once the pasta is shaped, it needs to be dried, and here, slow is the way to go. Drying quickly, using a lot of heat, is more expedient for the producer but can slightly "cook" the starch in the pasta, making the noodle a bit brittle as well as compromising the flavor of the wheat. Slow-drying pasta allows the interior and exterior to dry thoroughly and preserves the integrity and flavor of the high-quality flour.

PASTA BRANDS I RECOMMEND

To help you choose a good pasta, here are some of my favorites. Obviously, the Italians make superb pasta, but I'm thrilled to report that I'm seeing more high-quality American pasta noodles on the market as well; see the Resources (page 380) for suppliers.

→ **THE ITALIAN BRANDS I LOVE:**

- Mancini Pastificio Agricolo
- Martelli
- Molino e Pastificio
- Monograno Felicetti
- Morelli
- Pastificio Faella
- Pastificio Gentile

→ **THE AMERICANS MAKE GREAT PASTA, TOO:**

- Della Terra Pasta
- Flour + Water
- Sfoglini

Pastas with More Than Flour and Water

A second type of dried pasta is made from flour and water plus eggs or egg yolks; the eggs add a rich flavor and tender texture. Usually this takes the form of a wide, flat noodle, such as pappardelle or tagliatelle. You'll sometimes see these noodles shaped into nests and packaged in cellophane-covered cardboard trays. Rustichella d'Abruzzo and Bionaturae are two excellent, widely available brands.

Egg pappardelle is the classic partner for a meat-based ragu.

Flavored Pastas

Dried pastas made with flavorings, such as spinach, lemon, squid ink, or saffron look great in their boxes, but I don't use them very often. The flavors are either undetectable or not so nice. I'd much rather taste the flavor of beautifully farmed wheat.

Gluten-Free Pasta

I know many people either can't or choose not to eat gluten. If that's you, here's some good news: Gluten-free pasta has come a long way. Honestly, if you didn't tell someone the noodles were gluten-free, they might not even notice. The texture and flavor vary depending on the grain (I think the best tasting are made from quinoa, rice, or corn, or a combo), but a good gluten-free noodle can come close to delivering that signature pasta feel—tender yet chewy, springy, and resilient. As long as you understand that gluten-free pasta is its own thing—not an exact substitute for wheat-based pasta—you can achieve excellent results with these recipes.

Gluten-free pasta doesn't release as much starch during cooking as wheat pasta does, so you lose some of that silky, sauce-binding magic that starchy pasta water provides. But here's a trick that helps: Follow the process for adding pasta water to the noodles and sauce, but give the noodles a bit more time than the recipe specifies, so they soak up the flavors. Finishing the dish with butter and cheese also creates that desired silky consistency.

Some of my favorite gluten-free pasta brands include Edison Grainery organic quinoa pasta, La Fabbrica della Pasta di Gragnano's rice and corn pasta (from a renowned pasta-making town near Naples), Jovial's organic brown rice pasta, and Giadzy's slow-dried pasta from Alto Adige, also made with rice and corn.

MATCHING SHAPE TO SAUCE

If I could give you an exact set of rules for how to match pasta noodle shapes with sauce, I would. But that would take the fun out of experimenting with whatever crazy shape you come across when you're shopping for noodles. There are, of course, traditional regional pairings—carbonara with spaghetti, broccoli rabe and sausage with orecchiette, pesto with trofie—which also follow a commonsense logic: Delicate sauces work well with thinner, more delicate pastas, and chunky sauces work well with shapes that have curves and hollows.

One noodle shape that you should never use, however, is farfalle (bow-tie pasta). I hate it, as it is impossible to cook correctly. For the pinch in the middle of the bow to be properly cooked, the wings must be overdone, and vice versa. Please just pick another shape. End of rant.

Beyond that, I think the best noodle for your sauce is the one made from responsibly farmed durum wheat, shaped with bronze dies, and slowly air-dried to highlight the delicate wheat flavor and create the best texture. For the recipes in this book, I've listed the shape you see in the photos (where applicable), plus other options.

COOKING THE NOODLES

When dried noodle meets boiling water, things get interesting, and a bit nerve-racking, even for me. I've spent a lot of time standing over a boiling pasta pot, so my instincts are pretty good, and here's what I've learned.

I like to cook my pasta in at least 1 gallon (4 L) of water for 8 ounces (225 g) of dried pasta. My favorite pot is a 6-quart (6 L) stainless-steel All-Clad pot that has a perforated insert and a lid. A regular stockpot or a large enameled Dutch oven will work well, too.

I'm generous with the water for a few reasons. First, I want long noodles to be able to slide under the water even when they're still rigid—I don't want the last inch of linguine poking above the surface of the water while the rest of the noodle is cooking.

The noodles also need room to move around so they're not tempted to stick to each other or to the pot. And I want the boiling water to stay boiling even after I add the noodles, or at least to come back to a boil very quickly. This is where a lid can come in handy. Add the noodles, slap on the lid, and then, once the rolling boil resumes, remove the lid so you can monitor the progress of your pasta more easily.

I have built my pasta technique on the fixed feature of 1 gallon (4 L) of water, a large pot, and a specific amount of salt. The seemingly trivial fact of how much water you boil the noodles in has repercussions that go beyond the faucet.

BUCATINI
CALAMARATA
CONCHIGLIE
DITALINI
ELBOW MACARONI
ANELLI
LINGUINE
ORECCHIETTE
PENNE
RADIATORI
ROTELLE
RIGATONI

CAMPANELLE
CASARECCE
CAVATAPPI
FUSILLI COL BUCO
FUSILLI
GEMELLI
LUMACHE
MAFALDINE
SPAGHETTI
ZITI
TAGLIATELLE

Add plenty of salt to the cooking water so that each noodle will wind up perfectly seasoned.

WHY SALT IS SO IMPORTANT

Adding the salt is a crucial part of bringing the pasta water to a boil. By salting the boiling water, you are eventually salting the noodles themselves, and creating a "broth" that you'll use when building the pasta sauce. If your pasta water is too salty, you can wreck your sauce. Not salty enough, and your sauce will be underseasoned.

When to Salt?

It doesn't matter much whether you add the salt before the water boils or after, but it's key to develop a habit so that you don't forget. I always taste my pasta water before adding the noodles, just to verify that I haven't forgotten the salt.

And be aware that the salt-to-water ratio will change if you let the water boil down a bit, so don't add the salt and then get distracted, letting some of the water evaporate and making what's left too salty. But if this happens, you can top off the pot of pasta water with some fresh hot water.

HOW MUCH SALT IS ENOUGH?

I'm sure that in the past, I've said that pasta water should taste like ocean water, but in fact, that's a bit too salty.

For the recipes in this book, I call for 1 tablespoon (10 g) of kosher salt per quart/liter or 4 tablespoons (40 g) per gallon (4 L). This ratio is specific to the Diamond Crystal brand of kosher salt, which is the brand I used to test all the recipes. This amount will season your noodles nicely, and the pasta water will bring a generous amount of salt to your sauce. If you use another brand or type of salt, please adjust the measurement (see the chart below for guidelines).

When I cook pasta, I have a small pot of fresh water on a back burner, which I can use to finesse the final consistency of the sauce, or if my dish is becoming too salty, I'll switch to the plain water rather than add more salted pasta water (this is especially useful when making a pasta that contains salty ingredients, such as pancetta). If a third pot on the stove seems like too much traffic control for you, skip it, but know that hot tap water can help out in a pinch.

KNOW YOUR SALT

As you prepare to salt your pasta water, make sure you know how much salt is in your tablespoon, because salt brands vary widely in terms of the amount of salt per volume.

Some salt grains are dense and heavy, and others are lighter and fluffier. With dense, heavy grains, you can pack a lot of salt into a specific volume measurement, such as a tablespoon, while fluffier grains will fill that same tablespoon with less actual salt because there is more space between the grains.

Here are the salt quantities I suggest using in your pasta water:

For 8 ounces (225 g) dried pasta noodles:

SALT BRAND	WATER	SALT
Diamond Crystal kosher	1 gallon (4 L)	4 heaping tablespoons (40 g)
Jacobsen Salt Co. kosher	1 gallon (4 L)	4 heaping tablespoons (40 g)
Morton kosher	1 gallon (4 L)	2½ tablespoons (40 g)
Fine table salt	1 gallon (4 L)	Scant 2 tablespoons (40 g)

ADDING THE NOODLES TO THE WATER

The water is boiling, you've added the salt, and now it's time to add the noodles. Sounds easy, but I still have nightmares about my experiences as a young chef cooking pasta, dreaming that I would grab the wrong basket and put uncooked noodles in the sauce or, worse yet, putting noodles in a basket that already contains noodles of a different type.

I had to feed two hundred or more people a night with cooked-to-order pasta, so eventually, I got really good at it and learned a few truths, the most important of which is that to be proficient at cooking pasta, be patient and pay attention to detail right up to the point when you sit down to enjoy it. Here are a few more:

- Give the noodles a few big stirs during the first minutes to prevent them from glomming together. Then stir again once or twice during cooking to prevent the noodles from sticking to the pot.
- Don't break long noodles in half to make it easier to fit them into the pot. You'll miss out on all the fun of slurping up a 12-inch-long (30 cm) strand of linguine.
- Never add oil to the water. I see old recipes that suggest adding some oil to the cooking water to keep the noodles from gumming together after you drain them. This is not a good idea, as a coating of oil will make it difficult for the sauce to cling to the noodle, which is the opposite of the desired effect—noodles lightly cloaked in sauce so that every bite gets just enough of each element. (The exception is for pasta salads, for which you want to very lightly oil the noodles before they cool.)

Your noodles are now boiling, but I'm not yet going to discuss cooking time, doneness cues, or transferring noodles to sauce, because your sauce needs to be ready before your noodles are done. So read on to learn about the sauces in this book, and then we'll get back to the noodles. (Or jump ahead to the important marriage of noodle and sauce, page 64.)

The Sauces

You'll hear people say that the noodle is the most important part of a pasta dish. Okay, sure, but let's get real—noodles are grand, but it's the sauce that you'll be licking from your plate.

Most of the pasta dishes in this book use one of two types of sauce: a long-cooked ragu (perfect for cooking ahead and freezing) or a build-in-the-skillet sauce that you make while you're cooking the noodles. You can also make a quick sauce from condiments that you have on hand in the fridge or freezer. These consist of whipped ricottas, flavored butters, and pestos (see page 27). Often I use these condiments as components in more complex dishes, but even on their own—just flavored butter and noodles, for example—they make a fantastic quick pasta.

RAGUS

A ragu simmering on the stove is the promise of good things to come. This category is composed, for the most part, of long-cooked meat sauces, such as Pork Shoulder Ragu with Lemon (page 78) and Beef and Sweet Bell Pepper Ragu (page 86), though the Italian traditional ragu repertoire—and mine—also includes ragus based on poultry, seafood, vegetable, lentils, mushrooms, and more.

Spend a couple of hours (or less) cooking and making your kitchen smell great, then divide the finished ragu into portions; you can refrigerate some to use over the next few days and freeze the rest for future meals. Ragus make a complete dish on their own (with noodles, of course), finished with a simple shower of grated cheese, and they can also be paired with seasonal vegetables to create a more complex dish, such as Roasted Winter Squash with Nut Ragu (page 378).

Once you've spent up-front time and effort making a ragu, getting a plate of pasta on the table is a snap. See How to Sauce Pasta with a Ragu, page 64.

BUILD-IN-THE-SKILLET SAUCES

Most of the recipes in this book are build-in-the-skillet sauces. This is the way pasta sauces are made in restaurants, and once you learn the method, you can literally make a pasta dish from any ingredients you can think of, especially seasonal vegetables.

For this style of sauce, you usually start by sautéing some aromatic ingredients, such as garlic and dried chile flakes. Next you might add a meat, such as diced pancetta or sausage, followed by a vegetable and some kind of liquid—often canned tomatoes—in which to cook the vegetable and eventually to finish cooking the noodles. The sauce then gets a few more flavoring ingredients and is finished with a 50/50 blend of grated cheeses (half Parmigiano-Reggiano, half Pecorino Romano, grated in a food processor; see page 39). The exact details vary from recipe to recipe, but the sauce is essentially made to order in the skillet.

Ingredients vary, but the basic steps for most pasta dishes are the same: Sauté aromatics like garlic, chile flakes, and tomato paste to coax out their flavors. Add the main ingredients (here it's tomato) and simmer. Add the almost-al dente noodles and let them finish cooking in the sauce, drinking up the flavors as they do. Finish with a shower of cheese, using very low or no heat so that the cheese emulsifies easily with the sauce.

Noodle + Sauce

The moment when you add the noodles to the developing sauce is the most critical step in the pasta process. You are no longer cooking noodles or cooking a sauce; you are now cooking a pasta dish.

The process is both super simple and extremely complex, requiring many small judgments about doneness and the consistency of the sauce. Your "pasta IQ" will need to develop with experience, but once you've mastered the process, you'll start eating the best pastas of your life.

HOW TO GET THE NOODLES OUT OF THE WATER AND INTO THE SAUCE

The act of retrieving the noodles and transferring them to the sauce in the skillet can be high drama. Your noodles are essentially in a vat of boiling water, and you need to frequently sneak out hot noodles to test for doneness. Once you think you've reached the correct doneness, you need to move fast so that the remaining noodles don't overcook. The challenge is how to get slippery noodles out of rapidly boiling water and into the skillet, all while preserving enough precious pasta water. You have a few options.

When I'm cooking long noodles, such as spaghetti, I lift them out of the water with tongs, let the water drip off for a few seconds, and deposit them directly into the skillet with my sauce—no need for a colander.

It's harder to do this with short pastas or if you've cooked other ingredients, such as peas or broccoli, along with the pasta. In those cases, you can scoop up the shorties with a large slotted spoon or a wire spider. And, of course, if you have a pasta pot with an insert, lift the cooked pasta right out of the pot, let it drain for a few seconds, and pour it into the skillet.

Don't worry about draining off every last drop of water, as you'll be adding pasta water to the skillet anyway as you complete the final cooking.

The fourth option is to scoop out some pasta water from the pot using a large measuring cup, then drain the pasta into a colander and transfer the noodles from the colander to the skillet. The risk here is that (1) you might forget to scoop out your pasta water and end up with none, or (2) you might scoop out a cup but end up needing more. Which is not the end of the world, however; you can use plain hot tap water in a pinch.

DONENESS TESTS AND SETTING THE TIMER

While the process of boiling the noodles may be straightforward, the timing is not. The most important thing to understand is that you're only going to *partially* cook the noodles in the pot of boiling water. You will *finish* cooking the noodles in the sauce, bringing them to perfect al dente by allowing them to drink up some sauce. (What's perfect al dente? See page 22.)

This makes timing a bit tricky. You want to stop boiling the noodles about 2 minutes before they will be al dente. But when is a noodle at al dente? The suggested timing on the pasta package always includes a range, usually of 2 minutes—for example, "Cooks in 9 to 11 minutes." So for al dente, should you pull your noodles from the water at 7 minutes? 8 minutes? 9? Until you become familiar with a specific brand and shape of pasta noodle, you just won't know how long it takes to get to al dente, so

What Is al Dente and How Can You Get There?

Consistently cooking al dente pasta takes practice, and it also takes vigilance—you must test and evaluate even when using the same shape noodle from the same producer. Especially with good artisanal brands, but even with mass-produced noodles, cooking times will vary depending on how that particular batch was dried, how it was stored, the humidity in your kitchen, and other variables.

After making many bowls of pasta, you'll develop a sixth sense for doneness, but along the way, you must pay attention to the first five senses.

Hearing. In the early stages of boiling, the noodles are still brittle, and when you stir them with your tongs, they make almost a clicking sound as they hit the sides of the pot and each other. The closer they are to al dente, the more water they absorb, and the quieter they become.

Touch. When you start to test for doneness, the noodles will probably still feel a bit stiff, both as you pick them up to put them in your mouth and as you bite into them—you'll feel the center of a noodle crunch between your teeth even as the outside is getting softer. After a couple of test bites, you'll feel that the crunch in the center is gone but the noodles are still a bit firm and stick to your teeth. This is the "pre-al dente" stage, which is when you'll add the noodles to your sauce to finish cooking.

Smell and taste. I can actually smell when my noodles are getting close to done, as the fragrance coming from the pasta pot becomes rich with a good wheatiness. The noodles also begin to taste more of grain as they get closer to being done.

Sight. You can see when a noodle has been cooked correctly because overcooked noodles will slouch in the bowl, while a perfectly cooked batch sits up a bit and has more volume in the sauce. Take a look at the photos throughout the book to see what well-cooked noodles look like.

My philosophy is that it's better to eat noodles that are a bit too firm rather than those that are overcooked and flabby. Learn to ride that line and be comfortable with sometimes being too al dente.

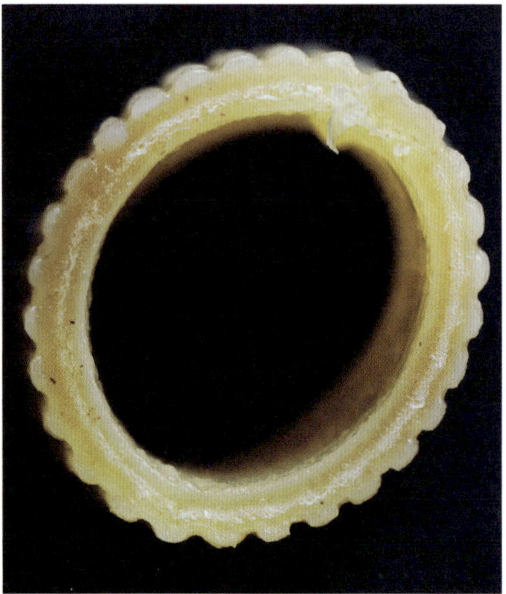

When you test your noodles for doneness, if you see a distinct white ring (left), keep cooking. If the ring is barely visible (right), finish the cooking in the sauce.

you'll want to err on the side of too soon rather than too late.

Here's how it should go: The package says your penne will cook in 9 to 11 minutes. Set your timer for 7 minutes. Get your sauce to the point that it's mostly complete and ready for the noodles, and then slide it off the burner so it doesn't keep cooking.

Note that as you get more familiar with your chosen recipe, you probably can start the sauce at the same time that you put the water on to boil, creating a satisfying choreography, but until then, it's always better to have your sauce ready to go so you're not scrambling. This is how I've sequenced the steps in the recipes in this book—sauce first, then noodles—because a sauce can wait, but noodles can't.

The timer you've set for your pasta rings, and now you can start to test . . . which means taste. Pull out a noodle (or two), blow on it to cool it as quickly as possible (the other noodles are continuing to cook, so hurry!), and taste. If it's super crunchy and chalky, you probably want to boil for another 45 seconds and then taste again.

You are aiming for pasta that has passed the point of crunchy but still has too much "tooth" to it—remember, you're going to stop boiling the noodles before they actually get to al dente.

When you think you're a minute or two away from al dente, retrieve your noodles—reserving some pasta water—and transfer them to the skillet with the sauce.

Here's where you'll begin working with the pasta water. The noodles are in the sauce, which includes some liquid but perhaps not enough to finish cooking the noodles, so, using a ladle, splash in some pasta water; ¼ cup (60 ml) is a good amount to start.

Adjust the heat so the noodles are simmering in the sauce. Your noodles won't be fully submerged in sauce, so to encourage even cooking, you'll need to gently agitate them, using tongs or shaking the skillet to flip the contents. As they simmer, continue to test for doneness, adding more pasta water as your first addition gets absorbed by the noodles.

When the noodles feel great to you, it's time to transition to the next phase, which is adding the cheese and other final ingredients.

FINAL STEPS: ENRICHING AND GARNISHING

It's important to know that in dishes that include cheese, adding it will thicken the sauce, and the sauce itself will thicken a bit further as it cools, so you need to take that into consideration as you evaluate the final sauce consistency. If the sauce feels very watery and loose, you'll want to continue to simmer for a few more seconds until it's more concentrated. Conversely, if the sauce feels quite concentrated and tight, you'll want to splash in just a bit more pasta water (or plain hot water, if the sauce is getting salty). At this stage, however, you should aim for a slightly loose consistency.

When adding grated hard cheese to your pasta, such as the half-and-half blend of Parmigiano-Reggiano and Pecorino Romano that I like to use (see page 39), the goal is for it to melt evenly and emulsify with the liquid ingredients in the sauce so that the result is creamy rather than oily and separated. Above all, you want to avoid a big glob of rubbery cheese stuck to your skillet.

The best way to achieve that ideal consistency is to lower the heat and incorporate the cheese bit by bit: Add some cheese, add a small splash of pasta water, and toss or stir until nicely blended. Repeat until all the cheese is added and blended. Check the viscosity of the sauce again, adding a few more drops of pasta water as needed, knowing that the sauce will stiffen a bit by the time it leaves the skillet and arrives in a bowl at the diner's place setting.

This is also the time for adjusting the final seasoning. Take a taste. The salt level should be fine, given the salted pasta water and salty cheese, but if you want more, add it now, along with more chile flakes, black pepper, lemon juice . . . whatever seasoning ingredients you've already used in the dish.

Now you need to move fast, because your noodles are perfect and your sauce is perfect. Ideally your pasta bowls are warmed (see Warm Bowls, Full Hearts, next). Tongs or a large spoon will do the trick for getting the pasta in those bowls, and definitely no twirling with forks to create perfect nests. A few generous heaps, a casual twist at the end—let the pasta speak for itself. I serve most of my pastas in shallow bowls, but I think long noodles can look fantastic on a flat plate, too.

Most of my pasta dishes are complete when they hit the pasta bowl, though I'll usually serve more grated cheese at the table. But some dishes get extra finishing touches. Shards of ricotta salata look dramatic. A dollop of whipped ricotta adds a creamy dimension. I plop the ricotta right on top of the plated pasta and then let the diner decide whether to toss everything together or just swoop their fork through the ricotta with every bite.

I finish some pastas with a bit of crunch, using breadcrumbs (page 36), or crunch plus spice, using Chile Crisp (page 37). I will also drizzle on some finishing-quality olive oil; I'm in love with lemony Agrumato (page 41). When added right before serving, oil isn't about giving the dish more fat or richness, it's about adding fragrance and a hit of bright flavor that enhances the other flavors in the dish, so make sure you use a restrained hand.

Now it's time to eat.

WARM BOWLS, FULL HEARTS

Warming your pasta bowl or plate is an extra step that ensures your pasta will arrive at the table in optimal condition and will stay warm as you eat it.

The goal is for the bowls to be warm, but not hot. You don't want to further cook the food, and you need to be able to handle the bowls; you're not going for the sizzling-fajita effect. I generally pop my bowls or plates in a low oven for a few minutes right before serving time. Some people heat their bowls in the microwave, though experts say that over time, that method can damage your oven; the microwave-safe dishes don't absorb many of the microwaves and therefore the energy is being absorbed by the appliance itself, which isn't great. Another method is to ladle some hot pasta water into the bowls as you finish your dish, then dump out the water right before you transfer the finished pasta to the bowl.

PASTA WATER IS MAGIC

Pasta cooking water is a critical—and magical—part of the dish. You will add it to the sauce to provide more liquid in which to finish cooking the noodles, regulate the consistency of the sauce, keeping it nicely fluid while also giving it some body from the residual starch in the pasta water, and emulsify with the cheese and any butter or oil that you add.

Finally, salted pasta water is your main seasoning. I find that I don't generally need to add any salt to finish a pasta dish because I get the right amount of seasoning from the noodles having been cooked in properly salted water and from the addition of the pasta water to the sauce. So pasta cooking water, which so many people just dump down the drain, is the unsung hero of the best pasta dishes. Always reserve at least 1 cup (240 ml) of pasta water to incorporate into the final dish.

Your Pasta Pantry

These are the ingredients you'll reach for frequently as you make the recipes in this book. Some should be homemade, others you'll buy, but all are essential.

Made from Scratch

Flavored butters, pestos, and whipped ricottas are favorite elements in my pasta tool kit; I use them to add dimension to a range of dishes, from classics such as Meatballs with Tomato Sauce, and More (page 128) to vegetable-forward pastas such as Cabbage with Whipped Lemon Ricotta and Chile Crisp (page 360), and I also use them as simple sauces on their own. See How to Sauce Pasta with Flavored Butter, Pesto, or Whipped Ricotta (page 31).

To contrast these creamy ingredients, think about adding texture with homemade breadcrumbs, crunchy croutons, or spicy-garlicky chile crunch. Most of these condiment-type ingredients will last for weeks or months in your fridge, freezer, or cupboard, so a few hours of up-front cooking gives you plenty of future pasta enjoyment.

FLAVORED BUTTERS

Also called compound butters, flavored butters are made from unsalted butter that's been blended with intensely flavored ingredients such as ramps, green garlic, or lemon. I often use flavored butters to add complexity and richness to dishes featuring seasonal vegetables, such as Green Beans with Pickled Ramp Butter and Chile Crisp (page 257).

And because everybody loves buttered noodles, dinner can be as simple as noodles, a flavored butter, and a grating of cheese. This three-ingredient pasta treatment is a testament to the power of real, good ingredients. See How to Sauce Pasta with Flavored Butter, Pesto, or Whipped Ricotta (page 31).

Flavored butters freeze beautifully, making them a truly convenient building block in your pasta repertoire. To make these butters easy to incorporate into meals, divide the finished butter into logical portions and freeze them on a sheet pan until firm, then pile the solid butter bits into a freezer container for easy retrieval.

Garlic Butter

Makes about 1½ cups (330 g)

1½ ounces (45 g) garlic cloves (about 12 large), smashed

1 cup (30 g) lightly packed fresh flat-leaf parsley leaves and tender stems

2 tablespoons lightly packed roughly chopped fresh oregano leaves

8 ounces (225 g) unsalted butter, at room temperature

2 tablespoons extra-virgin olive oil

¼ teaspoon kosher salt (preferably Diamond Crystal; see page 17)

⅛ teaspoon dried chile flakes

Put the garlic, parsley, and oregano into a food processor and pulse until everything's chopped into very small bits, scraping down the sides of the bowl as needed.

Combine the butter, olive oil, salt, and chile flakes in a medium bowl. Add the chopped garlic and herbs and fold together with a

silicone spatula until all the seasonings are well distributed.

If you have time, chill the butter for up to an hour so the flavors of the seasonings can infuse the butter.

Store the butter, tightly wrapped, in the refrigerator for up to 1 week or in the freezer (in one block or divided into portions; see page 27) for up to 3 months.

Green Garlic Herb Butter

Makes about 1½ cups (350 g)

8 ounces (225 g) unsalted butter, at room temperature

1 bunch green garlic (about 6 stalks), ½ inch (1.25 cm) of the green tops trimmed off, thinly sliced crosswise

1 cup (30 g) lightly packed fresh basil leaves, finely chopped

1 cup (30 g) lightly packed fresh flat-leaf parsley leaves and tender stems, finely chopped

Melt 1 tablespoon of the butter in a medium skillet over low heat, add the green garlic, and cook gently until it is soft and fragrant and some of the harshness has mellowed, about 10 minutes. Cool completely.

Combine the remaining butter, the basil, and the parsley in a medium bowl. Add the green garlic and the butter used for cooking it. Fold everything together with a silicone spatula until all the seasonings are well distributed.

If you have time, chill the butter for up to an hour so the flavors of the seasonings can infuse the butter.

Store the butter, tightly wrapped, in the refrigerator for up to 1 week or in the freezer (in one block or divided into portions; see page 27) for up to 3 months.

Green Garlic Herb Butter

Nettle Butter

Makes a generous 1 cup (250 g)

Leaves from 1 bunch nettles (about 2 cups/60 g)

8 ounces (225 g) unsalted butter, at room temperature

***Note:* Remember to wear gloves or otherwise avoid touching the nettles until they have been cooked.**

Bring a large pot of water to a boil, add the nettle leaves, and blanch until tender, about 1 minute. Drain the nettles and let cool until you can handle them.

Gently squeeze the nettles to remove as much water as possible. Give them a rough chop, then put them in a food processor along with the butter.

Using the pulse button, process the butter just until the nettles are finely chopped and incorporated into the butter.

If you have time, chill the butter for up to an hour so the nettle flavor can infuse the butter.

Store the butter, tightly wrapped, in the refrigerator for up to 1 week or in the freezer (in one block or divided into portions; see page 27) for up to 3 months.

Pickled Ramp Butter

Makes about 1½ cups (375 g)

½ cup (75 g) Pickled Ramps (recipe follows), drained

8 ounces (225 g) unsalted butter, at room temperature

1 teaspoon dried chile flakes

Blot off any excess pickling liquid from the ramps. Chop them very roughly, then put them in a food processor and pulse until the ramps are finely chopped but not coming close to a puree.

recipe continues →

Combine the chopped ramps, butter, and chile flakes in a medium bowl. Fold everything together with a silicone spatula until all the seasonings are well distributed.

If you have time, chill the butter for up to an hour so the flavors of the seasonings can infuse the butter.

Store the butter, tightly wrapped, in the refrigerator for up to 1 week or in the freezer (in one block or divided into portions; see page 27) for up to 3 months.

Pickled Ramps

Makes about 1 pint (500 ml)

1 pound (450 g) ramps

1 or 2 dried chiles, such as chiles de árbol

¾ cup (180 ml) water

¾ cup (180 ml) rice vinegar

3 tablespoons sugar

1 tablespoon plus 1 teaspoon kosher salt (preferably Diamond Crystal; see page 17)

1 tablespoon white wine vinegar

Trim the root ends off the ramps. Rinse the ramps well, especially between the leaves, then shake them dry. Stuff the whole ramps into a clean pint jar, leaving about 1 inch (2.5 cm) of headroom, and tuck in the dried chiles.

Combine the water, rice vinegar, sugar, salt, and white wine vinegar in a small saucepan and bring to a boil, stirring to dissolve the sugar and salt.

Pour the brine over the ramps, making sure they are fully covered. Cool, then seal the jar and refrigerate. Let the flavors develop for at least a couple of days before using the ramps, though you should let your taste be your guide.

Store in the refrigerator for up to 2 months.

Lemon Butter

Makes a generous 1 cup (240 g)

8 ounces (225 g) unsalted butter, at room temperature

2 tablespoons finely grated lemon zest

1 tablespoon preserved lemon paste

Note: Preserved lemon paste is available online (see Resources, page 380) or in specialty stores.

Combine the butter, lemon zest, and preserved lemon paste in a medium bowl. Fold everything together with a silicone spatula until the seasonings are well distributed.

If you have time, chill the butter for up to an hour so the flavors of the seasonings can infuse the butter.

Store the butter, tightly wrapped, in the refrigerator for up to 1 week or in the freezer (in one block or divided into portions; see page 27) for up to 3 months.

Brown-Butter Butter

Makes a generous 1 cup (225 g)

8 ounces (225 g) unsalted butter

Set a medium metal bowl over a large metal bowl filled with ice.

Melt the butter in a small saucepan over medium heat. When the butter has fully melted, keep cooking, swirling the pan frequently, until all the water has evaporated (the sizzling will stop), the milk solids at the bottom of the pan have turned deep gold, and the butter smells fragrant, 3 to 5 minutes.

Pour the brown butter into the medium bowl and, using a whisk or a flexible spatula, whip or stir the butter until it thickens and becomes creamy. Watch carefully as it starts to thicken so that it doesn't actually get so cold that it solidifies into chunks.

Store the butter, tightly wrapped, in the refrigerator for up to 1 week or in the freezer (in one block or divided into portions; see page 27) for up to 3 months.

Put the melted brown butter in a bowl over ice and whisk or stir with a flexible spatula until it firms up and becomes spreadable.

How to Sauce Pasta with Flavored Butter, Pesto, or Whipped Ricotta

Saucing your noodles with any of these three enrichments (butter, pesto, or whipped ricotta) is a genius way to create a quick and delicious pasta dish with minimal effort (provided you have the enrichment in your fridge or freezer already, of course). While each of these enrichments is made from different ingredients, they all share the fact that they are mostly fat: Flavored butters are, well, butter; pesto contains oil, cheese, and fatty nuts; and whipped ricottas include the fat from the ricotta plus additional olive oil.

To end up with a creamy, homogeneous sauce, which is the goal, you need to create an emulsion between the fats and the non-fat ingredients, which include the pasta water and perhaps other liquids, such as tomatoes or wine. The starch in the pasta water from the noodles will help the formation of the emulsion.

1. Transfer a few splashes of water from the pasta pot to your skillet and heat gently, then add your enrichment. For 8 ounces (225 g) dried pasta noodles, good starting amounts are 4 tablespoons (60 g) flavored butter (ideally cold), ¾ cup (180 g) pesto, or ¾ cup (180 g) whipped ricotta.

2. Swirl the pan to encourage the enrichment to blend with the pasta water; you can also use a whisk, but gently agitating the pan should accomplish the same thing. Ideally the mixture will look creamy rather than separated.

3. Cook your noodles until they are actually al dente; you won't finish them in the sauce as you do with most pastas in this book, to avoid breaking your emulsion. Also, high heat can damage the fragrance of the fresh herbs that are in some of the enrichments.

4. When your noodles are ready, add them to the sauce, along with grated cheese and perhaps a few more splashes of pasta water. Toss to incorporate the cheese and keep the sauce creamy and emulsified. Serve right away.

Basil Pesto

Sun-Dried Tomato and Almond Pesto

PESTOS

You've seen plenty of traditional Italian dishes that use basil-based pesto as the sauce, and for good reason—fragrant with herbal perfume and made rich with oily pine nuts and plenty of grated Parmigiano, pesto delivers great flavor and texture in one package.

Here is my version of that classic Italian pesto, plus one made from sun-dried tomatoes and almonds, with a sweet-tangy kick and nutty undertones, both rich and bright at the same time. Pestos keep well for about 5 days in the fridge and also freeze nicely. Basil pesto will darken a bit in storage, but that's just cosmetic. Scrape off the darkened surface, or stir it into the rest of the pesto; the flavor won't be affected. See How to Sauce Pasta with Flavored Butter, Pesto, or Whipped Ricotta (page 31).

Basil Pesto

Makes about 1½ cups (300 g)

3 cups (90 g) lightly packed fresh basil leaves

2 or 3 garlic cloves, smashed

⅓ cup (40 g) pine nuts (untoasted)

½ teaspoon kosher salt (preferably Diamond Crystal; see page 17)

½ cup (120 ml) extra-virgin olive oil, plus more for storage

½ cup (60 g) 50/50 cheese (half Parmigiano-Reggiano, half Pecorino Romano, grated in a food processor; see page 39)

Put the basil, garlic, pine nuts, and salt in a food processor and pulse a few times to make a coarse puree. With the motor running, slowly pour in the olive oil; stop once the oil is blended with the other ingredients. You may need to stop and scrape down the sides of the bowl a few times.

Add the cheese and pulse a few more times to incorporate, but don't process too much. Your goal is a pesto with a slight texture to it, rather than a completely smooth one, which would overwork the basil and muddy the flavor a bit.

Transfer the pesto to a small container, smooth the surface, float a thin layer of olive oil on top to create an air barrier, and refrigerate for up to 5 days or freeze for up to 3 months.

Sun-Dried Tomato and Almond Pesto

Makes just less than 2 cups (420 g)

⅔ cup (160 ml) extra-virgin olive oil

1½ ounces (45 g) garlic cloves (7 to 10 medium cloves), peeled

¼ teaspoon dried chile flakes

Several twists freshly ground black pepper

½ teaspoon kosher salt (preferably Diamond Crystal; see page 17), plus more to taste

¾ cup (140 g) sun-dried tomatoes packed in oil, drained

½ cup (75 g) whole skin-on almonds, lightly toasted

⅓ cup plus 2 tablespoons (50 g) finely grated Parmigiano-Reggiano

Combine the olive oil, garlic, chile flakes, black pepper, and salt in a small saucepan. The pan should be small enough that the oil covers the garlic.

Heat the mixture over medium-low heat until the garlic is very lightly caramelized, adjusting the heat so it ends up more golden than brown. Depending on the moisture in your garlic, this should take between 10 and 20 minutes. Let the oil cool.

Transfer the garlic with all the oil and spices to a food processor and add the sun-dried tomatoes, almonds, and grated cheese. Pulse until you have a fairly smooth puree (you'll still see bits of almond), scraping down the sides of the bowl as needed. Taste and add more salt if you like.

Transfer to an airtight container. Store in the fridge for up to 1 week or freeze for up to 3 months.

WHIPPED RICOTTAS

Whipping ricotta cheese with a few flavorings—salt and pepper at a minimum, preserved lemon paste at a maximum—and incorporating a small amount of olive oil creates a lush and deeply flavored condiment while preserving the simple milky flavor of plain ricotta.

One way to use whipped ricottas is to drop a big spoonful right in the center of a finished bowl of pasta, allowing the diner to integrate the ricotta with the other ingredients as they swipe their fork through it with each bite. You can also use whipped ricottas as a complete sauce, not just a garnish, as in Chard with Sausage and Whipped Ricotta (page 330).

Choose the best ricotta available, which means one made without gums or stabilizers. My favorite widely available brand is Calabro. Whipped ricottas keep for up to 1 week in the fridge; they're not great freezer material, as the ricotta becomes grainy after thawing. See How to Sauce Pasta with Flavored Butter, Pesto, or Whipped Ricotta (page 31).

Whipped Plain Ricotta

Makes about 1¼ cups (300 g)

1 cup (225 g) whole-milk ricotta

½ teaspoon kosher salt (preferably Diamond Crystal; see page 17), plus more to taste

Freshly ground black pepper

¼ cup (60 ml) extra-virgin olive oil, plus more as needed

Put the ricotta, salt, and about 20 twists of black pepper in a food processor. With the motor running, add the olive oil in a thin stream. Process until the ricotta is thick and creamy, scraping down the sides of the bowl as needed. Taste and adjust with more salt, pepper, or olive oil as needed.

Store in an airtight container in the fridge for up to 1 week.

Clockwise from top left: Whipped Basil Ricotta, Whipped Plain Ricotta, Whipped Tomato Ricotta, Whipped Lemon Ricotta

Whipped Basil Ricotta

Makes about 1¼ cups (300 g)

1 cup (225 g) whole-milk ricotta

2 cups (60 g) lightly packed fresh basil leaves

¼ teaspoon kosher salt (preferably Diamond Crystal; see page 17), plus more to taste

Freshly ground black pepper

¼ cup (60 ml) extra-virgin olive oil, plus more to taste

Put the ricotta, basil, salt, and about 20 twists of black pepper in a food processor. With the motor running, add the olive oil in a thin stream and process until the basil is well blended and the ricotta is thick and creamy, scraping down the sides of the bowl as needed. Taste and adjust with more salt, pepper, or olive oil as needed.

Store in an airtight container in the fridge for up to 1 week. The surface may darken with exposure to air after a day or so, but simply scrape that off; it won't affect the flavor.

Whipped Lemon Ricotta

Makes about 1¼ cups (300 g)

1 cup (225 g) whole-milk ricotta

2 tablespoons preserved lemon paste, plus more to taste

¼ teaspoon kosher salt (preferably Diamond Crystal; see page 17), plus more to taste

Freshly ground black pepper

¼ cup (60 ml) lemon Agrumato (lemony extra-virgin olive oil; see page 41), plus more to taste

Note: **Preserved lemon paste is available online (see Resources, page 380) or in specialty stores.**

Put the ricotta, preserved lemon paste, salt, and about 20 twists of black pepper in a food processor. With the motor running, add the Agrumato in a thin stream and process until the ricotta is thick and creamy, scraping down the sides of the bowl as needed. Taste and adjust with more lemon paste, salt, pepper, or olive oil as needed.

Store in an airtight container in the fridge for up to 1 week.

Whipped Tomato Ricotta

Makes about 1¼ cups (300 g)

¼ cup (50 g) sun-dried tomatoes packed in oil, drained

1 cup (225 g) whole-milk ricotta

2 tablespoons tomato paste

¼ teaspoon kosher salt (preferably Diamond Crystal; see page 17), plus more to taste

Freshly ground black pepper

¼ cup (60 ml) extra-virgin olive oil, plus more to taste

Put the sun-dried tomatoes in a food processor and process until you have a fairly smooth puree, scraping down the sides of the bowl as needed.

Add the ricotta, tomato paste, salt, and about 20 twists of black pepper. With the motor running, add the olive oil in a thin stream and process until the ricotta is thick and creamy, scraping down the sides of the bowl as needed. Taste and adjust with more salt, pepper, or olive oil as needed.

Store in an airtight container in the fridge for up to 1 week.

CRUNCHY TOPPINGS

Add another dimension to your pastas by finishing them with some crunch, or in the case of chile crisp, crunch plus spice. The breadcrumbs and croutons are quick to make; the chile crisp is not so quick, but it lasts for weeks when stored properly.

Dried Breadcrumbs

Makes about 1 cup (50 g)

Two 1-inch-thick (2.5 cm) slices good-quality bread

Heat the oven to its lowest setting, usually 250°F (120°C).

Cut the bread, complete with crust, into cubes. Spread the cubes in an even layer on a sheet pan and bake until they are fully dry but not browned, 1 hour or more, depending on how moist and dense the bread is.

Cool completely, then transfer the dried bread cubes to a food processor and pulse into crumbs. Aim for small crumbs that are all about the same size—think Grape-Nuts cereal. You don't want a lot of powdered crumbs, so shake the crumbs through a colander to remove the smallest particles and discard those.

Store the crumbs in an airtight container. If they're fully dry, they'll keep well at room temperature for a few weeks.

Torn Croutons

Makes about 2 cups (120 g)

2 large thick slices "country"-style bread (about 4 ounces/115 g total)

2 tablespoons extra-virgin olive oil

Kosher salt (preferably Diamond Crystal; see page 17)

Freshly ground black pepper

Heat the oven to 400°F (205°C).

Tear the bread, including the crust, into bite-size pieces. Toss with the olive oil and season lightly with salt and pepper.

Spread the croutons in an even layer on a sheet pan and bake until golden brown, checking every 4 to 5 minutes and stirring them around on the pan so they cook evenly. The cooking time will vary depending on your bread, but 10 to 20 minutes should do it.

Slide the croutons onto paper towels to absorb any extra oil; season again lightly with salt and pepper and leave until cool.

Store in an airtight container; they will stay good at room temperature for a couple of days, but you're likely to eat them as a snack before that.

Chile Crisp

Makes about 1½ cups (280 g)

1 pint (300 g) peeled garlic cloves (trim off the little nubs)

Extra-virgin olive oil

1 to 2 teaspoons dried chile flakes

Put the garlic in a food processor and pulse several times until broken down into pieces about the size of grains of rice. Add about ¾ cup (180 ml) olive oil and pulse several more times, scraping down the sides of the bowl as needed, until the garlic bits are more the size of black peppercorns and are suspended in the oil. The mixture should not be an actual puree; you should see the bits of garlic.

Scrape the mixture into a 10-inch (23 cm) nonstick skillet on a cold burner. The oil should just barely cover the garlic when spread out in the pan; if not, add a bit more.

Turn the heat to medium-low and cook the garlic slowly, stirring frequently with a heatproof spatula and scraping up any bits stuck to the pan, until the garlic is an even light brown. The goal is to reduce the moisture in the garlic without browning it too much, which would make it bitter.

As the garlic becomes crisp, you will hear it make a different sound as you scrape it with the spatula—think potato chip crumbs. Take the pan off the heat and stir in the chile flakes, adding the amount that corresponds with your heat tolerance. Leave until cool.

Scrape the chile crisp into a clean jar, cover tightly, and keep at room temperature for up to 1 month. Do not refrigerate, or the garlic will soften.

Store-Bought

With a well-stocked pantry (and by that I mean cupboard, refrigerator, and freezer), you can be quickly on your way to excellent pasta. Many of my fresh pantry items change with the seasons, but the following are my year-round staples, most of which you'll find at any decent grocery store; you can definitely find them all through online retailers.

Cheeses

Ninety-nine percent of the recipes in this book include cheese. If you are not a cheese eater, know that you can make most of my dishes sans fromage and still get a delicious result. But for me, the sweet-salty-milky allure of good cheese is an indispensable partner to pasta.

MY PREFERRED CHEESE BLEND: 50/50

Parmigiano-Reggiano and Pecorino Romano are both noble and delicious Italian cheeses, and I use them solo in all manner of dishes, but the cheese I use for most of my pasta dishes is a blend of the two that I call 50/50.

To make 50/50, I grate equal amounts of each cheese using a food processor (though the blender works, too) and combine them in a container that lives in my fridge. The Parmigiano provides a milky sweetness and the pecorino adds a bracing amount of saltiness—a good thing. The blend of these two cheeses isn't traditional in Italian cooking, but I swear that it makes any pasta taste better.

Many people like to grate their hard cheeses using a Microplane-type rasp grater, which is fine, but the rasp grater creates thin strands that can clump a bit as they melt, so I don't like using Microplaned cheese in my sauces.

Note that my 50/50 weighs about 4 ounces (120 grams) per 1 cup. Cheese grated using a Microplane or other type of grater isn't as dense and will take up more room in a measuring cup, so you'll get less cheese per cup measure. Generally, this isn't something to worry about when you make these recipes (and if you're using the metric measurements provided, ignore this); just know that you should feel free to add more cheese if you think your dish would benefit.

To make 50/50: Select pieces of each cheese that are approximately the same weight. Choose freshly cut pieces when possible, because older, prewrapped cheeses can be dried out, so they don't melt as well, and they have a more piquant flavor.

Crack the cheeses into nuggets by inserting the tip of a sturdy knife into each cheese and prying off pieces. Put the pieces in a food processor and pulse until the texture is fine-grained and light; the grains will look like tiny balls. Make sure you don't accidentally create a cheese puree, but process enough that you don't have lumps. Store the cheese blend in an airtight container in your fridge for up to a couple of weeks.

PARMIGIANO-REGGIANO

Firm, sweet, salty, and nutty, Parmigiano-Reggiano is integral to my cooking. Most people are familiar with "Parmesan" but may not realize that the real thing is a PDO (Protected Designation of Origin; in Italian, it's DOP, denominazione di origine protetta) product. This is a legal designation from the European Union that controls the production of the cheese, meaning everything from the type of cows that produce the milk, what they eat, and how they are milked through every step of the cheese making. The PDO stamp guarantees the quality and character of the cheese and also protects the true producers from knockoff cheeses. Parmigiano commands a high price, but I think it's worth it for the intense, umami-rich flavor and wonderful grainy-yet-creamy texture of the cheese. You'll find Parmigiano-Reggiano in various ages, from twelve months up to almost three years. I prefer younger ones for use in the kitchen and the super-aged ones for cheese boards.

Real Parmigiano offers the cook a bonus, too, in the form of the rind. Once you've grated as much cheese as you're going to get from a chunk of Parmigiano, you're left with the hard outer layer, which is also cheese but is too firm to grate. Give the rind a second life by adding a piece or two to long-simmered sauces, where it will slowly melt and contribute tons of umami savoriness without making your sauce overtly cheesy. Be sure to retrieve it before serving the sauce so no one gets an unexpected mouthful; the rind will be pretty mushy after a few hours, and smaller rinds may completely merge into your sauce, which is fine.

PECORINO ROMANO

Pecorino Romano is a firm, very salty sheep's-milk cheese from Italy that's also an excellent grating cheese. Pecorino Romano is sharper and less sweet than Parmigiano, so it's a perfect counterpoint to sweet spring vegetables, for example. Very young pecorino is tender and mild and in Italy is traditionally served in spring with fresh fava beans.

MOZZARELLA

Good fresh mozzarella should taste clean, simple, and sweet—like milk, but you don't need a glass. The texture should be tender, not rubbery. Fresh mozzarella has a high water content and is not a good melter. Too much heat, and fresh mozz's tender texture will become rubbery. To avoid that, I add it to pasta dishes only at the last minute, and I use it freely in pasta salads.

I like to rip rather than cut mozzarella, which creates a shaggy surface that helps the cheese integrate into the rest of the dish. I add the big shreds to my pasta, fold everything together once, and then plate the pasta and serve it ASAP. The diner will have the pleasure of discovering little pockets of mozzarella softening in the gentle heat of the pasta.

When you need the mozzarella to be part of a baked pasta, use the not-artisan type, something that comes in a block and might even come from Wisconsin, my home state. Look for whole-milk, low-moisture mozzarella for the best melting qualities. Don't ever use pregrated, which often is dusted with an anticlumping substance.

RICOTTA

Sweet, milky ricotta is one of my favorite ingredients for introducing some richness to a pasta dish. I prefer whole-milk ricotta. If you can find truly fresh ricotta from a local dairy, that will be your best choice, but the grocery store can yield some decent brands. Aim for ricottas made with no gums or stabilizers, which can create a pasty texture—exactly the opposite of good ricotta. Bellwether Farms ricotta has great flavor and texture. It comes in a little basket, which lets the excess whey drain off, producing a creamier result. Calabro is widely distributed, and though it's mass market, it's really good. Ricotta salata is a firm, dry, salty cheese that I like to grate or crumble onto my pastas as a final flourish.

Clockwise from top left: Parmigiano-Reggiano, Pecorino Romano, mozzarella, ricotta, ricotta salata

Fats

Some pasta dishes are rich, others are leaner, but all my pastas include some type of good fat.

EXTRA-VIRGIN OLIVE OIL

Pretty much every recipe in this book uses olive oil, and that's a very good thing. Extra-virgin olive oil is a key ingredient in all my cooking, but especially in pasta dishes, where I often use it to "bookend" the dish: I'll start by cooking aromatics in olive oil, whether a smashed garlic clove, some chopped pancetta, or a soffritto of celery, onion, and carrot. I'll then finish the dish with a final thread of oil, sometimes while the food is still in the skillet, sometimes after I've plated it. This finishing touch brings the flavors together and adds enrichment.

Ideally, use a moderately priced olive oil for cooking and a more expensive one for finishing, but they both need to be extra-virgin olive oil.

While there are plenty of mass-produced extra-virgin olive oils that are affordable and appropriate for glugging into the skillet, many olive oils on US market shelves that are labeled "extra-virgin" are in fact not extra-virgin in the way that most other olive oil–producing countries define the term.

True extra-virgin olive oil needs to meet a rigorous set of standards, created by the International Olive Council (IOC) and enforced through chemical analysis. The IOC is based in Madrid and governs most of the major global production—including oil from Spain, Italy, Greece, Portugal, and Turkey. Not the United States, however. California, notably, adheres to the IOC standards and has been encouraging the US Department of Agriculture to update US standards to the same level.

One of my all-time favorite extra-virgin olive oils is Frantoia, from Sicily. Its price is great for the quality, and it comes in a large tin as well. The Spanish oil called Graza comes in plastic squeeze bottles, making it super convenient to use, and the quality is excellent. They make two styles—the "drizzle" is intended for finishing and the "sizzle" is for cooking—so when you buy the pair, you've got your bases covered.

When I want to splurge on an olive oil that I won't glug into my skillet but will use to finish my pastas, I look to Italy, and I think the best of the best is Gianfranco Becchina Olio Verde.

My latest obsession is lemon Agrumato, a finishing oil that you'll see throughout the recipes. Made in Abruzzo, it's an extra-virgin-quality olive oil made by crushing the olives with lemons, producing an oil with an amazing lemon zest flavor that is dreamy as a finishing drizzle. The brand also makes blood orange, bergamot, tangerine, and citron flavors. You can order Agrumato online (see Resources, page 380) or find it in some specialty stores. Another new obsession is algae oil. . . . Yes, you read that right. New to the market, algae oil (page 381) is tasty (mild, buttery), has a super-high smoke point, is full of healthy fats, and is very gentle on the planet.

Whether budget or fancy, your oil needs to be as fresh as possible. Even though olive oil sits on a grocery store shelf in a bottle, it's actually a living, perishable agricultural product—fresh fruit juice, if you will. So buy as new an oil as possible. Some bottles list the harvest date (which is generally between November and January); look for those produced within the past year, if possible. Many producers just give a "best by" date, which could be two to three years after harvest. The oil will certainly still be usable but will lack the vitality and lovable qualities of a newer oil.

Once you get the oil home, store it away from heat and light. While it's natural to have your bottle of oil right next to the stove, it's not ideal. But if you go through olive oil as fast as I do, your oil won't have time to degrade, so keep the bottle wherever you want. If you are using a bottle that's been open in the cupboard for many months, taste the oil before you use it to verify that it has not gone rancid.

BUTTER

We've somehow been conditioned to think that butter is unhealthy for us. Which indeed it is, but only if you actually eat too much, too often. My belief is that when a dish calls for butter, you should use the amount that makes the dish taste amazing, and make sure it's a good-quality butter. For cooking, I use unsalted butter in order to control how much salt is getting into the dish. My favorite everyday butters are Kerrygold Pure Irish Butter, Vermont Creamery Cultured Butter, Cabot Creamery Premium Butter, and Vital Farms Grass-Fed Butter.

If you want to splurge, buy one of these: Ploughgate Creamery Cultured Butter, Rodolphe Le Meunier Beurre de Baratte Salted Butter, or Le Beurre Bordier.

Herbs and Spices

I'm all about creating delicious tension among the flavors in my dishes, and herbs and spices are key ingredients in that pursuit.

HERBS

I like fresh herbs, and I like them in large quantities. I'll often tear the leaves of fresh basil, mint, or parsley and add half early in the cooking process, so that they cook down and permeate the sauce with their flavor, then add the rest just as I'm about to plate the dish, letting their perfume waft directly from bowl to nose.

I don't often use dried herbs in pasta dishes. The one exception is dried oregano, which to me is its own thing rather than a substitute for fresh. I use a dried oregano from Calabria, still on the stem and packaged in a cellophane bag; it's easy to shake out the amount you need. One tablespoon of chopped fresh oregano equals about 1 teaspoon dried.

SALT

The recipes in this book were tested using Diamond Crystal kosher salt, a widely available brand that is frequently used by chefs; another common brand is Morton, and I like using kosher salt from Jacobsen Salt Co., produced in Oregon. "Kosher salt" is a catchall term for a coarse salt, usually mass-produced as opposed to a specialty artisanal salt. The grains of kosher salt are larger than those of table salt, also called fine salt, which makes them easier to pinch and sprinkle over a dish. Please refer to the chart on page 17 to see the correct amount of each brand or type to use for the recipes in this book—it matters!

In some recipes, I suggest salting to taste rather than giving you a specific measured amount, so use whatever salt you prefer and season to taste as usual. But when measuring the salt you'll add to your pasta water, if you use a brand of kosher salt other than Diamond Crystal or you use a fine/table salt, you should use half the amount called for. You can always add more, but you can't take any back.

BLACK PEPPER

Black pepper doesn't need to be used in every pasta dish, but when you do use it, you want it to deliver its full intriguing personality—sharp and hot, yes, but also beautifully floral and fragrant, characteristics that you'll never get from dusty old preground black pepper. So buy whole peppercorns—Tellicherry is a variety I like, but you'll find many black peppers on the market now—and grind them to order using a good pepper mill. For some of the pastas in this book, you'll need coarsely cracked peppercorns. You want the pepper bits to be of varying sizes, and you don't want a lot of finely ground pepper, which would make your dish too hot-spicy. The best way to achieve the desired mixed-texture consistency is to crack whole peppercorns with something heavy. Here's how I do it:

How to crack black peppercorns: Put the peppercorns in a heavy plastic bag (so they don't skitter away), fold a dish towel around the bag (to avoid creating holes in the bag), and place it on a cutting board. Now bash the peppercorns using whatever's handy—a pestle, a meat flattener, a hammer, the base of a heavy pot—checking the consistency frequently.

DRIED CHILE FLAKES

Dried chile flakes don't have to deliver a big dose of heat per se, but rather can provide some tension in the flavors of your pasta dish—the salt from cured meats and cheeses dances with the fruit from tomato, which dances with a touch of spicy heat from chile flakes.

Called by a few names—red pepper flakes, crushed red pepper—these are the flat dried seeds and crumbled flesh of spicy red chiles. As with all dried spices, make sure yours are fresh. If you bought your jar more than a year ago, think about picking up a new one or make your own flakes by crumbling a dried chile de árbol.

PRESERVED CHILES

Preserved chiles are great in pastas, and I'm especially fond of oil-packed Calabrian chiles, which come in jars. Nudge off the stem and scrape out the seeds with the point of a knife, then chop or slice as your recipe specifies. I also always give props to good ol' salad-bar-style peperoncini, which are small green pickled peppers. They'll add some mild heat and a nice tang to your dish. For a little more heat, I like pickled hot chiles, whether homemade or from a jar. The juice from any pickled chile is a brilliant way to add sparkle to a dish. Keep both oil-packed and pickled chiles in the refrigerator once you've opened the jar.

Tomato

Tomato is one of pasta's most important and traditional partners, and as with pasta noodles themselves, preserved tomato products (as opposed to fresh tomatoes) come in various forms and quality levels.

I generally use two types of prepared tomato—tomato paste and whole peeled tomatoes.

TOMATO PASTE

Tomato paste comes in small cans and tubes. I much prefer tubes because you can use the amount you want, screw the cap back on, and pop it into the fridge until next time. Tomato paste in a tube will last months, whereas an open can of tomato paste, even when refrigerated, tends to get moldy after a couple of weeks. You'll see tomato paste as either double or triple strength; use whichever you want, but the recipes in this book were developed with double.

The ideal is to make your own tomato paste, called conserva. You'll need a large quantity of good-quality tomatoes, preferably from your own garden or a farmers' market, and you'll need some time, but the process is easy and fun. The downside of homemade tomato paste is that you can't store it in a tube, but you can freeze it.

WHOLE PEELED TOMATOES

I like to start with the least processed of processed tomatoes, so I use whole peeled tomatoes rather than crushed or chopped varieties. Here's what I do to use them in most of my tomato-forward recipes:

Pour the contents of the can into a bowl. Pull off any skins still on the tomatoes or floating around; you'll sometimes find a surprising amount of skin in "peeled" tomatoes.

Next, crush the tomatoes, either with clean hands or using a sturdy wooden spoon (hands are better). The idea is to break them into smaller pieces, which will cook down nicely into a slightly chunky sauce. I always feel around for hard stem ends or unripe, stringy cores, which I either pinch off or cut out with a paring knife. Those tough bits can stay stubbornly hard even after cooking down in a sauce, so I get rid of them at the outset.

You can keep any leftover canned tomatoes in an airtight container in the fridge for up to 3 days or pop them in the freezer for next time.

You can also use already-squished tomato products, such as Pomi and other brands that come in a carton that lets you pour out the amount you want. These are convenient and certainly acceptable, but try to choose types that have some texture rather than perfectly smooth, strained tomatoes.

Conserva (Tomato Paste)

Tomato paste is a frequent player in my pasta recipes, and while there are plenty of good-quality tomato pastes on the market, homemade conserva is another thing altogether. Don't make it unless you have excellent ripe tomatoes from the farmers' market or your garden. Other recipes instruct you to use a paste- or Roma-style tomato, but what's most important to me is the flavor, so use tomatoes with a good balance of sweetness and acidity.

Makes about 2 cups (450 g)

About 8 pounds (3.6 kg) ripe tomatoes
Extra-virgin olive oil

Core the tomatoes and then roughly chop them. Pile them into a large stockpot, preferably one with a wide bottom, which will speed up cooking. Add about ¼ cup (60 ml) water to create some steam and get the tomato juices flowing. Bring to a boil over high heat, then reduce the heat to medium or whatever temperature keeps the tomatoes simmering (be careful not to let the tomatoes scorch on the bottom of the pot).

Cook until you've got the consistency of tomato sauce, 20 to 30 minutes; let cool slightly. Working in batches, puree the tomatoes in a blender and then work the puree through a food mill into a large bowl to remove the skins and seeds. (If you don't have a food mill, you can do this by pressing the puree through a fine-mesh sieve or very fine colander, but a food mill makes the job much easier.)

Heat the oven to 300°F (150°C).

Oil a rimmed sheet pan (or two, if needed) or a couple of 9 by 13-inch (22.5 by 32.5 cm) casserole dishes. Pour in the pureed tomatoes and bake for about 3 hours.

You'll need to tend to the conserva several times during cooking because the tomato close to the edges of the pan will brown more quickly. Use a heatproof silicone spatula to move the tomato from the edges of the pans into the center (and

vice versa) to promote even cooking and create deep flavors.

After 3 hours or so at 300°F (150°C), reduce the oven temperature to 200°F (95°C) and bake slowly for as long as you can, even overnight. You won't need to give the conserva as much attention at this lower heat, but you should check it now and then anyway.

The finished conserva should be very thick, like, um, tomato paste. Let cool completely before storing. Transfer to small freezer bags and freeze for up to 6 months, or scrape into small jars, top with olive oil, cover with lids, and refrigerate for up to 2 weeks.

When you want to create a full meal with pasta as the centerpiece, you can't beat these classic accompaniments.

Caesar Salad

A classic—and in my mind perfect—companion to pasta, Caesar salad is great as a refreshing first course or as a side dish served at the same time as your pasta main dish. When you're making a green salad, usually your goal is to avoid overdressing it, but here that goal goes out the window. With Caesar salad, excess is best. First, lightly dress the romaine leaves with lemon juice, olive oil, and grated cheese, and then bring in the Caesar dressing, along with breadcrumbs, croutons, and more cheese to create another layer of flavor and texture.

Serves 2

1 cup (60 g) Torn Croutons (page 37)

1 romaine heart (about 6 ounces/170 g), leaves separated

Lemon juice

Extra-virgin olive oil

Kosher salt (preferably Diamond Crystal; see page 17)

Freshly ground black pepper

50/50 cheese (half Parmigiano-Reggiano, half Pecorino Romano, grated in a food processor; see page 39)

¼ cup (60 ml) Caesar Dressing (recipe follows)

Lemon Agrumato (lemony extra-virgin olive oil; see page 41; optional)

Chunk of Parmigiano, for grating

Take about half the croutons and crush them until you have coarse crumbs; set aside the croutons and the crumbs separately.

Combine the lettuce and croutons in a bowl that's plenty large enough for tossing, and get ready to dress this salad using your hands.

Squeeze some lemon juice over the lettuce and toss, then drizzle on some olive oil and toss again. Season the lettuce lightly with salt and pepper, sprinkle on a few spoonfuls of 50/50 cheese, and toss thoroughly until the salad is lightly and evenly dressed. Drizzle the Caesar dressing around the inside of the bowl and toss the lettuce and croutons, scooping up the dressing from the sides of the bowl.

Add the crouton crumbs, more 50/50 cheese, and a few more twists of black pepper and toss again. If you have the Agrumato, drizzle some in and toss again.

Arrange the lettuce and croutons on large salad plates or bowls and grate a heavy shower of Parmigiano over everything. Serve right away, forks and knives optional.

Caesar Dressing

The addition of yogurt is not at all traditional, but I love the simultaneous tangy and creamy qualities it adds to the dressing. The dressing is quite garlicky; making it at least an hour ahead of serving lets the raw garlic settle down (or you can use a bit less garlic).

Make sure you use anchovies packed in oil, not the pickled white bocarones type. If you or your diners just can't abide anchovies, substitute 1 tablespoon drained brined capers to provide the all-important briny note. And in case lots of garlic and anchovies isn't lively enough for you, you can add chopped Calabrian chiles plus a splash of the oil from the jar.

Makes about 1½ cups (350 g)

Half a 2-ounce (56 g) can oil-packed anchovy fillets, drained, plus more to taste

1 ounce (30 g) garlic cloves (6 to 8 large cloves), smashed

1 cup (225 g) plain whole-milk Greek yogurt

⅓ cup plus 1 tablespoon (50 g) 50/50 cheese (half Parmigiano-Reggiano, half Pecorino Romano, grated in a food processor; see page 39)

2 tablespoons extra-virgin olive oil

1½ tablespoons fresh lemon juice, plus more to taste

1 tablespoon Dijon mustard, plus more to taste

1 tablespoon Worcestershire sauce, plus more to taste

1 teaspoon finely chopped oil-packed Calabrian chiles (from a jar; optional)

A few drops of oil from the jar of Calabrian chiles (optional)

Big pinch of fresh oregano leaves (optional)

¼ teaspoon kosher salt (preferably Diamond Crystal; see page 17), plus more to taste

Coarsely ground black pepper

Put the anchovies and garlic in a food processor and pulse until they are finely chopped, scraping down the sides of the bowl as needed (or finely chop them by hand).

Add the yogurt, 50/50 cheese, olive oil, lemon juice, mustard, Worcestershire, Calabrian chiles and their oil (if using), oregano (if using), salt, and many twists of black pepper to the processor bowl and pulse until all the ingredients are combined.

Taste and adjust the seasoning with more salt, pepper, lemon juice, or Worcestershire as needed.

Store in an airtight container in the refrigerator for up to 1 week.

Garlic Bread

Garlic bread is not called garlic toast, so do not overtoast it! The goal is to get the outside edges of the bread toasted, almost burnt, but to leave the center all gooey, like an underbaked cookie. I'm not listing specific amounts for the ingredients because so much depends on the size and shape of your bread. It's a feeling thing.

Makes the amount that you make

Garlic Butter (page 27), at room temperature

A small loaf of good bread, split in half lengthwise, cut into portion sizes; or thick slabs from a larger loaf

50/50 cheese (half Parmigiano-Reggiano, half Pecorino Romano, grated in a food processor; see page 39)

Chopped fresh flat-leaf parsley leaves, for finishing

Parmigiano-Reggiano, for finishing

Lemon Agrumato (lemony extra-virgin olive oil; see page 41) or extra-virgin olive oil and a squeeze of fresh lemon juice, for finishing

Heat the oven to 450°F (230°C).

Line a sheet pan with foil. Spread the garlic butter on the bread in a thick layer, as though you were frosting a cupcake. Top with a generous sprinkle of 50/50 cheese and arrange butter side up on the prepared pan. Bake in the hot oven until the edges are deeply toasted and the cheese is lightly browned, 8 to 10 minutes.

Take the bread out of the oven. Sprinkle chopped parsley over the top. Grate on Parmigiano and finish with a light drizzle of Agrumato or olive oil and a spritz of lemon juice. Cut the bread into smaller portions, if you like, and serve right away.

Made in France
Q41

Equipment

Pasta is one of the simplest dishes to cook and doesn't require much in the way of specialized equipment, but these pieces will make you more efficient.

Digital Scale

If you don't yet have a digital scale, buy one now and get ready for your life in the kitchen to change for the better.

Most American home cooks use sets of cups and spoons to measure ingredients by volume, but cooks in most other countries use a scale to measure by weight. Weight measurements are generally more consistent, and they eliminate the need to wrangle unwieldy ingredients into a measuring cup—think springy ribbons of kale or gangly julienned fennel. Are they "lightly packed" into the cup? "Firmly packed"? You can avoid all that by just weighing the ingredient.

And, of course, weighing out 8 ounces (225 g) of pasta noodles is a lot easier than eyeballing a 1-pound (450 g) package and hoping you're using half. But everyone should cook using the tools with which they're most comfortable.

In this book, we list the US measurements first, sometimes by weight, sometimes by volume, and metric measurements follow in parentheses, also by weight or volume, depending on the ingredient. Note that in metric-using kitchens, true liquids are measured by volume, in milliliters or liters, but ingredients that are semiliquid, such as ricotta and yogurt, are measured by weight, not volume. For example, in the United States, we might call for 1 cup ricotta, but in metric countries, we would call for 250 grams of ricotta, which is how much 1 cup of the stuff weighs.

Note that we list metric equivalents only for those US volume measurements that are ¼ cup or larger. Smaller amounts, such as 2 tablespoons, can easily be figured out by a non-US cook.

Large Pot, with or without Insert

I like to cook my pasta noodles in about 1 gallon (4 L) of water, or more if I'm cooking more than 8 ounces (225 g) of noodles. My personal favorite pot is an All-Clad 6-quart (6 L) pasta pot, with a lid and a perforated insert with which you can lift and drain the noodles in one efficient move. Many manufacturers make similar pasta pots, and you can always use a pot with no insert, but choose one that's tall and holds at least 6 quarts (6 L). If you don't have an insert, you'll probably want a . . .

Colander

I like a heavy stainless-steel colander with fairly large holes, which allows the water to drain quickly. A mesh strainer works well, too, but can be harder to clean because the pasta starch tends to gum up all those tiny mesh wires. The trick with mesh is to rinse it thoroughly right away.

With either style, the ideal is a colander that has handles that span your sink, thereby suspending the colander high above the drain and avoiding anything potentially icky in the sink.

Tongs

Tongs are indispensable, in my opinion, as you can perform just about any kitchen maneuver with a good set of spring tongs. I prefer the style that lets you lock the arms into a closed

Clockwise from top left: digital scale, pasta pot with insert, pepper "cannon," classic pepper mill, spider, pizza sauce spoon, tongs, and colander

position, making it easier to slide them into a drawer or utensil caddy, but the "always open" style is fine if that works for you. Longer tongs, such as those that are 16 to 18 inches (40 to 45 cm), allow you to reach deep into the pasta pot to stir up any stubborn noodles, but a 12-inch (30 cm) set is super easy to handle. You choose.

Slotted Spoon or Spider

A long-handled spoon with a wide perforated face allows you to scoop out vegetables that you've blanched in pasta water or short pasta shapes that aren't going to be drained in a colander. A spider is a cousin to a slotted spoon; made from wire or mesh, this tool is great for letting the water drain through quickly. In stores, spiders are often found with Asian utensils.

Ladle

You'll become good friends with a ladle as you work your way through the recipes in the book, because those final additions of starchy-salty pasta water have alchemical powers, allowing the noodles to cook to perfect al dente and bringing together the sauce ingredients and whatever cheese or butter you're adding into a balanced, nicely emulsified consistency. A ladle with a 4-ounce-capacity (120 ml) bowl is a good size. My favorite ladle is actually a pizza sauce spoon, perfect for pasta water, sauce, and delivering a finished pasta to a bowl.

Pepper Mill

A true essential, as using preground pepper is not okay. I love the classic wooden mills, but I'm obsessed with a heavy-duty mill from Männkitchen (page 381) called a "pepper cannon" . . . the name says it all.

Skillet

Most of the pasta sauces in this book are made to order in a skillet rather than made ahead in a big ol' pot, so having a skillet with the right diameter and side height, along with heavy construction and a lid, is imperative.

I like a 10-inch (25 cm) All-Clad, though any brand that has a heavy base (which creates even heat) will work. I use a sauté pan with straight sides that are about 2 inches (5 cm) high and a skillet/frying pan with sloped sides. Straight sides can accommodate a lot of liquid; sloped sides make tossing your ingredients easier. For dishes with ingredients that take up a lot of space (including some short noodle shapes, which are bulkier than skinny shapes like spaghetti), I'll use a 12-inch version of this skillet.

Graters

One of the greatest inventions of the twentieth century, a Microplane-style grater was originally used in woodworking, and now the culinary version makes formerly onerous chores—grating citrus zest, hard cheeses (but not the cheese for your sauce; see page 39), and even nutmeg—a breeze. I use a box grater for softer cheeses like Fontina.

Food Processor or Blender

You'll use one of these tools for pestos and purees and also for my signature 50/50 cheese blend (see page 39), which I make in large batches to have on hand in the fridge. I often use a handheld immersion blender, which has a chopping attachment, perfect for making 50/50 and whipped ricotta on the fly.

Timer

Yes, you can use your phone or your oven's built-in timer, but there's nothing like an actual timer to keep things on track.

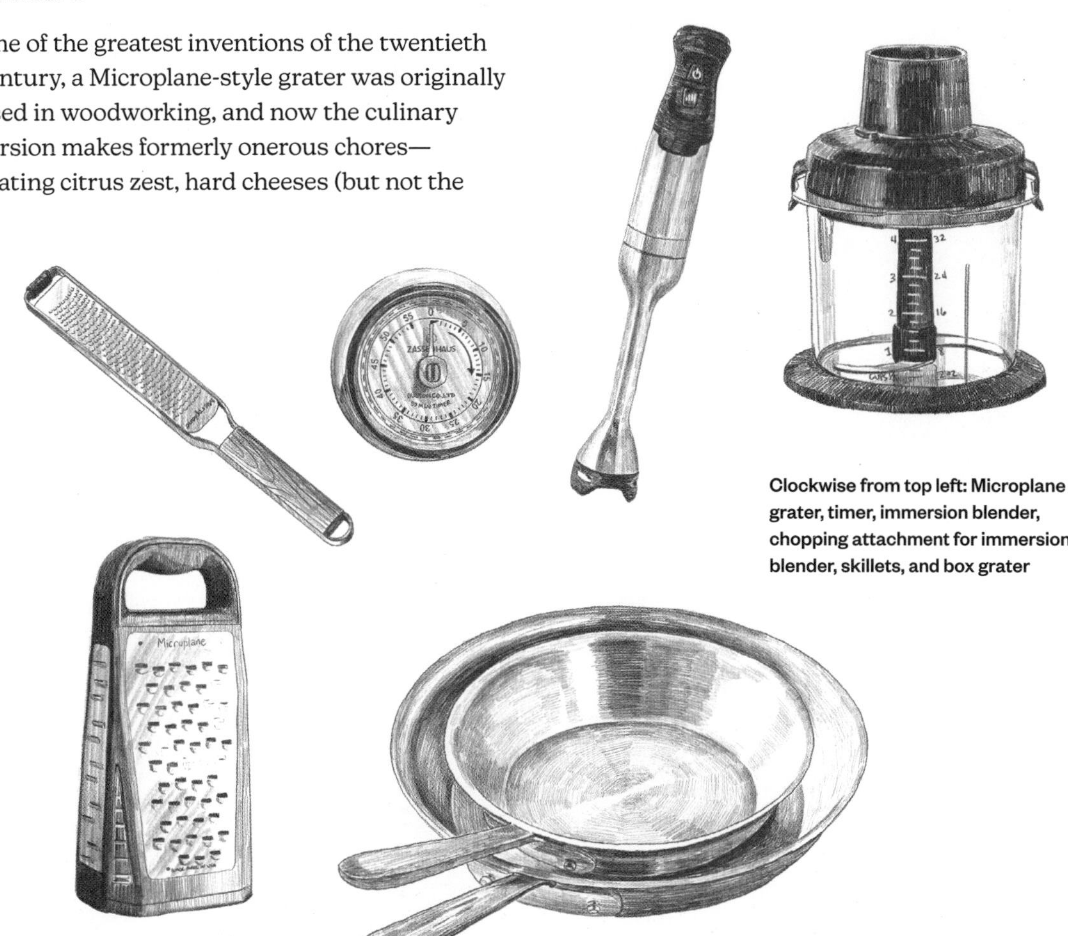

Clockwise from top left: Microplane grater, timer, immersion blender, chopping attachment for immersion blender, skillets, and box grater

Ragus

Charred Vegetable Ragu

This sauce is slightly magical. The texture cloaks your pasta noodles much like a traditional meat sauce does, and the flavors are deep and rich, but the sauce is vegetarian . . . vegan, actually! The key to success is cooking the vegetables hot and fast, so they char but don't fully cook and soften, which they will do once you're simmering the whole sauce. The other important point is to chop the vegetables, after charring, finely enough that they resemble the ground meat in a meat sauce yet not so finely that they become a puree. I use a food processor, but you might have more control with a big ol' chef's knife and a cutting board.

Inspired by a recipe from *Food & Wine* magazine, my version includes dried porcini (though it's optional), which enhances the smoky-meaty flavors of the charred vegetables, and I crisp up a bunch of kale leaves and add them to the mix, which brings a pleasant, slightly bitter note to the otherwise sweet vegetables.

Pappardelle rigate is a great noodle for this ragu, with its wide, slightly ridged surface. I also like bucatini for slurpability and rigatoni for when you want a short noodle, perhaps in a baked dish.

Makes about 6 cups (1.3 kg), enough to sauce 12 portions of pasta

½ ounce (15 g) dried porcini mushrooms (optional)

6 ounces (170 g) carrots (about 2 medium), cut into 2-inch (5 cm) chunks

6 ounces (170 g) celery (about 2 large stalks), peeled if fibrous and cut into 2-inch (5 cm) chunks

6 ounces (170 g) fennel (1 small bulb), trimmed, cored, and cut into 1-inch (2.5 cm) wedges

1 large onion (about 10 ounces/280 g), cut into thick slices

12 ounces (340 g) cremini mushrooms (or a mix of other mushrooms), stems removed

8 ounces (225 g) Tuscan kale (1 large bunch), thick stems cut or ripped out

Extra-virgin olive oil

4 or 5 garlic cloves, smashed

¼ cup (60 g) tomato paste

1 tablespoon chopped fresh rosemary

1 tablespoon chopped fresh thyme

1 tablespoon kosher salt (preferably Diamond Crystal; see page 17), plus more to taste

½ teaspoon freshly ground black pepper, plus more to taste

1 cup (240 ml) dry red wine

One 28-ounce (794 g) can whole peeled tomatoes, crushed by hand (see page 44), with their juices

If you're using the dried porcini, put them in a small bowl, cover with hot water, and soak until softened, 20 minutes to 1 hour. Gently wring out the softened mushrooms and chop finely. Set aside.

Heat the oven to 500°F (260°C) or as hot as you can get it without setting off your smoke alarm.

Arrange the carrots, celery, fennel, onion, and cremini mushrooms on two sheet pans in a single layer. Arrange the kale leaves on a separate sheet pan. Drizzle all the vegetables with olive oil and flip them all around so they're lightly and evenly coated with oil. Cook the vegetables in the hot oven until they are charred in spots and around the edges, 10 to 15 minutes for the kale, 20 to 35 minutes for the other vegetables. You're cooking the kale separately to avoid crowding the oven and creating too much moisture, which would inhibit the charring. Let the vegetables cool.

recipe continues →

Working in batches, pulse the vegetables in a food processor (or chop with a chef's knife) until they are in small bits. You want the texture to be varied, but with pieces no smaller than ¼ inch (6 mm) and no larger than about ⅓ inch (8 mm).

Heat ¼ cup (60 ml) olive oil in a large Dutch oven or large high-sided sauté pan over medium heat. Add the garlic and gently cook, breaking it up with your spatula, until it's soft and fragrant and starting to toast but not browned, 4 to 5 minutes.

Add the tomato paste, spreading it into a thin layer on the surface of the pan, and cook until it's darkened and slightly toasted, about 2 minutes.

Add the chopped vegetables, chopped porcini (if using), rosemary, thyme, salt, and black pepper. Increase the heat to medium-high, add the wine, and simmer until it has reduced by half, 3 to 4 minutes (it might be hard to see the wine, but use your best judgment).

Add the crushed tomatoes and their juices, reduce the heat to maintain a gentle simmer, and cook, stirring frequently, until the ragu is nicely thick and concentrated in flavor, about 45 minutes. Taste and adjust the seasoning with more salt or pepper as needed.

Let the ragu cool completely, then divide it into 1-cup (250 g) portions (enough to sauce 8 ounces/225 g dried noodles, or two servings). Use now (the ragu will last for up to 5 days in the refrigerator) or freeze for up to 4 months.

To serve, follow the process outlined in How to Sauce Pasta with a Ragu (page 64).

What Is a Soffritto?

Soffritto is an Italian cooking term that describes a mix of vegetables that is used to create an aromatic base for a sauce, soup, or braise. Probably every cuisine in the world has a similar component. An Italian soffritto usually includes onion, carrot, and celery (as does the French equivalent, mirepoix); the vegetables should be chopped quite finely and evenly for something like a ragu, which has a fairly fine-grained consistency. But you can make a coarser soffritto, with chunky rather than tiny dice, for a dish such as a stew.

Cook your soffritto slowly, usually in olive oil but sometimes in butter, because the goal is to coax out the sweetness of these foundational vegetables without actually browning them, which can introduce bitter notes.

Green Lentil Ragu

This vegetarian ragu is delicious in its hearty simplicity but equally delicious when teamed up with an "add-in" (see below), which could be sautéed vegetables or mushrooms or a meat such as juicy cotechino sausage or chopped prosciutto.

Green lentils are ideal, as they will hold their shape. I wouldn't make this with regular brown lentils, which break down rapidly.

Season this ragu lightly—no fresh herbs or chile flakes, for example—so that you can customize it according to your mood or the moment when you pair it with noodles.

Noodles with twists and turns to capture the lentils, such as shell-shaped lumache and the frilly bells of campanelle, are ideal. For a longer shape, I like one of the long fusillis (fusilli lunghi), which combine length and curls.

Makes about 7 cups (1.7 kg), enough to sauce 14 portions of pasta

Extra-virgin olive oil

¼ cup (35 g) finely diced carrot

¼ cup (35 g) finely diced celery

¼ cup (40 g) finely diced onion

2½ tablespoons tomato paste

3 cups (525 g) dried green lentils

4 garlic cloves, smashed

1 quart (1 L) homemade (page 143) or low-sodium store-bought vegetable broth, chicken broth, or water

One 15-ounce (425 g) can whole peeled tomatoes, crushed by hand (see page 44), with their juices

2 or 3 bay leaves

Kosher salt (preferably Diamond Crystal; see page 17)

Heat a generous glug of olive oil in a large heavy-bottomed pot, such as a Dutch oven, over medium heat. When the oil is hot, add the carrot, celery, and onion and cook, stirring frequently, until the vegetables are translucent and fragrant, 3 to 4 minutes; don't let them brown.

Increase the heat to medium-high, add the tomato paste, spreading it thinly on the surface of the pot, and cook until it toasts a bit, 3 to 5 minutes.

Add the lentils and garlic and stir to coat them with the tomato paste. Add the broth, crushed tomatoes and their juices, and bay leaves. Bring everything to a boil, then quickly adjust the heat to maintain a simmer. If you see large chunks of tomato, smash them with your spoon. Season lightly with salt and a big glug of olive oil.

Simmer gently, uncovered, stirring frequently, until the lentils are just tender but still holding their shape, 30 to 45 minutes. Note that you'll be cooking the lentils further when you use the ragu in a pasta dish, so keeping them intact now is a good idea. You don't want them hard or crunchy, just al dente and not losing their shape, so pay attention during the final minutes of cooking.

Taste the lentils and add more salt if you like, keeping it light since you'll be seasoning the ultimate dish you'll be making. Give the ragu one more generous drizzle of olive oil.

Let the ragu cool completely, then remove the bay leaves. Divide the ragu into 1-cup (250 g) portions (enough to sauce 8 ounces/225 g dried noodles, or two servings). Use now (the ragu will last for up to 5 days in the refrigerator) or freeze for up to 4 months.

To serve, follow the process outlined in How to Sauce Pasta with a Ragu (page 64).

Note that, unlike other ragus in this book, this lentil ragu will need to be thawed before you reheat it or the lentils could become mushy.

MORE WAYS

Sauté finely diced pancetta or roughly chopped prosciutto along with the carrot, celery, and onion and fold into the finished ragu.

Brown links of sweet or hot sausage, slice thinly, and fold into the finished ragu (make sure the sausage is cooked through).

Toss diced butternut squash with olive oil, salt, and pepper and roast in a hot oven until browned and tender. Fold into the finished ragu.

SAUSAGE RAGU
SHORT RIB RAGU
PORK + BEEF RAGU W/ KALE +
10.01
CHIX RAGU
CHIX RAGU
SHORT RIB RAGU W/
BEEF RAGU W/
10.01

ALL ABOUT RAGUS

The term *ragu* has multiple meanings (including being the brand name of a red sauce that lives in a jar), but I use *ragu* to mean any long-cooked sauce that can be served with pasta noodles, either on its own or with the addition of garnishes such as artichoke hearts, sautéed vegetables, sliced sausages, or anything that complements the main flavors in the sauce.

The building blocks of most ragus comprise three elements—a flavor base, a meat or other protein, and a liquid. The flavor base starts with a mix of aromatic vegetables called a *soffritto* in Italian (see page 59), with onion, carrot, and celery being a standard combo. Leeks, shallots, fennel, peppers, or other vegetables that soften and sweeten with long, gentle cooking would also be at home in soffritto for a ragu. Garlic, dried chiles, and fresh or dried herbs such as bay leaf or rosemary can also be part of the flavor power base.

Next is the protein, usually meat or poultry, most often cuts that start out tough but yield into melting tenderness after a few hours in a Dutch oven over low heat. Short ribs and chuck roast are excellent beef cuts, with their deep beefiness and plenty of collagen and other compounds that tenderize with long cooking and contribute a lushness of texture. Pork and lamb shoulder cuts are similar—deeply flavored and, after long cooking, producing meat that's silky and tender.

In Chicken Ragu Bianco (page 72), you'll use a mix of breast meat and darker, fattier chicken thighs, and you'll leave the skin on until the chicken is cooked and the meat is pulled from the bones. The skin will add fat, which you'll probably want to skim off, but it adds a lot of flavor as well.

I sometimes use ground meat, which is a bit easier to manage than large cuts. My favorite approach is to combine ground meat and pieces of a larger cut, which yields a complex texture of fine-grained meat and tender shreds or small chunks.

Liquids include wine, tomatoes, broth, and even milk in the Pork Shoulder Ragu with Lemon (page 78), but often plain water is plenty, allowing the flavors of the main ingredients to take the lead.

Note that my ragu recipes give timing and instructions for stovetop cooking, but you can also cook your ragus at low temperature (275° to 300°F/135° to 150°C) in a covered Dutch oven. The oven method is mostly hands-off, other than checking for doneness once in a while.

Most ragus are best the day after you make them, the delay allowing you to chill the ragu so the fat congeals on the surface, making it easy to skim off. A little fat is necessary for flavor, but too much meat fat can make the ragu heavy and overly rich, especially when finished with cheese.

You can also make meatless ragus, with nuts (page 71), lentils (page 60), and vegetables (page 56) in the lead roles, all with enough depth of character to make meat irrelevant.

A big plus to a ragu is that it freezes well, so making a big pot is not only a pleasurable way to spend time in the kitchen and prepare dinner for tonight, it's also a way to have long-cooked benefits in just a few minutes, weeks or months later. (All these ragu recipes can be easily doubled as well.)

I usually divide my ragus into 1-cup (250 g) portions—a good amount for two 4-ounce (115 g) portions of dried pasta. I package them in reusable freezer containers and label them. See more about storing ragus and using them with pasta on page 64.

A ragu is an excellent starting point for a baked pasta, providing a complex flavor base. Just add ricotta or mozzarella, a few vegetables, and then the pasta shape of your choice. See How to Invent Your Own Baked Pasta, page 358.

How to Sauce Pasta with a Ragu

While a ladleful of red sauce cascading over a bowl filled with spaghetti may be what springs to mind when you think "ragu," that's not how saucing pasta works, at least not in my pasta reality. And thank goodness, because the proper way to sauce your pasta yields much more delicious and easy-to-eat results.

First, Italians don't drown their pastas with sauce, and neither should you. A well-made sauce has enough intensity of flavor that a small amount is adequate. And, of course, a huge part of the pleasure of pasta is, well, the pasta—the noodles themselves. You want enough ragu or other sauce to lightly coat all the noodles and to have plenty of the added ingredients per bite, but you never want a pool of sauce at the bottom of the bowl. For the ragus in this book, a 1-cup (250 g) amount is enough to sauce 8 ounces (225 g) of dried pasta, which is generally a perfect amount for two people (for more on portion size, see page 9).

Bringing a ragu to the perfect noodle-cloaking consistency uses pasta water (see page 25), that magic ingredient that helps integrate all the components of a pasta dish—the noodles, the sauce, the cheese, and sometimes butter or olive oil. Here are the steps to make this happen.

1. Get your salted pasta water boiling.

2. Put a splash of the pasta water into a large skillet over medium-high heat. Add 1 cup (250 g) of the ragu of your choice; if it's still frozen, allow a few extra minutes for it to thaw (the exception is Green Lentil Ragu, page 60, which should be thawed before being reheated to avoid a mushy situation).

3. Add 8 ounces (225 g) of the dried noodles of your choice to the pot of boiling water and set a timer for 2 minutes less than the shortest suggested cooking time on the package of pasta. Stir the noodles several times during the first 2 minutes of cooking to prevent them from clumping.

4. When the noodles seem like they are 1½ to 2 minutes away from a perfect al dente, transfer them to the ragu in the skillet; make sure you reserve at least 1 cup (240 ml) of the pasta water.

5. Finish cooking the noodles, tossing and adding plenty of splashes of the reserved pasta water, until they are perfectly al dente. If you think the ragu and noodles look a bit watery, simmer for another few seconds to tighten up the consistency, bearing in mind that adding cheese will thicken the mixture. If the sauce seems dry, add a bit more pasta water.

6. Reduce the heat to low, add about ⅓ cup (40 g) freshly grated 50/50 cheese (half Parmigiano-Reggiano, half Pecorino Romano, grated in a food processor; see page 39), and toss to incorporate and emulsify, adding splashes of pasta water if needed to keep the consistency creamy and prevent the cheese from clumping. Divide the pasta between two warm bowls and serve right away, with more cheese to add at the table.

Marinara Sauce

For dishes that need a lot of sauce, such as a baked pasta, this marinara is my go-to. It's hard to beat spaghetti as the best noodle shape for marinara; I might look for spaghetti alla chitarra, which has a more hand-cut look with squared-off edges rather than the rounded shape of a regular spaghetti strand. And because marinara is ideal for baked pastas, ziti and penne are also great noodle partners.

Makes about 6 cups (1.5 kg), enough to sauce 12 portions of pasta

½ cup (120 ml) extra-virgin olive oil

1½ cups (225 g) finely chopped yellow onion

½ cup (65 g) finely chopped or grated carrot

¼ cup (35 g) finely chopped or grated celery

½ teaspoon kosher salt (preferably Diamond Crystal; see page 17), plus more to taste

¼ teaspoon dried chile flakes, plus more to taste

4 or 5 garlic cloves, finely chopped

2 tablespoons tomato paste

Two 28-ounce (794 g) cans whole peeled tomatoes, crushed by hand (see page 44), with their juices

Large handful of fresh basil or flat-leaf parsley leaves, or a mix

Big pinch of fresh oregano leaves

1 bay leaf

Heat the olive oil in a large, wide, heavy-bottomed saucepan or large, deep sauté pan over medium heat. Add the onion, carrot, celery, salt, and chile flakes and cook, stirring occasionally, until soft, fragrant, and lightly golden, 10 to 15 minutes. Add the garlic and cook for another 30 seconds (don't let it brown).

Add the tomato paste, spreading it thinly on the surface of the pan, and cook until it's lightly toasted, about 1 minute. Add the crushed tomatoes with their juices, basil (tear the leaves into a few pieces), oregano, and bay leaf. Reduce the heat to maintain a low simmer and cook, uncovered, stirring every once in a while, until the sauce is reduced, glistening with oil, and concentrated in flavor. Taste as you go. It should take between 30 and 40 minutes.

Taste and adjust the seasoning with more salt or chile flakes if you like.

Let the sauce cool completely, then remove the bay leaf. Divide the sauce into 1-cup (250 g) portions (enough to sauce 8 ounces/225 g dried noodles, or two servings). Use now (the ragu will last for up to 5 days in the refrigerator) or freeze for up to 4 months.

To serve, follow the process outlined in How to Sauce Pasta with a Ragu (page 64). Or freeze the whole batch to use in American-Style Lasagna (page 139) or Baked Ziti with Broccoli Rabe (page 356).

MORE WAYS

Sauté chopped red bell pepper or other sweet pepper along with the onion, carrot, and celery.

Marcella's Tomato-Butter Sauce with Long-Cooked Kale

The Marcella in this recipe title is, of course, Marcella Hazan, the grande dama of Italian cookbook writers, whose simple sauce of canned tomato, onion, and lots of butter is legendary. I've put my own twist on her signature sauce by adding what some people say is my signature vegetable—kale. You'll simmer the kale (preferably Tuscan kale, also called black kale, cavolo nero, or lacinato kale) with the other ingredients until it's quite tender and then puree everything (minus the onion) so that the sauce is flecked with bits of kale, taking on a slightly deeper, earthier flavor that complements the bright tomato. This sauce works brilliantly as a basic tomato sauce, portions of which can live in the freezer until you or your kids want a quick bowl of pasta.

Because I think of this ragu as a solid go-to tomato sauce, I use the same noodles I would with a marinara sauce—classic long shapes like spaghetti and linguine, and classic short shapes like penne, ziti, and rigatoni.

Makes about 1 quart (1 kg), enough to sauce 8 portions of pasta

Three 15-ounce (425 g) cans whole peeled tomatoes, with their juices

6 cups (150 g) lightly packed ¾-inch (1.75 cm) ribbons of kale, heavy stems cut out

1 medium onion (8 ounces/225 g), peeled and halved

7 tablespoons (100 g) unsalted butter

1 tablespoon kosher salt (preferably Diamond Crystal; see page 17), plus more to taste

Pour the tomatoes and their juices into a Dutch oven or other large heavy-bottomed pot. With clean hands, squish them until they're nicely broken up, removing any hard stem ends or unripe, stringy centers (you can also use a wooden spoon or potato masher, but your hands will be the most efficient tool).

Add the kale, onion, butter, and salt. Bring everything to a simmer and cook, stirring and scraping the sides of the pot occasionally, until the kale is very tender, the onion has softened, and the tomatoes have reduced and concentrated slightly, 1 to 1½ hours.

Let the sauce cool slightly, then remove the onion (discard it, add it to your compost, or save it to eat in another manner). Transfer the sauce to a blender and blend until the kale is reduced to little green flecks. Taste and add more salt if needed.

Let the sauce cool completely, then divide it into 1-cup (250 g) portions (enough to sauce 8 ounces/225 g dried noodles, or two servings). Use now (the ragu will last for up to 5 days in the refrigerator) or freeze for up to 4 months.

To serve, follow the process outlined in How to Sauce Pasta with a Ragu (page 64).

Nut Ragu

I came up with this crazy creation around ten years ago at an Italian restaurant I owned in Portland, Oregon. I don't think of it as substitute for a meat ragu, nor do I really think of it as a vegan dish (though it is). It's simply a nut ragu, a unique recipe that is happy to be its own delicious thing.

Take your time while you toast the nuts in olive oil. You don't want to overcook them, because too dark equals bitter, and nuts are expensive, so you don't want to have to start over.

This sauce is delicately chunky (no, that's not an oxymoron), so I like a noodle that has curls and crevices for the nuts to grab on to. Some favorites include busiate, which are tight short spirals, and strozzapreti, which are looser, hand-rolled medium-short tubes that capture ragus nicely.

Makes about 3 cups (725 g), enough to sauce 6 portions of pasta

½ cup (60 g) raw almonds (skinless if possible)

½ cup (60 g) raw cashews

½ cup (60 g) raw hazelnuts (skinless, if possible)

½ cup (60 g) raw pistachios

½ cup (60 g) raw walnuts

½ cup (120 ml) extra-virgin olive oil

4 or 5 garlic cloves, smashed

½ teaspoon finely chopped fresh rosemary

½ teaspoon finely chopped fresh thyme

¼ teaspoon freshly ground black pepper, plus more to taste

⅛ teaspoon dried chile flakes, plus more to taste

Kosher salt (preferably Diamond Crystal; see page 17)

1½ tablespoons tomato paste

2½ cups (625 g) canned whole peeled tomatoes, crushed by hand (see page 44), with their juices

Chop the almonds, cashews, hazelnuts, pistachios, and walnuts with a chef's knife or a mezzaluna until they are fairly fine but not at all powdery. You want bits of varying sizes. You can also chop them by pulsing them in a food processor.

Heat the oven to 300°F (150°C).

Heat the olive oil in a heavy-bottomed ovenproof pot with a lid, such as a Dutch oven, over medium heat. Add the garlic and cook gently until it softens, 4 to 5 minutes, breaking it up a bit with your spatula; don't let it actually brown.

Add the chopped nuts and cook gently, stirring frequently, until the nuts are beginning to toast, 3 to 5 minutes; they should be fragrant and very light brown but not super toasty, as they will continue to cook in the sauce. Take care that the garlic isn't starting to get too brown; if it is, reduce the heat a bit.

Add the rosemary, thyme, black pepper, chile flakes, and 1 teaspoon kosher salt.

Add the tomato paste, spreading it around on the surface of the pan, and cook until it's slightly darkened (but make sure you're not overbrowning the nuts or garlic). Stir until the nuts are evenly coated with the tomato paste.

Add the crushed tomatoes and their juices and stir to combine everything. Bring to a simmer and cook for 2 to 3 minutes, then cover the pot with a lid (or foil) and transfer to the oven.

Cook until the nuts are very soft, the tomato sauce has reduced and concentrated in flavor, and the whole thing is a nicely integrated sauce, 1½ to 2 hours. Check a few times during cooking to give everything a stir and add a bit of water if it seems like the sauce is drying out.

Let the sauce cool slightly, then transfer about one-quarter of the sauce to a blender. Blend until smooth, then fold back into the sauce. (You can also use a handheld immersion blender and just eyeball it.) Taste and adjust the seasoning with more salt, pepper, or chile flakes if needed.

Let the ragu cool completely, then divide it into 1-cup (250 g) portions (enough to sauce 8 ounces/225 g dried noodles, or two servings). Use now (the ragu will last for up to 5 days in the refrigerator) or freeze for up to 4 months.

To serve, follow the process outlined in How to Sauce Pasta with a Ragu (page 64).

Chicken Ragu Bianco

This ragu is dead simple and as good as it gets—just chicken, soffritto, herbs, and water come together to make a deeply flavored but light-on-its-feet ragu. I like the consistency of this ragu even better the next day, once everything has settled in, so if you have time, make it a day ahead. And like all these ragus, this one does well in the freezer.

The ragu is slightly brothy, with shreds of chicken; it's delicate but not finely textured. A short noodle with large holes, such as paccheri or large rigatoni, or a longer noodle with a grabby texture, such as ruffly mafaldine, works well.

Makes about 6 cups (1.2 kg), enough to sauce 12 portions of pasta

3 pounds (1.35 kg) bone-in, skin-on chicken pieces (a good combo is 2 pounds/900 g thighs and 1 pound/450 g breasts)

Kosher salt (preferably Diamond Crystal; see page 17)

Extra-virgin olive oil

¾ cup (100 g) finely diced carrot

½ cup (70 g) finely diced celery

½ cup (75 g) finely diced onion

½ cup (70 g) finely diced shallot

2 or 3 sprigs fresh thyme

One 4-inch (10 cm) sprig fresh rosemary

1 bay leaf

1 small dried chile, such as chile de árbol, or ¼ teaspoon dried chile flakes

Season the chicken pieces generously with salt on all sides. Heat a deep heavy-bottomed pot, such as a Dutch oven, over medium-high heat, pour in a glug of olive oil, and when the oil is hot, add the chicken, skin side down.

Cook the chicken until the first side is deeply browned, about 15 minutes (don't try to move the pieces for the first couple of minutes to allow a crust to form, which will prevent the skin from sticking). Flip the chicken, cook for another 10 minutes or so to brown the other side a bit, then transfer the chicken pieces to a plate.

Carefully pour off all but about 2 tablespoons of the grease from the pot. Reduce the heat to medium. Add the carrot, celery, onion, and shallot and cook, stirring and scraping occasionally so the moisture from the vegetables "deglazes" the chicken juices cooked onto the bottom of the pot, until the vegetables are beginning to brown and soften, about 10 minutes.

Return the chicken and any accumulated juices to the pot. Add 1 quart (1 L) water and the thyme, rosemary, bay leaf, and chile. Bring the water to a lively simmer and cook, with the lid on but partially cracked, until the chicken is completely tender and falling off the bone, about 1 hour. (Alternatively, bring the liquid to a simmer on the stovetop and then transfer the partially covered pot to a 350°F/175°C oven.)

Once the chicken is cooked, let it cool for a few minutes, then take it out of the liquid (but keep the cooking liquid in the pot) and let it cool until you can comfortably handle it. Pull off and discard the skin, then pull off the meat in large shreds (chop the larger ones) and return it to the cooking liquid.

Simmer the chicken and liquid until the liquid has reduced a bit and you have the consistency of a chunky sauce. Remove and discard the thyme and rosemary sprigs, the bay leaf, and the chile. Taste the ragu and add more salt if needed.

Let the ragu cool completely, then divide it into 1-cup (250 g) portions (enough to sauce 8 ounces/225 g dried noodles, or two servings). Use now (the ragu will last for up to 5 days in the refrigerator) or freeze for up to 4 months.

To serve, follow the process outlined in How to Sauce Pasta with a Ragu (page 64).

MORE WAYS

Add a piece of Parmigiano-Reggiano rind when you add the dried chile. Remove the rind before shredding the chicken.

Instead of plain water, use chicken broth as your liquid for a richer flavor.

Lamb Ragu

In Italy, this super-versatile ragu is typically made in spring and summer, hence the green garlic in the recipe. Green garlic is immature garlic, harvested before the plant has developed into bulbs with separate cloves; it looks like a chubby scallion and has a sweeter, mellower flavor than mature garlic. A combo of scallions and regular garlic can be a fine substitute.

I make this sauce using both chunks of lamb shoulder meat and ground lamb to create a complex texture, a trick I learned when I cooked in Italy. Make sure you use lamb shoulder and not "stew meat," which is usually cut from leg of lamb; leg meat is lean and tight and won't develop the melting texture that long-cooked shoulder meat has.

The combo texture of this ragu does well with a noodle shape that has enough curls to hold the sauce. Try the curly, corkscrewy Vesuvio (also called girelle), or consider radiatore, which has many nooks and slots for sauce. For a long noodle, try the long, skinny-but-curly fusilli col buco.

Makes about 3 cups (750 g), enough to sauce 6 portions of pasta

Extra-virgin olive oil

1 pound (450 g) lamb shoulder, cut into 1-inch (2.5 cm) chunks

⅓ cup (45 g) finely diced carrot

⅓ cup (45 g) finely diced celery

⅓ cup (50 g) finely diced onion

⅓ cup (50 g) finely diced shallot

3 ounces (85 g) green garlic, finely chopped, or 4 scallions and 4 garlic cloves, finely chopped

8 ounces (225 g) ground lamb

Kosher salt (preferably Diamond Crystal; see page 17)

2 quarts (2 L) homemade (page 143) or low-sodium store-bought chicken broth or water

3 sprigs fresh thyme

One 4-inch (10 cm) sprig fresh rosemary

2 or 3 bay leaves

1 small dried chile, such as chile de árbol, or a pinch of dried chile flakes

Heat a glug of olive oil in a large deep skillet that has a lid or a Dutch oven over medium-high heat. When the oil is hot, add the lamb shoulder chunks and cook, undisturbed, for 2 minutes, then cook until nicely browned on all sides; this should take about 10 minutes total.

Reduce the heat to medium. Add the carrot, celery, onion, shallot, and green garlic and cook, stirring frequently, until the vegetables are soft and fragrant but not browned, about 5 minutes.

Add the ground lamb and cook until the lamb is no longer pink, breaking it up into small bits with your spatula. Season lightly with salt.

Add the chicken broth, thyme, rosemary, bay leaves, and chile. Partially cover the pan and bring to a very gentle simmer. Cook, stirring once in a while, until all the meat is very tender, the lamb shoulder chunks are falling apart, and the liquid has reduced quite a bit, 2 to 3 hours. (Alternatively, bring the ragu to a simmer on the stovetop and then transfer to a 325°F/160°C oven.) The ragu should look like very small bits of meat and vegetables generously cloaked in a rich liquid; it should not be soupy. Taste and add more salt if needed. Retrieve and discard what's left of the herb sprigs, bay leaves, and chile.

Let the ragu cool completely, then divide it into 1-cup (250 g) portions (enough to sauce 8 ounces/225 g dried noodles, or two servings). Use now (the ragu will last for up to 5 days in the refrigerator) or freeze for up to 4 months.

To serve, follow the process outlined in How to Sauce Pasta with a Ragu (page 64).

MORE WAYS

Marry the ragu with spring vegetables such as snap peas, shelled English peas, or baby carrots, or fold in a handful of nettles and toss until wilted.

Pork Shoulder Ragu with Lemon

One of my favorite ragus, this sauce is at once rich and light, brightened with a touch of lemon. The milk may seem unusual, especially as you watch the sauce developing a slightly "broken" consistency from the milk separating, but this hearkens to maiale al latte, a traditional Italian dish of pork loin braised in milk. The milk gives the ragu a slight creaminess as well as a nutty flavor from the caramelized milk solids.

As with all these ragus that use tough cuts of meat, give yourself plenty of time for slow-cooking the pork shoulder to the point of fork-tender. Not all pork shoulder cooks the same, and you can't rush this process. The magic happens only toward the very end of cooking, when the meat seems to cross a threshold from tender-but-still-chewy to so-tender-I-don't-need-a-knife.

This ragu loves some surface area and shape to hold the tender shreds of pork, so I like the wide diameter of paccheri, the open corkscrew shape of cavatappi, or, for a long pasta, the width of a pappardelle, rigate or not.

Makes about 5 cups (1.2 kg), enough to sauce 10 portions of pasta

1 small red onion (about 6 ounces/170 g), cut into chunks

4 or 5 medium celery stalks (about 4 ounces/115 g), cut into chunks

Kosher salt (preferably Diamond Crystal; see page 17)

2½ pounds (1.1 kg) pork shoulder, cut into 2-inch (5 cm) chunks

Extra-virgin olive oil

5 or 6 garlic cloves, finely chopped

1 tablespoon finely chopped fresh rosemary

2½ cups (600 ml) dry white wine

1½ cups (360 ml) whole milk

Piece of Parmigiano rind (optional)

One 4-inch (10 cm) strip lemon zest

1 tablespoon fresh lemon juice, plus more to taste

Put the onion into a food processor and pulse until it is finely and evenly chopped; don't let it turn into a puree. Transfer to a measuring cup—you should have about 1 cup (160 g). Do the same with the celery; you should have about 1 cup (115 g). Set the vegetables aside.

Generously salt the pork chunks. Heat a glug of olive oil in a Dutch oven or other large heavy-bottomed pot over medium-high heat. When the oil is hot, add enough pork chunks to make an even single layer, not too crowded; you'll cook the pork in batches. Cook, undisturbed, until the pork forms a nice browned crust on the bottom, then turn it and brown the other sides, adjusting the heat as necessary to prevent the juices from burning. One batch of pork should take 10 to 15 minutes to brown. Transfer the pork to a bowl or plate. Cook the rest of the pork in the same way.

When all the pork has been browned, if there is a lot of grease in the pot, pour off all but about 2 tablespoons. Reduce the heat to medium, add the onion and celery, and cook, scraping the bottom of the pan and letting the moisture from the vegetables "deglaze" the pork juices. Add the garlic and rosemary and continue cooking until the vegetables are soft and fragrant but not browned, about 8 minutes total.

Increase the heat to medium-high and add the wine. Simmer until the wine has reduced by about half, 8 to 10 minutes.

Return the pork to the pot and add the milk, Parmigiano rind, if using, and strip of lemon zest. Adjust the heat so that the liquid simmers very gently when the pot is covered. Simmer, covered, until the pork is so tender you can crush it between your fingers, 2 to 3 hours, depending on your pork. When you think it's ready, be sure to taste a few chunks to verify that the pork is fully tender.

recipe continues →

Transfer the meat to a bowl or plate, and when it's cool enough to handle, break the chunks into shreds and smallish pieces, removing any bits of fat or gristle. Return the meat to the sauce, simmer for a few minutes to unify everything, then add the lemon juice. Taste and add more salt or lemon juice if needed. Remove the Parmigiano rind, if using, which will be very soft by now, and the strip of lemon zest, though it may have disintegrated, which is just fine.

Let the ragu cool completely, then divide it into 1-cup (250 g) portions (enough to sauce 8 ounces/225 g dried noodles, or two servings). Use now (the ragu will last for up to 5 days in the refrigerator) or freeze for up to 4 months.

To serve, follow the process outlined in How to Sauce Pasta with a Ragu (page 64).

Beef and Pork Ragu

Beef and pork can be fatty, so I like to make this meat sauce at least 1 day ahead, chill it overnight, and then spoon off the solidified fat. Don't get me wrong; fat is great! That's where so much of the flavor is, but too much meat fat can feel heavy and too rich.

The finished ragu has a slightly chunkier texture than a classic ragu Bolognese, but you can use it in much the same way—on wide egg noodles such as pappardelle or in a lasagna (pages 135 and 139) are two of my favorite options.

Makes about 2 quarts (2 kg), enough to sauce 16 portions of pasta

- 2 pounds (900 g) boneless chuck roast, big pockets of fat and any silver skin or gristle removed, cut into 1½-inch (3.5 cm) chunks
- Kosher salt (preferably Diamond Crystal; see page 17)
- Freshly ground black pepper
- Extra-virgin olive oil
- 1 pound (450 g) ground pork
- 2 cups (300 g) finely chopped onion
- ½ cup (65 g) finely diced carrot
- ½ cup (65 g) finely diced celery
- 4 garlic cloves, smashed and finely chopped
- 4 fresh medium sage leaves
- 4 sprigs fresh thyme
- Three 4-inch (10 cm) sprigs fresh rosemary
- 3 tablespoons unsalted butter
- 1 cup (240 ml) dry white wine
- One 28-ounce (794 g) can whole peeled tomatoes, crushed by hand (see page 44), with their juices

Season the chuck with salt and pepper (see page 82). Heat a glug of olive oil in a very large deep skillet or Dutch oven over medium-high heat. Blot the beef chunks with paper towels to dry them and, when the oil is hot, add them to the pan in an even layer with plenty of room between the chunks. You'll probably need to do this in batches or use two pans.

Cook, undisturbed, for 2 minutes, then turn the meat and cook until all sides of the chunks are nicely browned, about 15 minutes for the whole batch. Take your time to develop some nice browning, which will add so much flavor to the ragu; reduce the heat if your juices start to blacken in the pan. You do *not* want that to happen. Transfer the browned beef to a tray and set aside.

Pour off all but about 2 tablespoons of the grease from the pan. Break the ground pork into a couple of large chunks, add to the pan, and cook all surfaces well so they get deeply browned and slightly crusty, 5 to 10 minutes; once the pork has browned, break it into smaller bits.

Add the onion, carrot, and celery and cook, stirring to dissolve the cooked-on meat juices in the pan, until the vegetables are soft and fragrant, about 5 minutes. Add the garlic and cook for another minute, then add the sage, thyme, and rosemary.

Put the beef and any accumulated juices back into the pan and add the butter. Cook, stirring everything around, until the butter has melted and is starting to brown a bit, 3 to 4 minutes.

Add the wine and simmer until it has reduced by about half, 2 to 3 minutes. Then add the crushed tomatoes and their juices, along with 2 teaspoons salt.

Adjust the heat so the ragu simmers merrily but not hard when covered. Letting the sauce actually boil will toughen the beef, which is not what you want. Simmer, covered, stirring every

20 minutes or so, until the sauce has reduced and has a nice slick of oil on top and, most important, the beef is completely tender and starting to fall apart; you should be able to shred the chunks with a fork and crush them between your fingers. This can take between 1 and 3 hours, depending on your beef. It's critical to leave yourself enough time to cook the ragu until the beef gets to this point; otherwise, you'll have chewy beef, which, even if you were to cut it into smaller pieces, just won't be succulent.

Taste and adjust the final flavoring with more salt or pepper. Remove and discard the herb sprigs, if you like.

Let the ragu cool completely; if time allows, chill the ragu for several hours so the fat solidifies on top, then skim off the fat and discard it. Divide the ragu into 1-cup (250 g) portions (enough to sauce 8 ounces/225 g dried noodles, or two servings). Use now (the ragu will last for up to 5 days in the refrigerator) or freeze for up to 4 months.

To serve, follow the process outlined in How to Sauce Pasta with a Ragu (page 64).

MORE WAYS

Use a fruity but dry red wine, such as an Italian red, instead of white wine.

Salting Beef to Up the Beefy

For any of these beef-forward ragus, salt your beef up to a day ahead to enhance the beefy flavor. Sprinkle the pieces generously with kosher salt and spread the beef on a large tray, or ideally on a rack set over a tray. Let it sit at room temperature for up to 2 hours; if you're going to "age" it longer, put it in the fridge. When you're ready to cook the meat, blot off any moisture from the surface and proceed with the recipe, bearing in mind that you've already salted the meat and won't need to add much more salt when cooking.

Pork and Beef Ragu with Kale and Chile

We're definitely stepping outside the Italian tradition with this ragu, which features kale and fish sauce along with soffritto, ground beef and pork, and canned tomatoes. Though fish sauce is an Asian seasoning, the Italians have a counterpart called colatura di alici, a garum also made from fermented anchovies and salt. I always have fish sauce in my cupboard (or fridge, once the bottle is opened). It's an excellent and inexpensive way to add a hit of umami to any dish, but if you have colatura, use it in place of the fish sauce.

The amount of chile in the recipe, both dried flakes and fresh hot chiles, is fairly restrained, so if you like chile heat, go ahead and add more, especially the fresh ones. Unclassic in flavor but classic in its meat-sauce texture, this ragu likes a long noodle—spaghetti, bucatini, tagliatelle, or linguine.

Makes about 7 cups (1.4 kg), enough to sauce about 14 portions of pasta

Extra-virgin olive oil

1 cup (150 g) chopped sweet or yellow onion

9 or 10 garlic cloves, smashed

2 to 4 tablespoons minced fresh chile, such as serrano or jalapeño, depending on your heat preference (core and seed it before mincing)

1 to 2 tablespoons dried chile flakes, depending on your heat preference

1 pound (450 g) ground pork

1 pound (450 g) ground beef

10 cups (340 g) lightly packed ¾-inch (1.75 cm) ribbons of kale, thick stems cut out (from about 2 bunches)

One 15-ounce (425 g) can whole peeled tomatoes, crushed by hand (see page 44), with their juices

¼ cup (60 ml) fish sauce, plus more to taste

3 tablespoons tomato paste

Note: **Look for the Red Boat brand of fish sauce, my favorite (see Resources, page 380).**

Heat a generous glug of olive oil in a Dutch oven or other large heavy-bottomed pot over medium-high heat. When the oil is hot, add the onion, garlic, fresh chile, and chile flakes and cook until the onion is soft and fragrant but not browned, 4 to 5 minutes.

Add the ground pork and beef and cook until there is no more pink, 7 to 8 minutes. Spoon off any visible grease and discard.

Add the kale (you may need to add a few handfuls at a time and let it begin to wilt before you add more) and cook, stirring, until wilted, 8 to 10 minutes.

Add the crushed tomatoes and their juices, fish sauce, and tomato paste. Stir everything together, adjust the heat to maintain a low simmer, and cook, uncovered, until the kale is fully tender, the meats are broken down to a more granular texture, and the flavors have melded and concentrated, 1 to 2 hours. Taste and adjust the final seasoning to your liking with more chile flakes or fish sauce.

Let the ragu cool completely, then divide it into 1-cup (250 g) portions (enough to sauce 8 ounces/225 g dried noodles, or two servings). Use now (the ragu will last for up to 5 days in the refrigerator) or freeze for up to 4 months.

To serve, follow the process outlined in How to Sauce Pasta with a Ragu (page 64).

MORE WAYS

Add a big handful of fresh mint leaves, torn into a few pieces, as you adjust the final seasoning.

Beef and Sweet Bell Pepper Ragu

Imagine a comforting pot roast reincarnated as pasta; that's what this pasta is all about.

This ragu is best with sturdy shorter noodle shapes, such as rigatoni, penne, or, for something curvier, lumache. For the best texture, be sure to shred or chop the beef into small pieces.

Makes about 1 quart (1 kg), enough to sauce 8 portions of pasta

Kosher salt (preferably Diamond Crystal; see page 17)

2 pounds (900 g) boneless chuck roast, big pockets of fat and any silver skin or gristle removed

Extra-virgin olive oil

3 or 4 garlic cloves, smashed

1 medium onion (8 ounces/225 g), sliced

½ teaspoon dried chile flakes

2 pounds (900 g) red bell peppers, cored, seeded, and sliced about ½ inch (1.25 cm) thick

2 tablespoons tomato paste

1 cup (240 ml) dry white wine

1 cup (250 g) canned whole peeled tomatoes, crushed by hand (see page 44), with their juices

3 or 4 sprigs fresh thyme

Generously salt the beef all over and let it sit for about 1 hour; this will make the meat taste a bit more "beefy" (see page 82).

Heat the oven to 300°F (150°C).

Heat a generous glug of olive oil in a large Dutch oven or other heavy-bottomed ovenproof pot with a lid over medium-high heat. Blot any surface moisture off the beef with a paper towel and, when the oil is hot, put it in the pot. You may need to cut the meat into a couple of smaller pieces to fit.

Brown the beef on all sides; aim for a rich brown crust without burning the bottom of the pot, which should take 15 to 25 minutes total. Transfer the beef to a plate and set aside.

Pour off the rendered beef fat from the pot, add a fresh glug of olive oil, and reduce the heat to medium. Add the garlic and cook until it starts to soften, 1 to 2 minutes. Add the onion and chile flakes and cook until the onion is soft, fragrant, and starting to turn golden, 8 to 10 minutes.

Add the bell peppers, season lightly with salt, and cook, stirring and scraping the pot often, until the peppers are also soft and starting to brown, 10 to 15 minutes. Add the tomato paste and cook, spreading it thinly on the surface of the pot, until it's lightly toasted, 1 to 2 minutes.

Increase the heat to medium-high, add the wine, and simmer until the wine has reduced by about half, 2 to 3 minutes. Add the crushed tomatoes and their juices, the thyme, and ½ cup (120 ml) water and bring to a simmer. Put the beef back in the pot, nestling it among the peppers and spooning some peppers and tomato on top.

Cover the pot and cook in the oven until the beef is fall-apart tender, the sauce has reduced a bit, and the peppers are a lovely sloppy mess; this could take between 1½ and 3 hours, depending on the shape of the beef.

Let everything rest until cool enough to handle, then transfer the beef to a plate or cutting board and spoon off any excess grease from the sauce remaining in the pot. Pull the beef into shreds, cutting any larger pieces and removing big bits of fat or gristle. Fold the beef back into the peppers. Taste the ragu and add more salt as needed.

Let the ragu cool completely, then divide it into 1-cup (250 g) portions (enough to sauce 8 ounces/225 g dried noodles, or two servings). Use now (the ragu will last for up to 5 days in the refrigerator) or freeze for up to 4 months.

To serve, follow the process outlined in How to Sauce Pasta with a Ragu (page 64).

MORE WAYS

Instead of, or in addition to, the red bell peppers, use a mix of sweet pepper varieties—Jimmy Nardellos, lipstick peppers, pimentos—or even a few hotter chiles such as Anaheims or poblanos.

Sausage Ragu

Whether mild or spicy, depending on your choice of sausage, this ragu is definitely hearty. Look for well-made Italian sausage, meaning one without corn syrup or tons of preservatives.

I love pairing sausage with orecchiette—sturdy, shallow little cups that hold sauce nicely. Garganelli, an egg-enriched pasta, is lovely as well. The shape is made from small squares of ridged pasta that are loosely rolled into pointy tubes.

Makes about 3 cups (750 g), enough to sauce 6 portions of pasta

1 pound (450 g) bulk Italian sausage, sweet or hot (or half and half)

Extra-virgin olive oil

2 tablespoons finely chopped garlic

½ teaspoon coarsely ground black pepper, plus more to taste

¼ teaspoon dried chile flakes, plus more to taste

⅓ cup (45 g) finely chopped carrot

⅓ cup (45 g) finely chopped celery

⅓ cup (50 g) finely chopped onion

2 teaspoons chopped fresh rosemary

2 teaspoons dried thyme

2 tablespoons tomato paste

One 15-ounce (425 g) can whole peeled tomatoes, crushed by hand (see page 44), with their juices

2 teaspoons kosher salt (preferably Diamond Crystal; see page 17), plus more to taste

Shape the sausage into 4 patties. Heat a glug of olive oil in a Dutch oven or other large heavy-bottomed pot over medium-high heat. When the oil is hot, add the sausage and sear, smashing the patties down from time to time with your spatula; don't move them until a nice crust forms on the bottom, about 5 minutes. Flip the patties and continue cooking, now breaking them into smaller pieces, until the sausage is mostly cooked, 3 to 5 minutes more.

Add the garlic, black pepper, and chile flakes and cook, stirring, until the garlic is fragrant, taking care not to let it brown, 1 to 2 minutes.

Add the carrot, celery, and onion and cook, stirring frequently, until the vegetables have softened, about 5 minutes.

Add the rosemary and thyme to the pot, stirring to combine with the sausage and vegetables.

Push the ingredients to one side of the pot and add the tomato paste to the cleared space. Spread the tomato paste over the surface of the pot and cook for about 1 minute to caramelize it slightly, then stir it into the sausage mixture.

Add the crushed tomatoes and their juices along with the salt and stir everything together. Bring the sauce to a simmer, then reduce the heat to low and let it simmer gently, uncovered, stirring occasionally, until the flavors have married nicely, the sausage is well integrated, and the sauce has thickened, 1 to 1½ hours. Taste and adjust the seasoning to your liking with more chile flakes, black pepper, or salt.

Let the ragu cool completely, then divide it into 1-cup (250 g) portions (enough to sauce 8 ounces/225 g dried noodles, or two servings). Use now (the ragu will last for up to 5 days in the refrigerator) or freeze for up to 4 months.

To serve, follow the process outlined in How to Sauce Pasta with a Ragu (page 64).

Short Rib Ragu with Black Peppercorns

This ragu is a play on peposa, a Tuscan beef dish with a long history and a lot of black pepper. Some recipes use crushed (not finely ground) pepper, but I like using whole black peppercorns. After you've simmered the dish long enough for the short ribs to be fully tender, the peppercorns become tender as well. When you bite down on one, you'll definitely get a pop of pepper heat—I liken the effect to dishes containing Sichuan peppercorns—but overall, the dish isn't killer hot. If you're concerned, use a smaller amount of peppercorns the first time you make this, but don't be too cautious or you'll miss the point of the dish.

You'll use a different technique for the soffritto here, finely chopping the vegetables in a food processor rather than cutting them into a fine dice with a knife. This way the soffritto melts into the sauce, adding its flavors but not much texture.

This bold ragu works best with a curled noodle shape that can capture the chunks and shreds of meltingly tender beef short ribs; think spiraled gemelli or rotini.

Makes about 5 cups (1.2 kg), enough to sauce 10 portions of pasta

- Kosher salt (preferably Diamond Crystal; see page 17)
- 3 pounds (1.3 kg) bone-in short ribs
- 1 small red onion (about 6 ounces/170 g), cut into chunks
- 2 or 3 medium celery stalks (about 3 ounces/85 g), cut into chunks
- 1 medium fennel bulb (about 8 ounces/225 g), cut into chunks
- Extra-virgin olive oil
- 6 or 7 garlic cloves, finely chopped
- 2 cups (480 ml) dry white wine
- One 28-ounce (794 g) can whole peeled tomatoes, crushed by hand (see page 44), with their juices
- 2 bay leaves
- 2 tablespoons whole black peppercorns
- One 5-inch (12.5 cm) sprig fresh rosemary

Generously salt the short ribs and let them sit for up to 1 day (see page 82; if you're leaving them for longer than 2 hours, refrigerate them). If you don't have time, you can simply salt the short ribs and proceed with the recipe.

Put the onion in a food processor and pulse until it is finely and evenly chopped; don't let it turn into a puree. Transfer to a measuring cup—you should have about 1 cup (150 g).

Do the same with the celery and fennel, chopping them together in the food processor; you should have about 1½ cups (200 g). Set all the vegetables aside.

Heat a glug of olive oil in a Dutch oven or other large heavy-bottomed pot over medium-high heat. Blot the short ribs dry with a paper towel. When the oil is hot, add the short ribs in an even single layer (cook the ribs in batches, if necessary). Cook, undisturbed, until a nice browned crust forms on the bottom, then turn them and brown the other sides, about 15 minutes total; adjust the heat as necessary to prevent the juices from burning on the bottom of the pot. Transfer the ribs to a bowl or plate.

You'll probably have a lot of grease in the pot; pour off all but about 2 tablespoons. Reduce the heat to medium, add the onion, celery, and fennel, and cook, scraping the bottom of the pot and letting the moisture from the vegetables "deglaze" the meat juices. Add the garlic and continue cooking until the vegetables are soft and fragrant but not browned, about 8 minutes total.

Increase the heat to medium-high and add the wine. Simmer until the wine has reduced by about half, 8 to 10 minutes. Return the short ribs to the pot and add the crushed tomatoes and their juices, bay leaves, peppercorns, and rosemary.

Adjust the heat so that the liquid simmers very gently when the pot is covered. Simmer, covered, until the bones easily slip out of the short ribs and the meat is so tender you can crush it

between your fingers, 2 to 4 hours, depending on your meat. Be sure to taste a few pieces to verify that the meat is fully tender.

Transfer the meat to a bowl or plate and, when it's cool enough to handle, break it into shreds and smallish pieces, removing any bits of fat or gristle. (Each rib will have a heavy piece of connective tissue around the bone that should be removed because it's very chewy.)

Spoon off as much of the beef fat as possible from the sauce remaining in the pot, and then taste the sauce. It should be richly flavored and the peppercorns should be soft. If not, simmer the sauce for another 20 minutes or so and taste again. When the sauce seems ready, remove the bay leaves and rosemary sprig, return the meat to the sauce, and simmer for a few minutes to unify everything. Taste and add more salt if needed.

Let the ragu cool completely, then divide it into 1-cup (250 g) portions (enough to sauce 8 ounces/225 g dried noodles, or two servings). Use now (the ragu will last for up to 5 days in the refrigerator) or freeze for up to 4 months.

To serve, follow the process outlined in How to Sauce Pasta with a Ragu (page 64).

White Bolognese with Cream

As with so many classic dishes, ragu alla Bolognese (the parent to this ragu) comes with variants, misconceptions, and many strong opinions. The primary debate is whether Bolognese sauce is a tomato sauce or not. From what I know, "not" is the most accurate answer, though outside of Italy, ragu alla Bolognese has somehow morphed into what might be called "spaghetti sauce," a very tomatoey sauce with ground meat.

Most traditional Italian versions of ragu alla Bolognese focus on the meats, which can include a range—beef, pork, veal, prosciutto. The sauce generally includes finely ground meats and finely chopped soffritto (see page 59), and the flavor is intense and luxurious. In recipes that include tomato—whether as paste, canned, or both—it is not the principal ingredient. The no-tomato version is often called white or bianco.

While I'm all for tradition, I also like to push the edges a bit, which is why this version of white Bolognese, inspired by one made by Australian food writer Odette Williams, caught my attention. Here the "white" refers to not only the absence of tomato but also to a generous addition of cream. The sauce is made even creamier by blending a portion of it and then folding it back in. I add dried porcini to the mix, intensifying the umami savoriness.

This elegant ragu is beautiful when served simply with classic long noodles such as pappardelle, tagliatelle, or fettucine. It is fantastic with handfuls of greens tossed in at the very end, especially nice bitter greens such as escarole or dandelion.

Makes a generous 6 cups (1.5 kg), enough to sauce 12 portions of pasta

½ ounce (15 g) dried porcini mushrooms (optional)

Extra-virgin olive oil

5 ounces (140 g) pancetta, finely chopped

1 pound (450 g) ground beef

1 pound (450 g) ground pork

4 cups (8 ounces/225 g) finely chopped cremini mushrooms

⅔ cup (85 g) finely diced carrot

⅔ cup (85 g) finely diced celery

⅔ cup (100 g) finely chopped onion

3 or 4 garlic cloves, finely chopped

1 cup (240 ml) dry white wine

2 teaspoons finely chopped fresh rosemary

1 teaspoon finely chopped fresh sage

1 teaspoon finely chopped fresh thyme

2 or 3 bay leaves

1 quart (1 L) homemade or low-sodium beef or chicken broth

¾ cup (180 ml) heavy or whipping cream

¼ teaspoon freshly ground black pepper

Freshly grated nutmeg

Kosher salt (preferably Diamond Crystal; see page 17)

If you're using the dried porcini, put them in a small bowl, cover with hot water, and soak until softened, 20 minutes to 1 hour. Gently wring out the softened mushrooms and chop finely. Set aside.

Heat a glug of olive oil in a large, deep, heavy-bottomed pot, such as a Dutch oven, over medium heat. When the oil is hot, add the pancetta and cook until it is crisp and most of the fat has melted out, 5 to 6 minutes, then remove it with a slotted spoon and set it aside.

Pour off all but about 3 tablespoons of the fat from the pan (the fat will add wonderful flavor, but you don't want so much that the sauce becomes too heavy). Increase the heat to medium-high, add the ground beef and pork, and cook, breaking the meat up into bits with your spoon, until it's browned on the surface and no longer pink inside, 5 to 6 minutes. Transfer the meat with a slotted spoon to a bowl and set aside.

recipe continues →

Add the cremini mushrooms, carrot, celery, onion, garlic, and chopped porcini, if using, and cook, stirring frequently so the moisture from the vegetables "deglazes" any cooked-on meat juices, until the vegetables are tender and most of the liquid released by the mushrooms has evaporated, 8 to 10 minutes. Don't actually brown the vegetables but aim to get them lightly caramelized.

Add the white wine, rosemary, sage, thyme, and bay leaves, then return all the meat to the pan and simmer until the wine has reduced almost entirely. Add the broth and simmer gently, stirring frequently, until it's reduced by half, 1 to 1½ hours.

Add the cream and simmer until the cream has reduced a bit and incorporated into the sauce, 4 to 5 minutes.

Retrieve the bay leaves and discard them. Add the black pepper, several gratings of fresh nutmeg (a Microplane-style grater works well for this), and a pinch of salt.

Scoop out about one-quarter of the sauce, transfer to a blender, and blend until it's mostly smooth and emulsified (it will remain a bit granular). You can also use an immersion blender to puree the sauce right in the pot. Return it to the pan with the rest of the sauce and stir to combine. Taste and add more salt if you like, but remember that you'll be adding cheese when you use this sauce to make your pasta dish.

Let the ragu cool completely, then divide it into 1-cup (250 g) portions (enough to sauce 8 ounces/225 g dried noodles, or two servings). Use now (the ragu will last for up to 5 days in the refrigerator) or freeze for up to 4 months.

To serve, follow the process outlined in How to Sauce Pasta with a Ragu (page 64).

Any Season

Aglio e Olio

The name of this dish simply means "garlic and oil," and the recipe couldn't be simpler, making this a go-to that you can always make with ingredients you likely have on hand. Most of the time I don't even add cheese to the sauce or grate cheese over the finished dish, but feel free to do so, as there's nothing wrong with a little grated cheese.

The most important part of this dish—in addition to the garlic—is the salty, starchy pasta water, which you add to the partially cooked noodles once they're in the skillet; it's like you're making a quick broth that you emulsify with a generous amount of olive oil (see page 109).

Serves 2

Kosher salt (preferably Diamond Crystal; see page 17)

⅓ cup (80 ml) extra-virgin olive oil

5 or 6 garlic cloves, smashed

½ teaspoon dried chile flakes, or 1 fresh hot chile, such as jalapeño, cored, sliced into thin rings, and the seeds flicked out, plus more to taste

8 ounces (225 g) spaghetti, spaghetti alla chitarra, or linguine

½ cup (15 g) roughly chopped fresh flat-leaf parsley leaves (optional)

50/50 cheese (half Parmigiano-Reggiano, half Pecorino Romano, grated in a food processor; see page 39), for serving (optional)

Fill a large pot (at least 6 quarts/L) with 1 gallon (4 L) of water; add 4 tablespoons (40 g) kosher salt, cover the pot, and bring the water to a boil while you make your sauce. If the water begins to boil before your sauce is ready, turn down the heat, but don't let the volume of the pasta water reduce by boiling off.

Heat the olive oil in a large skillet over medium heat. Add the garlic and cook, smashing it a bit to break it up and to flavor the oil, until it's nicely toasted but not actually browned, 3 to 4 minutes. Take your time with this, reducing the heat a bit if needed.

Add the dried chile flakes or fresh chile and cook for another minute or so to infuse the garlicky oil with the spice. Splash a bit of the water from the pasta pot into the skillet to stop the garlic from cooking further (watch out, as the oil might spatter) and slide the skillet off the heat.

Get the pasta water boiling again, add the noodles, and set your timer for 2 minutes less than the shortest suggested cooking time on the package of pasta; this will ideally be 2 minutes before the pasta is al dente. Stir the noodles several times during the first 2 minutes of cooking to prevent them from sticking to the bottom of the pot or otherwise clumping together.

When the timer goes off, start tasting the noodles. When they seem like they are 1½ to 2 minutes away from a perfect al dente (see page 22), drain and transfer them to the sauce in the skillet using your preferred method (see page 21), making sure to reserve at least 1 cup (240 ml) of the pasta water.

Slide the skillet back onto medium heat and finish cooking the noodles, tossing them and adding plenty of splashes of the starchy pasta water to emulsify with the olive oil, creating a cloaking consistency. When the pasta is ready, you should have a luxuriously moist pasta but no more actual liquid in the pan.

Add the parsley, if using, toss, taste the pasta, and add more salt or chile flakes if you like. Divide the pasta between two warm bowls and serve right away. Add cheese if you like, too.

Pasta Knowledge: TOASTING GARLIC

Instead of finely chopping garlic and then adding it to the pan, I start by smashing a whole clove (which makes the skin easy to remove, by the way) and, from there, adjusting my technique depending on my desired result. I cook the slightly broken-up cloves slowly, to develop toasty flavors and to infuse the oil with garlic flavor; this is difficult to do with finely chopped garlic, which burns quickly. With this method, I can remove the garlic once the oil has taken on its flavor or leave it in the dish for more flavor, breaking up the now-softened cloves into smaller bits that integrate easily into the sauce.

Here's my method: Place the side of your chef's knife on a clove (or more than one, if you can manage it) and pound the knife blade with your fist to smash the garlic. This should flatten it out a bit, and the clove will either stay whole or break into a couple of pieces. Pull off the skin. Add the garlic to moderately hot oil in your pan and cook slowly, smashing it down with your spoon and tilting the pan now and then so the garlic gets bathed in the hot oil, until it has softened and is a nice toasty brown (but not *too* brown), 3 to 4 minutes. If the garlic stays in the pan for the whole sauce-making process, it will eventually break up into little bits that blend with the sauce, but take care that it doesn't burn early on. If needed, scoop it out and return it to the pan later in the process when there are more ingredients to buffer the heat, or leave it out altogether.

Amatriciana

Amatriciana is a classic Italian pasta dish that originates from the town of Amatrice in the Lazio region of Italy, which is on the west side of the country. The dish is made with spaghetti, canned tomatoes, a fatty bit of cured pork cut into strips called lardons, Pecorino Romano cheese, and dried chile flakes.

I sometimes grind the cured pork rather than cut it into lardons, which gives the sauce a really nice, fine consistency, but truly any size or shape is fine as long as the pork is rendered and crisp. And *do not* discard the fat from the pork. It adds incredible flavor and a lush texture to the finished dish.

Onions aren't traditional in amatriciana, but I add them anyway, because I like the taste and texture of onions in the sauce and I'm the cook. So are you, so you get to choose.

Serves 2

Kosher salt (preferably Diamond Crystal; see page 17)

Extra-virgin olive oil

3½ ounces (100 g) guanciale or pancetta, cut into small strips or diced

½ very small red onion (about 2½ ounces/70 g), cut into ¼-inch-thick (6 mm) slices

½ teaspoon dried chile flakes, plus more to taste

1 tablespoon tomato paste

1 cup (250 g) canned whole peeled tomatoes, crushed by hand (see page 44), with their juices

8 ounces (225 g) rigatoni, penne, or spaghetti

⅓ cup (40 g) 50/50 cheese (half Parmigiano-Reggiano, half Pecorino Romano, grated in a food processor; see page 39), plus more for serving

Finishing-quality extra-virgin olive oil, for serving

Fill a large pot (at least 6 quarts/L) with 1 gallon (4 L) of water; add 4 tablespoons (40 g) kosher salt, cover the pot, and bring the water to a boil while you make your sauce. If the water begins to boil before your sauce is ready, turn down the heat, but don't let the volume of the pasta water reduce by boiling off.

Heat a glug of olive oil in a large skillet over medium heat. When the oil is hot, add the guanciale and cook until the fat starts to run and everything is sizzling nicely, about 2 minutes. Add the red onion and cook until the guanciale is getting crisp and the onion is frying, softening, and lightly browning, another 8 minutes or so.

Add the chile flakes, then add the tomato paste and cook, stirring and spreading the tomato paste thinly on the pan so it toasts and darkens a bit, for 30 seconds to 1 minute. Add the crushed tomatoes and their juices and cook, stirring sort of constantly, until the sauce has reduced by half, 4 to 5 minutes. At this point you should have a really nice pork-flavored spicy tomato sauce. Slide the skillet off the heat.

Bring the pasta water (back) to a boil, add the noodles, and set your timer for 2 minutes less than the shortest suggested cooking time on the package of pasta; this will ideally be 2 minutes before the pasta is al dente. Stir the noodles several times during the first 2 minutes of cooking to prevent them from sticking to the bottom of the pot or otherwise clumping together.

When the timer goes off, start tasting the noodles. When they seem like they are 1½ to 2 minutes away from a perfect al dente (see page 22), drain and transfer them to the sauce in the skillet using your preferred method (see page 21), making sure to reserve at least 1 cup (240 ml) of the pasta water.

Slide the skillet back onto medium heat and finish cooking the noodles, tossing and adding plenty of splashes of pasta water until the noodles are perfectly al dente and the sauce is nicely juicy. If the sauce seems watery, simmer for another few seconds to tighten it up, bearing in mind that the cheese will thicken it.

Reduce the heat to very low. Add the grated cheese and toss to emulsify it with the other sauce ingredients, adding splashes of pasta water (or plain hot water, if things are getting

too salty) if needed to keep the consistency creamy and prevent the cheese from clumping. Taste and add more salt or chile flakes if you like.

Divide the pasta between two warm bowls, drizzle with a nice glug of good olive oil, and sprinkle more cheese on top.

Pasta Knowledge: CURED PORK

Many pasta recipes call for a small amount of cured pork as a flavoring and a source of fat and richness. The two most common are guanciale and pancetta. Guanciale is cured pork jowl, which has a fantastic porky flavor and a lot of fat compared to the meaty part. Its kin, pancetta, is cured pork belly, which is the same cut you'd use to make American bacon, but unlike bacon, pancetta is not smoked; it's often cured with spices as well as salt. Be careful if using American bacon in place of pancetta, because the smokiness can overwhelm the dish.

Traditionally, you would cut guanciale or pancetta into lardons, which are ¼-inch-thick (6 mm) strips, about 1 inch (2.5 cm) long. To create lardons of this size, you need to start with a ¼-inch-thick (6 mm) piece of the cured pork, but that option isn't common in ordinary grocery stores. More often, you'll see packaged thinly sliced guanciale or pancetta, or finely diced pancetta. If this is what's available, no worries; it will work fine. Simply chop or cut the slices into ¼-inch-thick (6 mm) strips or use the diced pancetta as is. Both guanciale and pancetta freeze well.

Cacio e Pepe

As with all classic Italian pasta dishes, this one provokes passionate opinions and proclamations of dos and don'ts. While my cooking leans toward classic, I'm not even close to being a purist in the cacio (cheese) department, as I like to cut the traditional pecorino with Parmigiano-Reggiano.

As for the pepe (pepper) part of the recipe, you want some larger-than-you-would-think chunks of black pepper. You do not want the pepper bits to be all the same size, and you don't want a lot of finely ground black pepper, which would make the dish too hot-spicy and one-note. (See how I do this on page 43.) Use a pepper mill only if you have one that can produce the right consistency.

Serves 2

Kosher salt (preferably Diamond Crystal; see page 17)

1½ teaspoons (4 g) whole black peppercorns

Extra-virgin olive oil

8 ounces (225 g) spaghetti, bucatini, or linguine

½ cup (60 g) 50/50 cheese (half Parmigiano-Reggiano, half Pecorino Romano, grated in a food processor; see page 39), plus more for serving

2 tablespoons unsalted butter (optional)

Fill a large pot (at least 6 quarts/L) with 1 gallon (4 L) of water; add 4 tablespoons (40 g) kosher salt, cover the pot, and bring the water to a boil while you make your sauce. If the water begins to boil before your sauce is ready, turn down the heat, but don't let the volume of the pasta water reduce by boiling off.

As the water is coming to a boil, crack the peppercorns following the method on page 43.

Set a large heavy-bottomed skillet over medium heat. Add the cracked black pepper to the dry pan and toast, stirring, until you smell a lovely black pepper fragrance, 15 to 30 seconds. Don't go too far or the pepper will become bitter.

Add a generous glug of olive oil to the skillet and heat gently for 1 minute to infuse the pepper into the oil. Slide the pan off the heat.

Bring the pasta water (back) to a boil, add the noodles, and set your timer for 2 minutes less than the shortest suggested cooking time on the package of pasta; this will ideally be 2 minutes before the pasta is al dente. Stir the noodles several times during the first 2 minutes of cooking to prevent them from sticking to the bottom of the pot or otherwise clumping together.

When the timer goes off, start tasting the noodles. When they seem like they are 1½ to 2 minutes away from a perfect al dente (see page 22), scoop out 1 cup (240 ml) of the pasta water and add it to the pepper-oil mixture in the skillet. Transfer the noodles to the sauce in the skillet using your preferred method (see page 21), reserving another 1 cup (240 ml) of the pasta water.

Slide the skillet back onto medium heat and finish cooking the noodles, tossing until the noodles are perfectly al dente and have absorbed the peppery water and the sauce is nicely juicy. Add more pasta water if needed to achieve this result, bearing in mind that the cheese will thicken the sauce.

Reduce the heat to very low. Add the grated cheese and toss to emulsify it with the other sauce ingredients, adding splashes of pasta water (or plain hot water, if things are getting too salty) if needed to keep the consistency creamy and prevent the cheese from clumping.

If it seems like you have too much water, you can increase the heat slightly for a few seconds at a time, but be vigilant to avoid the cheese sticking to the bottom of the pan too much. If using the butter, add it now and continue to swirl and toss the pasta. Take a quick taste and add more salt or pepper if you like.

When the cheese and water and oil have emulsified into a silky sauce that coats all the noodles, divide the pasta between two warm bowls and serve right away, with more cheese to add at the table.

Pasta Knowledge: EMULSIFICATION

A final—and critical—step in most of the recipes in this book involves emulsifying the fat ingredients (cheese, butter, oil, fat from meat products) with the non-fat liquids, such as pasta water or tomato juices. But what does *emulsify* actually mean? At its simplest, emulsification is when non-fat liquids are broken into tiny droplets that get dispersed in fats, or vice versa—when tiny fat droplets blend into the non-fats. In either case, the result is a blended, creamy consistency.

The process happens more easily, and the creaminess lasts longer, when you have an ingredient that holds the two together: an emulsifier. In these pasta recipes, the starch in the pasta water is the main emulsifier.

The process also requires some agitation to break the liquids into droplets. For a vinaigrette, you'd use a whisk or blender. With pasta, the gentle action of tossing noodles with tongs, shaking the pan, and otherwise messing about with the noodles in the skillet will do the trick.

If your emulsion "breaks" and you find yourself with a slick of butterfat or olive oil, you can try to repair it by whisking in more non-fat liquid, such as another splash of starchy pasta water.

Pasta Knowledge: INCORPORATING GRATED CHEESE

The addition of grated cheese to a pasta dish is the final step that unites all the other ingredients and determines the ultimate consistency of the sauce, so it's critical that you do it right. Your goal is to allow the cheese to slowly melt while it blends into and emulsifies with the water-based ingredients in the sauce, such as pasta water and/or tomato juices. To help control the process, work over very low or no heat and add the cheese and the pasta water a bit at a time. It's key to recognize the point at which the sauce will generously coat the noodles; you're looking for a silky sauce that is not so loose that it's thin or drowning the noodles nor so tight that the pasta becomes dry as the sauce cools and thickens. This is a skill you'll gain through close observation over time.

Cacio e pepe is deceptively simple. You need few ingredients but plenty of technique: Crack—don't grind—your peppercorns for the best texture. Allow the pepper to gently infuse into the oil. Add plenty of starchy pasta water to build the base of the sauce. Add the cheese over very low heat so it doesn't clump. And toss, toss, toss until you have a creamy—not soupy—sauce that cloaks every noodle.

Carbonara

Many people love to eat pasta carbonara but are intimidated by the thought of making it. How do you get the eggs in the sauce to be creamy and rich, not scrambled or, at the other end of the scale, uncooked? I learned to make carbonara classically when I lived in Rome, and I ate it every place I could, gathering carbonara experiences to draw from as I eventually developed my own method . . . which is easier to control than the classic method.

Guanciale is the ideal pork product for the dish, but pancetta is easier to find and works, too. Pecorino Romano is the classic cheese choice, given that the dish was supposedly created by shepherds feeding themselves during the herding season, but I prefer using my standard 50/50 cheese blend of Parmigiano-Reggiano and Pecorino Romano.

And, last, I add scallions—definitely not classic, but a move I learned from Mark Ladner, a chef I worked for and truly admire. The scallions add a pop of color, but they're mostly there as a flavor note and a grassy contrast to the rich sauce.

Serves 2

Kosher salt (preferably Diamond Crystal; see page 17)

1½ teaspoons (4 g) whole black peppercorns, plus more to taste

Extra-virgin olive oil

3 ounces (85 g) guanciale or pancetta, thinly sliced

½ cup (40 g) sliced scallions (about 4 large, white and light green parts only)

8 ounces (225 g) rigatoni, bucatini, or fettucine

1 egg

2 egg yolks

⅓ cup (40 g) 50/50 cheese (half Parmigiano-Reggiano, half Pecorino Romano, grated in a food processor; see page 39), plus more for serving

Fill a large pot (at least 6 quarts/L) with 1 gallon (4 L) of water; add 4 tablespoons (40 g) kosher salt, cover the pot, and bring the water to a boil while you make your sauce. If the water begins to boil before your sauce is ready, turn down the heat, but don't let the volume of the pasta water reduce by boiling off.

Crack the black peppercorns following the method on page 43.

Heat a glug of olive oil in a large skillet or Dutch oven over medium heat. When the oil is hot, add the guanciale and cook slowly until crisp and evenly cooked, 5 to 7 minutes. Remove the skillet from the heat (don't pour off the fat), add the cracked black pepper and the scallions, and set aside to let the pepper and scallions infuse their flavor into the oil.

Bring the pasta water (back) to a boil, add the noodles, and set your timer for 2 minutes less than the shortest suggested cooking time on the package of pasta; this will ideally be 2 minutes before the pasta is al dente. Stir the noodles several times during the first 2 minutes of cooking to prevent them from sticking to the bottom of the pot or otherwise clumping together.

After the noodles have cooked for 2 or 3 minutes, scoop out ½ cup (120 ml) of the pasta water and set aside to cool. Continue cooking the noodles.

Meanwhile, combine the egg and egg yolks in a medium bowl and whisk with a fork until nicely blended. Now, check the temperature of the oil in the skillet—it should not be actually hot, but it must still be warm to the touch. If it's too cool, put the skillet back on the burner for a few seconds.

Add the reserved ½ cup pasta water (which should be at warm room temperature now; if it is still hot, add a few drops of cold water) to the skillet and swirl to blend. Then whisk in the egg

mixture and set aside. (Adding the eggs to warm, not hot or cold, ingredients helps temper it—that is, it gets the eggs used to some heat and begins their thickening process.)

When the timer goes off, start tasting the noodles. When they seem like they are a perfect al dente (see page 22), drain and transfer them to the sauce in the skillet using your preferred method (see page 21), making sure to reserve at least 1 cup (240 ml) of the pasta water.

Your goal now is to gently heat the mixture so that the eggs are cooked (and safe to eat) and thicken to a light custardy texture, but not cook them so much that they coagulate and scramble. Use a silicone spatula or a spoon to stir and scrape the skillet, and regulate the heat by moving the pan on and off the burner; you can also loosen the consistency with a little pasta water. This process will take around 5 minutes.

When the egg-guanciale mixture is looking good, add the grated cheese and toss to emulsify it with the other sauce ingredients, adding splashes of pasta water (or plain hot water, if things are getting too salty) if needed to keep the consistency creamy and prevent the cheese from clumping. Taste and add more salt or pepper if you like.

Divide the pasta between two warm bowls and serve right away, with more cheese to add at the table.

Pasta Knowledge: MANAGING AN EGG-BASED SAUCE

Eggs are great thickeners, creating a lush consistency in a sauce if they are handled properly. That's a big *if*, however: If heated too much or too quickly, the proteins in the eggs will bond together tightly, creating a curdled texture. To avoid the dreaded scrambled-egg effect, never add eggs directly to very hot ingredients; either temper the eggs first by whisking a small amount of hot liquid into them or dilute them by whisking with other liquids (such as the warm pasta water in the carbonara recipe), then whisk that tempered mixture into your sauce. Take your time and cook your egg sauce over low heat, using a silicone spatula to constantly scrape the pan to prevent eggy buildup, until you've achieved the proper creamy consistency.

The key to making carbonara is managing the temperature by adding warm-but-not-hot pasta water to the skillet before whisking in the egg mixture. This means you'll have enough heat to begin thickening the eggs but not so much that they coagulate and become lumpy.

Al Limone with Cream

Essentially a lemony Alfredo, this sauce is simple and elegant and needs a delicate touch. Traditional Alfredo sauce is made from butter, heavy cream, and grated Parmigiano cheese; the al limone version includes both lemon zest and lemon juice. You can make it with regular lemon, but when Meyer lemons are in season, use them for their sweeter perfume and flavor. Note that I add the zest early in the process, so that it can infuse into the cream, but I add the juice only once the sauce is off the heat in order to avoid a cooked-lemon flavor, which to me tastes sort of like lemonade.

Serves 2

Kosher salt (preferably Diamond Crystal; see page 17)

½ cup (120 ml) heavy or whipping cream

2 tablespoons finely grated lemon zest

8 ounces (225 g) mafaldine, fettucine, or pappardelle

1 tablespoon unsalted butter

⅓ cup (40 g) 50/50 cheese (half Parmigiano-Reggiano, half Pecorino Romano, grated in a food processor; see page 39), plus more for serving

2 tablespoons fresh lemon juice, plus more to taste

Finishing-quality extra-virgin olive oil, for serving (optional)

Fill a large pot (at least 6 quarts/L) with 1 gallon (4 L) of water; add 4 tablespoons (40 g) kosher salt, cover the pot, and bring the water to a boil while you make your sauce. If the water begins to boil before your sauce is ready, turn down the heat, but don't let the volume of the pasta water reduce by boiling off.

Heat a large skillet over medium-high heat. Pour in the cream and add the lemon zest. Adjust the heat so the cream bubbles gently and cook until it has reduced and thickened slightly, 2 to 4 minutes. Slide the skillet off the heat.

Bring the pasta water (back) to a boil, add the noodles, and set your timer for 2 minutes less than the shortest suggested cooking time on the package of pasta; this will ideally be 2 minutes before the pasta is al dente. Stir the noodles several times during the first 2 minutes of cooking to prevent them from sticking to the bottom of the pot or otherwise clumping together.

When the timer goes off, start tasting the noodles. When they are a perfect al dente (see page 22), drain and transfer them to the sauce in the skillet using your preferred method (see page 21), making sure to reserve at least 1 cup (240 ml) of the pasta water. You probably won't need any reserved pasta water unless your cream has overreduced and gotten thick, but leave yourself the option.

Pasta Knowledge: WORKING WITH CREAM-BASED SAUCES

Cream sauces for pasta are some of the easiest to make. The key is controlling the thickness of the sauce to produce a satiny cloak of rich cream and not a thick, heavy sauce from which the butterfat is about to break out.

Use a cooking temperature that keeps the cream simmering but not boiling hard; a fast boil can reduce the cream so quickly that you can't monitor it, and if you truly overreduce the cream, you'll break the emulsion and the butterfat will separate out. Remember that a cream sauce will thicken with the addition of cheese and/or starchy pasta water, and the sauce will thicken as it cools.

Before you unite pasta and sauce in your skillet, cook the noodles in your pasta pot all the way to al dente rather than finishing them in the sauce with multiple additions of pasta water (as you do in most of the recipes in this book). This avoids a lot of boiling of the sauce, which can be too aggressive for a very delicate sauce like this one.

Slide the skillet back onto medium heat, toss the noodles in the cream to coat, then add the butter.

Reduce the heat to very low. Add the grated cheese and toss to emulsify it with the cream, adding a few small splashes of pasta water if needed to keep the consistency creamy and prevent the cheese from clumping.

Take the skillet off the heat, add the fresh lemon juice, and toss the noodles again. If you like, add a big drizzle of good olive oil. Taste and add more salt or lemon juice if you like.

Divide the pasta between two warm bowls, shower with more grated cheese, and serve right away.

"Penne" alla Vodka

This is one of the best Italian American pasta recipes of all time, but the penne is the least important part. There are better options for this sauce—fusilli (as pictured) comes to mind (as do rigatoni and paccheri). I'm not alone in my opinion, as I've seen countless menus that list "penne alla vodka" and then serve a dish made with rigatoni.

So the penne's not critical, and frankly, neither is the vodka. It does add a slight edge to the flavor and possibly creates some good chemistry among the other ingredients, but you'll still have a delicious sauce if you leave out the vodka.

What is critical here is the tomato paste, which is the only source of tomato in this recipe. The large amount of tomato paste does some heavy lifting, flavor-wise, meaning you want the sweet fruitiness of tomato as well as the deeper toasty umami flavors that can also come from tomato.

Serves 2

Kosher salt (preferably Diamond Crystal; see page 17)

Extra-virgin olive oil

¾ cup (75 g) thinly sliced onion (slice the onion, then cut the slices in half to make them shorter)

1 or 2 garlic cloves, smashed and thinly sliced

1 teaspoon thinly sliced oil-packed Calabrian chiles (from a jar; remove their seeds before slicing)

1 tablespoon unsalted butter

¼ cup plus 1 tablespoon (75 g) tomato paste

⅓ cup plus 1 tablespoon (90 ml) heavy cream

2 tablespoons vodka (optional)

8 ounces (225 g) fusilli, rigatoni, or penne

⅓ cup (40 g) 50/50 cheese (half Parmigiano-Reggiano, half Pecorino Romano, grated in a food processor; see page 39), plus more for serving

Fill a large pot (at least 6 quarts/L) with 1 gallon (4 L) of water; add 4 tablespoons (40 g) kosher salt, cover the pot, and bring the water to a boil while you make your sauce. If the water begins to boil before your sauce is ready, turn down the heat, but don't let the volume of the pasta water reduce by boiling off.

Heat a glug of olive oil in a large skillet over medium heat. When the oil is hot, add the onion and garlic, and cook until they become translucent and fragrant, 4 to 5 minutes; reduce the heat as needed to prevent them from browning.

Add the chiles and butter and cook for a couple of minutes until the butter has melted and the chiles have shared their flavor with the other ingredients.

Increase the heat to medium-high and add the tomato paste. Cook for another 1 to 2 minutes, spreading the tomato paste thinly on the surface of the pan so it toasts a bit.

Reduce the heat to medium. Scoop out about ½ cup (120 ml) of water from the pasta pot and stir it into the skillet. Add the cream and stir until blended. Add the vodka, if using, and simmer to cook off both the alcohol from the vodka and the raw cream flavor. Slide the skillet off the heat.

Bring the pasta water (back) to a boil, add the noodles, and set your timer for 2 minutes less than the shortest suggested cooking time on the package of pasta; this will ideally be 2 minutes before the pasta is al dente. Stir the noodles several times during the first 2 minutes of cooking to prevent them from sticking to the bottom of the pot or otherwise clumping together.

When the timer goes off, start tasting the noodles. When they are almost a perfect al dente (see page 22), drain and transfer them to the sauce in the skillet using your preferred method (see page 21), making sure to reserve at least 1 cup (240 ml) of the pasta water.

recipe continues →

5
6

Slide the skillet back onto medium heat and finish cooking the noodles, tossing and adding plenty of splashes of pasta water until the noodles are perfectly al dente and the sauce is nicely juicy. If the sauce seems watery, simmer for another few seconds to tighten it up, bearing in mind that the cheese will thicken it.

Reduce the heat to very low. Add the grated cheese and toss to emulsify it with the other sauce ingredients, adding splashes of pasta water (or plain hot water, if things are getting too salty) if needed to keep the consistency creamy and prevent the cheese from clumping. Note that this dish should be a bit saucier and looser than most other pasta dishes. Taste and add more salt if you like.

Divide the pasta between two warm bowls and serve right away, with more cheese to add at the table.

Pasta Knowledge: TOASTING TOMATO PASTE

A spoonful of tomato paste becomes a flavor powerhouse when you toast it. In addition to tomato's fruity notes, you'll get rich caramelized flavor and savory umami notes thanks to tomato's sugar and glutamate content. To unlock the full effect, add the tomato paste to the skillet in which you're making the sauce and smear it around the surface of the pan using your spatula to create a thin layer. As the tomato paste begins to darken around the edges, scoot it around and re-smear it, essentially toasting the sugars and creating deeper flavors. Don't go overboard, of course, because those sugars can go from caramelized to burnt and bitter pretty quickly.

These are the key steps to making penne alla vodka, with or without the penne or the vodka! Simmer the cream with the aromatics (onion, garlic, chiles, and tomato paste). Add the vodka—but it's optional. Cook for a few minutes to reduce and blend the flavors, and to evaporate the alcohol, if using vodka. Add the almost-al dente noodles; here fusilli plays the role of the penne. Cook for a few minutes until the noodles are on point. Reduce the heat and add the cheese, along with a few splashes of water as needed. And there you have it—an excellent penne alla vodka.

Pomodoro

This may be the most hotly debated noodle dish on the planet. You should/shouldn't include garlic, always/never use tomato paste, don't/always add herbs. And no matter how you make yours, my grandmother's version is better. My grandmother actually didn't make this pasta, so I am free to make it however I want, meaning with lightly toasted garlic, tomato paste (and canned tomatoes), and a big ol' handful—or two—of fresh herbs.

This dish is a fine destination for a bottle of excellent, finishing-quality extra-virgin olive oil (see my favorites on page 41). Incorporating a nice big glug at the end will add a silken texture and grassy depth of flavor.

Serves 2

- Kosher salt (preferably Diamond Crystal; see page 17)
- Extra-virgin olive oil
- 5 to 7 garlic cloves, smashed
- Big pinch of dried chile flakes, plus more to taste
- 1 tablespoon tomato paste
- One 15-ounce (425 g) can whole peeled tomatoes, crushed by hand (see page 44), with their juices
- Small handful of fresh basil leaves
- 8 ounces (225 g) spaghetti, bucatini, or penne
- 2 tablespoons unsalted butter
- Small handful of fresh mint leaves (optional)
- 50/50 cheese (half Parmigiano-Reggiano, half Pecorino Romano, grated in a food processor; see page 39), for serving (optional)
- Finishing-quality extra-virgin olive oil, for serving (optional)

Fill a large pot (at least 6 quarts/L) with 1 gallon (4 L) of water; add 4 tablespoons (40 g) kosher salt, cover the pot, and bring the water to a boil while you make your sauce. If the water begins to boil before your sauce is ready, turn down the heat, but don't let the volume of the pasta water reduce by boiling off.

Heat a glug of olive oil in a large skillet over medium heat. Add the garlic and cook, smashing it a bit to break it up and flavor the oil, until it's nicely toasted but not actually browned, 4 to 6 minutes. Take your time with this, reducing the heat a bit if needed.

Add the chile flakes and tomato paste and cook for a minute or two, spreading the tomato paste thinly on the surface of the pan, until it thickens and darkens a bit. Add the crushed tomatoes and their juices and increase the heat to medium-high. Tear about half the basil leaves into a few pieces and add them to the sauce. Cook until the tomatoes have reduced by about half, 3 to 4 minutes. Slide the skillet off the heat.

Bring the pasta water (back) to a boil, add the noodles, and set your timer for 2 minutes less than the shortest suggested cooking time on the package of pasta; this will ideally be 2 minutes before the pasta is al dente. Stir the noodles several times during the first 2 minutes of cooking to prevent them from sticking to the bottom of the pot or otherwise clumping together.

When the timer goes off, start tasting the noodles. When they seem like they are 1½ to 2 minutes away from a perfect al dente (see page 22), drain and transfer them to the sauce in the skillet using your preferred method (see page 21), making sure to reserve at least 1 cup (240 ml) of the pasta water.

Slide the skillet back onto medium heat and finish cooking the noodles, tossing and adding plenty of splashes of pasta water until the noodles are perfectly al dente and the sauce is nicely juicy. If the sauce seems watery, simmer for another few seconds to tighten it up.

Take the skillet off the heat and add the butter, the remaining basil leaves, and the mint, if using (tear up the herbs a bit). Taste and add more salt or chile flakes if you like.

Divide the pasta between two warm bowls. If using, shower with grated cheese and drizzle with some excellent olive oil, and serve right away.

Pasta Knowledge: ADDING FRESH HERBS

I think of fresh herbs more as leafy greens than as ingredients that get added by the teaspoon. I either keep my herb leaves whole or tear them into just a few pieces, which releases some fragrance, and I often add the herbs in two stages—early in the sauce-making process, which allows those leaves to fully integrate into the sauce and contribute their flavor, and then toward the end of cooking, so that their raw flavor and fragrance can still pop. I'll also add torn-up leaves to the finished pasta once it's in the bowl, letting the heat of the dish release the perfume of the herb.

Sausage and Tomato

Hearty and filling, this sauce is a natural springboard for variations. Choose sweet or hot sausage, use dried chile flakes alone or supplement with pickled chiles (and a splash of their pickling liquid), and finish with basil, a shower of breadcrumbs (page 36), or even a dollop of creamy whipped ricotta (page 34). All these variations support rather than overshadow the main player: the sausage.

Serves 2

Kosher salt (preferably Diamond Crystal; see page 17)

6 ounces (180 g) bulk Italian sausage, sweet or hot

Extra-virgin olive oil

3 garlic cloves, smashed

Pinch of dried chile flakes, plus more to taste

1 cup (250 g) canned whole peeled tomatoes, crushed by hand (see page 44), with their juices

8 ounces (225 g) orecchiette, lumache, or rigatoni

1 tablespoon unsalted butter

⅓ cup (40 g) 50/50 cheese (half Parmigiano-Reggiano, half Pecorino Romano, grated in a food processor; see page 39), plus more for serving

Fill a large pot (at least 6 quarts/L) with 1 gallon (4 L) of water; add 4 tablespoons (40 g) kosher salt, cover the pot, and bring the water to a boil while you make your sauce. If the water begins to boil before your sauce is ready, turn down the heat, but don't let the volume of the pasta water reduce by boiling off.

Shape the sausage into 2 patties. Heat a glug of olive oil in a large skillet over medium-high heat. When the oil is hot, add the sausage and sear, smashing the patties down from time to time with your spatula to create a nicely browned crust on the bottom, about 5 minutes.

Flip the patties, add the garlic, and continue cooking until the sausage has browned and the garlic is nicely toasted and softened but not too dark, another 3 to 4 minutes.

Add the chile flakes, then add the crushed tomatoes and their juices and simmer, breaking up the sausage and garlic into smaller bits, until thickened and concentrated, another 3 to 4 minutes. Slide the skillet off the heat.

Bring the pasta water (back) to a boil, add the noodles, and set your timer for 2 minutes less than the shortest suggested cooking time on the package of pasta; this will ideally be 2 minutes before the pasta is al dente. Stir the noodles several times during the first 2 minutes of cooking to prevent them from sticking to the bottom of the pot or otherwise clumping together.

When the timer goes off, start tasting the noodles. When they seem like they are 1½ to 2 minutes away from a perfect al dente (see page 22), drain and transfer them to the sauce in the skillet using your preferred method (see page 21), making sure to reserve at least 1 cup (240 ml) of the pasta water.

Slide the skillet back onto medium heat and finish cooking the noodles, tossing and adding plenty of splashes of pasta water until the noodles are perfectly al dente and the sauce is nicely juicy. If the sauce seems watery, simmer for another few seconds to tighten it up, bearing in mind that the cheese will thicken it.

Reduce the heat to very low. Add the butter and the grated cheese and toss to emulsify them with the other sauce ingredients, adding splashes of pasta water if needed to keep the consistency creamy and prevent the cheese from clumping. Taste and add more salt or chile flakes if you like.

Divide the pasta between two warm bowls, drizzle with a bit of good olive oil, and sprinkle with a bit more cheese. Serve right away.

Pasta Knowledge: COOKING SAUSAGE

My goal when cooking sausage is to develop as much browning as possible, which will ultimately dissolve into the sauce and produce deep, savory flavor. Rather than simply crumbling the sausage directly into the pan, I use a patty method: Shape the sausage into patties to create the maximum surface area. Brown the patties on one side, flip them, brown the second side, and only then break up the patties with a spatula to create smaller bits that are appropriate for a sauce.

'Nduja and Tomato

The excitement in this dish comes from 'nduja, a spicy spreadable sausage originally from Italy's Calabria region. 'Nduja is typically served uncooked, spread on bread or crackers as an appetizer, but you can definitely cook it as well. You'll find plenty of options for buying 'nduja online, including several American-made products (I am a big fan of Underground Meats from Wisconsin; see Resources, page 380). 'Nduja has a long shelf life—around one year unopened and four months once opened, provided you keep it airtight in the refrigerator—which means you can keep some on hand to use whenever you have the urge for some fiery noodles.

Serves 2

Kosher salt (preferably Diamond Crystal; see page 17)

Extra-virgin olive oil

3 garlic cloves, smashed

3 ounces (85 g) 'nduja

1 tablespoon tomato paste

1 cup (250 g) canned whole peeled tomatoes, crushed by hand (see page 44), with their juices

8 ounces (225 g) rigatoni, penne, or ziti

½ cup (60 g) 50/50 cheese (half Parmigiano-Reggiano, half Pecorino Romano, grated in a food processor; see page 39), plus more for serving

1 tablespoon unsalted butter

Fill a large pot (at least 6 quarts/L) with 1 gallon (4 L) of water; add 4 tablespoons (40 g) kosher salt, cover the pot, and bring the water to a boil while you make your sauce. If the water begins to boil before your sauce is ready, turn down the heat, but don't let the volume of the pasta water reduce by boiling off.

Heat a glug of olive oil in a large skillet over medium-high heat. When the oil is hot, add the garlic and cook gently, breaking it up a bit with your spatula, until it is nicely toasted and fragrant but not too brown, 3 to 4 minutes.

Add the 'nduja and smash it down a bit, then cook until it starts to get slightly browned and the oil separates out, about 4 minutes.

Add the tomato paste and cook, stirring and smearing the tomato paste onto the surface of the pan, until it has darkened, 2 minutes.

Add the crushed tomatoes and their juices and simmer, stirring frequently, until reduced by about half, another 4 minutes or so. Slide the skillet off the heat.

Bring the pasta water (back) to a boil, add the noodles, and set your timer for 2 minutes less than the shortest suggested cooking time on the package of pasta; this will ideally be 2 minutes before the pasta is al dente. Stir the noodles several times during the first 2 minutes of cooking to prevent them from sticking to the pot or clumping together.

When the timer goes off, start tasting the noodles. When they seem like they are 1½ to 2 minutes away from a perfect al dente (see page 22), drain and transfer them to the sauce in the skillet using your preferred method (see page 21), making sure to reserve at least 1 cup (240 ml) of the pasta water.

Slide the skillet back onto medium heat and finish cooking the noodles, tossing and adding plenty of splashes of pasta water until the noodles are perfectly al dente and the sauce is nicely juicy. If the sauce seems watery, simmer for another few seconds to tighten it up, bearing in mind that the cheese will thicken it.

Reduce the heat to very low. Add the grated cheese and toss to emulsify it with the other sauce ingredients, adding splashes of pasta water (or plain hot water, if things are getting too salty) if needed to keep the consistency creamy and prevent the cheese from clumping. Add the butter and toss to blend. Taste and add more salt if you like.

Divide the pasta between two warm bowls and serve right away, with more cheese to add at the table.

Pasta Knowledge: INTRODUCING 'NDUJA

'Nduja (pronounced "en-DOO-ya") is a spicy pork sausage originally from the Calabria region of southern Italy. 'Nduja can be difficult to find in the United States, as it's a relatively new thing here, hitting the scene only about ten years ago. It is made with a combination of pork meat and fat, as well as a heavy dose of high-heat Calabrian chiles. Lightly fermented and sometimes lightly smoked, 'nduja has a specific and addictive flavor, full of umami balanced by a light sour tang. Most often served uncooked, as a spread, 'nduja can also be lightly sautéed and incorporated into cooked dishes. The idea is simply to warm and loosen it so that it blends with the other ingredients; you're not aggressively browning it the way you would brown a typical pork sausage. As you cook 'nduja, the fat will separate from the meaty part, carrying with it the luscious pork and chile flavors.

Meatballs with Tomato Sauce, and More

Spaghetti and meatballs is a classic, and when it's made with care, the dish is close to perfect. Of course I mess with it a little bit, because why not try to improve on perfection? First, think of the "spaghetti" loosely. Spaghetti noodles are great, but so are busiate, mafaldine, fusilli col buco, bucatini, and pappardelle. And think about using a couple of finishing touches that will exceed expectations—a dollop of creamy whipped ricotta with a contrasting shower of crunchy breadcrumbs. Both are optional, both fantastic.

Serves 2 or 3

Extra-virgin olive oil

6 to 9 uncooked Beef and Pork Meatballs (page 131; 3 per person, or as many as you like)

3 or 4 garlic cloves, smashed

¼ teaspoon dried chile flakes (or more if you like)

2 tablespoons tomato paste

One 15-ounce (425 g) can whole peeled tomatoes, crushed by hand (see page 44), with their juices

2 tablespoons unsalted butter

Kosher salt (preferably Diamond Crystal; see page 17)

Freshly ground black pepper

Small handful of fresh basil leaves (optional)

8 ounces (225 g) busiate, mafaldine, or fusilli col buco

⅓ cup (40 g) 50/50 cheese (half Parmigiano-Reggiano, half Pecorino Romano, grated in a food processor; see page 39), plus more for serving

2 or 3 spoonfuls Whipped Plain Ricotta (page 34; optional)

2 to 3 tablespoons Dried Breadcrumbs (page 36; optional)

Heat a generous glug of olive oil in a large skillet or Dutch oven over medium-high heat. When the oil is hot, add the meatballs, working in batches if needed to avoid crowding the pan. Sear the meatballs until browned on all sides, 2 to 3 minutes per side (if something round can have "sides"). Set aside.

Pour off the fat from the pan, but don't scrape out the browned bits from the meatballs (unless they are burned). Add another generous glug of olive oil to the pan and heat over medium heat. When it's hot, add the garlic and cook gently, smashing the cloves with your spatula and scraping up any browned bits so they don't burn, until soft and lightly toasted but not browned, 3 to 4 minutes. Add the chile flakes (use more if you like it spicy) and cook for another few seconds.

Add the tomato paste and cook, spreading it on the surface of the pan, until lightly toasted, 1 to 2 minutes. Add the crushed tomatoes and their juices, butter, 1 teaspoon salt, several twists of freshly ground black pepper, and, if you like, fresh basil leaves, tearing them into pieces.

Bring to a simmer and cook, stirring frequently, until the sauce has reduced and thickened a bit, about 10 minutes. Taste and adjust the seasoning, knowing that the sauce will get tastier as the meatballs cook.

Return the browned meatballs and any accumulated juices to the pan, nestling them into the sauce. Cover the pan and simmer gently, stirring occasionally, until the meatballs are thoroughly cooked and the sauce has reduced and concentrated even more, 30 to 40 minutes. (You can also cook the meatballs in a 300°F/150°C oven.) Stir things around a few times during cooking, scraping down the sides of the pan to capture the tasty sauce along the edges.

recipe continues →

Note: **You can cook the meatballs to this point up to 1 day ahead; refrigerate everything if waiting more than 2 hours to finish the dish. Then, when you're ready to continue, reheat until the sauce is simmering and the meatballs are heated through.**

Fill a large pot (at least 6 quarts/L) with 1 gallon (4 L) of water; add 4 tablespoons (40 g) kosher salt, cover the pot, and bring the water to a boil. If the water begins to boil before your sauce is ready, turn down the heat, but don't let the volume of the pasta water reduce by boiling off.

When the meatballs are done cooking (or are heated through, if you're reheating them), transfer them to a small saucepan, leaving most of the sauce behind, and keep them warm over low heat. This is so they won't get in the way while you're finishing the noodles in the tomato sauce. Slide the skillet with the sauce off the heat.

Bring the pasta water (back) to a boil, if needed. Add the noodles and set your timer for 2 minutes less than the shortest suggested cooking time on the package of pasta; this will ideally be 2 minutes before the pasta is al dente. Stir the noodles several times during the first 2 minutes of cooking to prevent them from sticking to the bottom of the pot or otherwise clumping together.

When the timer goes off, start tasting the noodles. When they seem like they are 1½ to 2 minutes away from a perfect al dente (see page 22), drain and transfer them to the sauce in the skillet using your preferred method (see page 21), making sure to reserve at least 1 cup (240 ml) of the pasta water.

Slide the skillet back onto medium heat and finish cooking the noodles, tossing and adding plenty of splashes of pasta water until the noodles are perfectly al dente and the sauce is nicely juicy. If the sauce seems watery, simmer for another few seconds to tighten it up, bearing in mind that the cheese will thicken it.

Reduce the heat to very low. Add the grated cheese and toss to emulsify it with the other sauce ingredients, adding splashes of pasta water (or plain hot water, if things are getting too salty) if needed to keep the consistency creamy and prevent the cheese from clumping. Return the meatballs to the pan and cook gently for a few seconds to reacquaint them with the sauce.

Divide the pasta and meatballs between two or three warm bowls. Top with a dollop of whipped ricotta and a shower of breadcrumbs, if using. Serve right away, with more grated cheese to add at the table.

Beef and Pork Meatballs

If you are a meat-eater, you probably love a good meatball, which is why you should always have a batch of these (uncooked) in the freezer.

Makes about 2 dozen 1-ounce (30 g) meatballs

½ cup (25 g) breadcrumbs (panko-style or homemade; see page 36)

¼ cup (60 ml) whole milk

Extra-virgin olive oil

½ cup (65 g) finely chopped onion

¼ cup (50 g) finely diced pancetta

8 ounces (225 g) ground beef

8 ounces (225 g) ground pork

⅓ cup (40 g) 50/50 cheese (half Parmigiano-Reggiano, half Pecorino Romano, grated in a food processor; see page 39)

1 egg, lightly beaten

2 tablespoons finely chopped fresh flat-leaf parsley leaves

1 tablespoon minced garlic

1 teaspoon dried oregano

½ teaspoon dried chile flakes, plus more to taste

1 teaspoon kosher salt (preferably Diamond Crystal; see page 17), plus more to taste

¼ teaspoon freshly ground black pepper, plus more to taste

Line a sheet pan with parchment paper or foil so it's ready to receive the shaped meatballs.

Put the breadcrumbs in a small bowl, pour the milk over them, and soak for a few minutes until the milk has been absorbed. Set aside.

Heat a small glug of olive oil in a small skillet over medium heat. When the oil is hot, add the onion and pancetta and cook until the onion is soft and golden and the pancetta has rendered most of its fat and is getting brown and crisp, 8 to 10 minutes. Set aside to cool.

Combine the ground beef, ground pork, pancetta and onion, soaked breadcrumbs, grated cheese, egg, parsley, garlic, oregano, chile flakes, kosher salt, and black pepper in a large bowl. Using your hands, mix gently until everything is well combined. You want all the ingredients evenly dispersed, but you don't want to squeeze or compact the mixture, which could make your meatballs too dense.

Check to see that you're happy with the seasoning level by frying a teaspoon or so of the mixture and tasting. If needed, add more salt, pepper, or chile flakes.

Using your hands, gently shape the mixture into 1-ounce (30 g) meatballs, about the size of a walnut in the shell. If things get sticky as you work, rinse your hands in cool water. Place the rolled meatballs on the prepared sheet pan.

If you want to freeze the meatballs to use later in a sauce, put the sheet pan in the freezer, uncovered, and leave until the meatballs are firm, then transfer them to ziplock freezer bags or other freezer containers. Because they were frozen solid before being piled together, they will separate easily, so you can retrieve however many you want to use and leave the rest frozen.

To use frozen meatballs, either thaw them in the refrigerator overnight or let them sit at room temperature until the meat at the surface has thawed, about an hour. Then brown and finish them in the sauce of your choice, as directed in the related recipes. You'll need to cook still-frozen meatballs for a bit longer than what the recipes call for to make sure they are cooked through.

Meatballs in Kale Sauce

This is a lighter, fresher, and greener version of a classic spaghetti-and-meatball supper. For this recipe, I suggest cooking the meatballs on a sheet pan in the oven, instead of in the sauce as I do in the other meatball recipes; the kale sauce doesn't want to be simmered for too long.

Serves 2 or 3

Extra-virgin olive oil

6 to 9 Beef and Pork Meatballs (page 131; 3 per person, or as many as you like)

1 or 2 garlic cloves, smashed

Big pinch of dried chile flakes

1 recipe Kale Sauce (page 341)

Kosher salt (preferably Diamond Crystal; see page 17)

8 ounces (225 g) pappardelle rigate, fettucine, or spaghetti

⅓ cup (40 g) 50/50 cheese (half Parmigiano-Reggiano, half Pecorino Romano, grated in a food processor; see page 39), plus more for serving

2 or 3 spoonfuls Whipped Lemon Ricotta (page 35; optional)

Heat the oven to 350°F (175°C) and line a small sheet pan with parchment paper or foil.

Heat a generous glug of olive oil in a large skillet or Dutch oven over medium-high heat. When the oil is hot, add the meatballs, working in batches if needed to avoid crowding the pan. Sear the meatballs until browned on all sides, 2 to 3 minutes per side (if something round can have "sides"). Transfer the meatballs to the prepared sheet pan (don't clean the skillet) and bake until cooked through, 18 to 25 minutes.

Pour off the fat from the skillet, but don't scrape out the browned bits (unless they are burned). Add a generous glug of olive oil to the skillet and heat over medium heat. Add the garlic and cook gently, smashing the cloves with your spatula and scraping up any browned bits so they don't burn, until soft and lightly toasted but not browned, 3 to 4 minutes. Add the chile flakes and cook for another few seconds.

Add the kale sauce, stir everything together, and bring to a simmer. Return the cooked meatballs and any accumulated juices to the pan, nestling them into the sauce. Simmer until the meatballs are thoroughly warmed through and integrated into the sauce. Slide the skillet off the heat.

Fill a large pot (at least 6 quarts/L) with 1 gallon (4 L) of water; add 4 tablespoons (40 g) kosher salt, cover, and bring the water to a boil. Add the noodles and set your timer for 2 minutes less than the shortest suggested cooking time on the package of pasta; this will ideally be 2 minutes before the pasta is al dente. Stir the noodles several times during the first 2 minutes of cooking to prevent them from sticking to the pot or otherwise clumping together.

When the timer goes off, start tasting the noodles. When they seem like they are almost a perfect al dente (see page 22), drain and transfer them to the sauce in the skillet using your preferred method (see page 21), making sure to reserve at least 1 cup (240 ml) of the pasta water.

Slide the skillet back onto medium heat and finish cooking the noodles, tossing and adding plenty of splashes of pasta water until the noodles are perfectly al dente and the sauce is nicely juicy, taking care not to break up the baked meatballs. If the sauce seems watery, simmer for another few seconds to tighten it up, bearing in mind that the cheese will thicken it.

Reduce the heat to very low. Add the grated cheese and toss to emulsify it with the other sauce ingredients, adding splashes of pasta water (or plain hot water, if things are getting too salty) if needed to keep the consistency creamy and prevent the cheese from clumping.

Divide the pasta and meatballs between two or three warm bowls. Dollop with whipped lemon ricotta, if using, and serve right away, with more cheese to add at the table.

Bolognese-Style Lasagna (Customizable)

Lasagna alla Bolognese is an iconic dish, rich and elegant, constructed from multiple fine layers of pasta, meat sauce, and béchamel, with copious amounts of grated Parmigiano. I think you can't eat true lasagna alla Bolognese unless you're in Bologna. And for chefs like me who love tradition but also can't resist improvising, this style of lasagna is a perfect springboard for a small amount of customization, as you'll see at the end of this recipe.

For this lasagna, I like to use no-boil lasagna noodles because they are thinner and flatter than the typical ruffle-edged lasagna noodles. While no-boil means, well, you don't need to boil them before using them, actually you *do* need to with this recipe. The sauces in this style of lasagna are fairly dry, compared to a marinara sauce in an American-style lasagna, and they don't contribute quite enough moisture to the no-boil noodle to give it the right texture. So boil the noodles quickly before use, not to fully cook them but to give them a boost of hydration. Yes, boiling a no-boil noodle might seem like a hassle, but it's worth the small effort.

Makes one 9 by 13-inch (22.5 by 32.5 cm) lasagna, enough to serve 6

For the Béchamel:

6 tablespoons (90 g) unsalted butter

4 tablespoons (32 g) all-purpose flour

3 cups (720 ml) whole milk

½ teaspoon kosher salt (preferably Diamond Crystal; see page 17)

Freshly ground black pepper

Freshly grated nutmeg

For Assembly:

4 cups (900 g) ragu of your choice (see suggestions on page 136; recipes begin on page 56)

Kosher salt (preferably Diamond Crystal; see page 17)

9 ounces (250 g) no-boil lasagna noodles (about 15 sheets)

1½ cups (180 g) 50/50 cheese (half Parmigiano-Reggiano, half Pecorino Romano, grated in a food processor; see page 39)

2 tablespoons unsalted butter, cut into small bits

Make the béchamel: Melt the butter in a medium saucepan over medium heat. Add the flour, stir to make a smooth, liquidy paste, and cook for about 3 minutes so the raw flour flavor cooks out. Add the milk, whisking vigorously to avoid lumps . . . but don't worry if things do get lumpy, as most of the lumps will cook out or you can put the sauce through a strainer.

Bring the sauce to a simmer, then whisk in the salt, several twists of black pepper, and a small grating of fresh nutmeg. Simmer the béchamel until the texture is velvety smooth and the flavor is rich and creamy, about 20 minutes, scraping down any sauce from the sides of the pan and whisking it in.

When it's ready, let the sauce cool to room temperature. If the sauce develops a skin, whisk it into the sauce before using.

Assemble the lasagna: If the ragu is straight from the fridge, warm it gently in a pan so that it's spreadable; if it still seems stiff, loosen the ragu with a few drops of water.

recipe continues →

Line a sheet pan with parchment paper and set it next to your stove. Bring a large pot of water to a boil and add a generous amount of salt.

Add about 5 lasagna sheets to the pot (cooking in batches prevents the flat sheets from sticking together). Boil for 3 minutes, then lift them out, let the water drip off, and lay them flat on the prepared sheet pan. Repeat with the remaining sheets. Do not overlap the boiled sheets on the pan; add another layer of parchment if needed.

Heat the oven to 400°F (205°C).

Spread a few tablespoons of béchamel over the bottom of a 9 by 13-inch (22.5 by 32.5 cm) baking dish; this is just so the noodles don't stick to the dish.

Arrange three sheets of pasta side by side in the baking dish to create the first layer. It's okay if the noodles don't totally fill the dish, as they will swell up a bit and fill it out better later.

Gently spread about ½ cup (125 g) béchamel over the noodles, taking care not to dislodge them.

Spread about 1 cup (250 g) ragu over the béchamel. It's easiest to distribute small dollops of the ragu over the surface and then use your spoon to nudge them closer together. You don't need to have total coverage; just do your best.

Sprinkle on about ¼ cup (30 g) of the cheese, then arrange a second layer of 3 pasta sheets on top.

Repeat the process until you have used all the pasta and ragu; you should end with a layer of noodles. Spread the final portion of béchamel on the noodles, sprinkle with the remaining cheese, and dot the top with the butter.

Bake the lasagna until it's fully heated through, browned on top, and merrily bubbling around the edges, 25 to 35 minutes. Let it cool for at least 15 minutes before cutting and serving. Keep any leftovers tightly covered in the refrigerator for up to 3 days; reheat using the tips in Neater Slices, Crispier Edges (page 138).

MORE WAYS

Keep the basic elements of ragu, béchamel, pasta noodle, and cheese and make variations within that framework.

Ragus. The ragus that work best in lasagna are those with a fine-ish consistency, with evenly sized bits of vegetable and/or meat and no big chunks, which will allow you to stack up the pasta and keep neat, even layers. Try the White Bolognese with Cream (page 94), Sausage Ragu (page 89), or Lamb Ragu (page 77), or either of a pair of the meatless ones—Nut Ragu (page 71) or Charred Vegetable Ragu (page 56).

Béchamel. A basic béchamel (white sauce) will be delicious with any of these ragus, but you can modify this component as well, seasoning it with fresh herbs, using a rich chicken or meat broth along with or instead of the milk, or upping the cheese quotient by adding grated cheese to the béchamel itself.

Neater Slices, Crispier Edges

Lasagna, no matter what style, is so much about texture, with distinct layers of tender noodle and filling, and especially the crisp edges where the cheese has browned and bubbled.

The first way to optimize your lasagna's texture is to do nothing. Meaning when you take the baked lasagna out of the oven, don't cut it—don't even touch it—for 15 to 20 minutes. During this waiting period, the cheeses and béchamel will go from super runny to still tender but firm enough to hold their shape when you cut a slice, ensuring that every bite will contain the right ratio of creamy-cheesy to the other ingredients.

The ideal scenario is to bake the lasagna the day before you want to serve it, let it cool entirely (in the fridge, once it's at room temp), and then reheat it. You'll still need to let the dish sit for a few minutes when you pull it out of the oven, but the overnight rest will have firmed everything up, allowing the noodles to drink up flavors from the sauce and become altogether better.

The ultimate reheating scenario—this is how restaurants do it—is to bake the lasagna, cool it completely, cut slices, and then reheat the slices in a hot oven, drizzled with some good olive oil and showered with more grated Parmigiano. All four sides (and the top) will get that crisping kiss of heat.

American-Style Lasagna (Slightly Customizable)

In addition to the Italian style of lasagna, I also love to make what I call "American" lasagna, of which every family probably has a version. This type of lasagna uses a tomato sauce, with or without meat, and plenty of cheese—ricotta, mozzarella, and Parmigiano are the basics, but you could use whatever you like as long as it's a good melter, meaning it's whole-milk (not "part-skim") and fairly low in moisture.

American lasagna is adaptable, though it's pretty perfect in its simplicity. The best places to customize are the tomato sauce, adding ground meat if you like, making it spicier with dried chile flakes, or adding fennel, red bell pepper, or some fresh hot chile to the soffritto of onion, carrot, and celery. I also sometimes use whipped basil or tomato ricotta in the filling, but I mix it half and half with plain ricotta to keep the consistency light and to preserve the milkiness of the plain ricotta.

Because I'm not trying to create a multilayered confection like the Bolognese-Style Lasagna (page 135), I use regular lasagna noodles here, not the thinner no-boil noodles. This lasagna has only three layers of noodles, so you want each one to have some presence.

Makes one 9 by 13-inch (22.5 by 32.5 cm) lasagna, enough to serve 6

Extra-virgin olive oil

Kosher salt (preferably Diamond Crystal; see page 17)

1 pound (450 g) lasagna noodles (not no-boil)

2 cups (450 g) whole-milk ricotta, or 1 cup (225 g) ricotta plus 1 cup (225 g) Whipped Basil Ricotta (page 35) or Whipped Tomato Ricotta (page 35)

1 cup (120 g) 50/50 cheese (half Parmigiano-Reggiano, half Pecorino Romano, grated in a food processor; see page 39)

1 teaspoon finely grated lemon zest

½ cup (15 g) finely chopped fresh flat-leaf parsley leaves

1 recipe Marinara Sauce (page 67)

1 pound (450 g) whole-milk, low-moisture mozzarella (from Wisconsin, if possible—my home state), shredded on the large holes of a box grater (don't use pregrated)

1½ tablespoons unsalted butter (optional)

Heat the oven to 375°F (190°C). Lightly oil a sheet pan.

Fill a large pot (at least 6 quarts/L) with 1 gallon (4 L) of water; add 4 tablespoons (40 g) kosher salt, cover the pot, and bring the water to a boil. Add the lasagna noodles and set your timer for 2 minutes less than the shortest suggested cooking time on the package of pasta; this will ideally be 2 minutes before the pasta is al dente. Stir the noodles several times during the first 2 minutes of cooking to prevent them from sticking to the bottom of the pot or otherwise clumping together.

When the timer goes off, start tasting the noodles. When they seem like they are not quite al dente (see page 22), drain in a colander or otherwise get them out of the water and lay them on the prepared sheet pan. Avoid overlapping them if possible so they don't stick together; add another layer of parchment if needed.

Combine the ricotta, half the 50/50 cheese, the lemon zest, and the parsley in a large bowl and mix until blended.

recipe continues →

Spread about one-quarter of the marinara sauce over the bottom of a 9 by 13-inch (22.5 by 32.5 cm) baking dish. Arrange the noodles in an even layer on top, cutting and piecing them as needed to cover the surface.

Spread another quarter of the sauce over the noodles. Dollop half the ricotta mixture over the sauce and gently spread it to make as even a layer as possible (don't worry if you can't cover all the gaps). Sprinkle on about one-third of the mozzarella.

Arrange a second layer of noodles over the cheeses. Spread another quarter of the sauce over the noodles. Dollop the remaining ricotta mixture over the sauce and spread it. Sprinkle on another third of the mozzarella.

Arrange a final layer of noodles over the mozzarella. Spread the remaining sauce over the noodles. Distribute the remaining mozzarella over the sauce. Sprinkle the remaining ½ cup (60 g) 50/50 cheese over everything. Cut the butter, if using, into little pieces and dot the surface with them.

Set the baking dish on a sheet pan to catch any drips. Bake until it's hot, bubbling, and browned on top and around the edges, about 45 minutes. Let cool for at least 15 minutes before cutting and serving, which lets the cheeses set up a bit so they don't run out from the noodles. Keep any leftovers tightly covered in the refrigerator for up to 3 days; reheat using the tips in Neater Slices, Crispier Edges (page 138).

Chicken Noodle Soup

At its heart, chicken noodle soup is a pasta dish, too. Sure, meaty chicken is important, and rich savory broth is key, but most critical are the noodles—tender, plentiful, and of course slurpable.

I add a variety of seasonal vegetables to my chicken broth, cooking them in the liquid right before serving the soup. They should be added in the order of cooking time needed (longest-cooking to quickest-cooking), and as always, think about the size—smaller pieces cook faster.

I cook the noodles separately in salted water rather than in the broth, which would make the noodles tasty but would drink up too much broth. And by noodles, I don't mean those short "egg noodles" that are typically used in chicken noodle soup. I use long pasta noodles—bucatini, fettucine, spaghetti, pappardelle, tagliatelle, linguini, even mafaldine. I add the al dente noodles to the soup bowls, ramen-style, right before I'm ready to serve and then I pour on the hot broth, chicken, and vegetables.

And because I'm a huge fan of Vietnamese pho, I adopted the idea of serving a sidecar of pho-inspired customizable add-ins at the table—fresh basil, fresh mint, fresh tarragon (this chicken soup is tarragon's reason for being), citrus wedges, chile oil, and more.

Spring (top)

Early summer (bottom)

Chicken Noodle Soup (Customizable)

If the chicken has giblets, use all of them except the liver (sauté that up with some onion, chop it, and spread it on toast as a cook's snack). If you can get your hands on some spare parts, such as chicken necks, backs, feet, or wings, use them in addition to the whole chicken as a way to supercharge the flavor and body of the broth.

I don't list specific amounts for the seasonal veg add-ins or the at-the-table aromatics because that depends on how many people you're serving and what you have available, so figure that all of that is "to taste."

Makes about 3 quarts (3 L) soup broth with chicken, to serve 6

For the Broth and Chicken:

One 3½- to 4-pound (1.5 to 1.8 kg) whole chicken, including neck and other giblets but not the liver

2 medium carrots, quartered

2 celery stalks, quartered

2 medium onions, quartered

3 or 4 garlic cloves, smashed

10 whole black peppercorns

Small handful of fresh parsley stems

1 sprig fresh thyme

1 small dried red chile, such as chile de árbol

1 medium jalapeño, quartered (optional)

1 tablespoon kosher salt (preferably Diamond Crystal; see page 17)

For the Aromatics:

Extra-virgin olive oil

1 cup (120 g) diced carrot

1 cup (120 g) diced celery

1 cup (120 g) diced fennel (optional)

1 cup (150 g) diced onion

Pinch of kosher salt (preferably Diamond Crystal; see page 17)

For the Noodles:

Kosher salt (preferably Diamond Crystal; see page 17)

About 2 ounces (60 g) dried pasta noodles per serving, preferably a long shape

Add-Ins for the Table (optional):

Small handfuls of fresh basil, mint, and/or tarragon leaves

Sliced radishes

Small handful of lettuce leaves (the crunchier, the better)

Lemon or lime wedges

Sliced fresh chiles

Chile Crisp (page 37)

Chile oil

Finishing-quality extra-virgin olive oil

Lemon Agrumato (lemony extra-virgin olive oil; see page 41)

Make the chicken broth: Put the chicken and any giblet pieces in a large pot with plenty of room for water; if you need to cut the chicken into pieces, that's fine. Add the carrots, celery, onions, garlic, peppercorns, parsley stems, thyme, dried chile, and jalapeño, if using.

Add about 4 quarts (4 L) water and the kosher salt; you want the chicken to be covered, so if it's not, add more water. The goal is to end up with about 3 quarts (3 L) rich broth after reducing.

Bring the water to a simmer and simmer until the chicken is fully cooked, 1 to 1½ hours, skimming off the foam that develops during the first 30 minutes or so of cooking. Be sure the meat is fully cooked.

Remove the chicken from the pot and let it cool in a large bowl or on a sheet pan. When it's cool enough to handle, pull off all the meat and set the meat aside.

Return the chicken bones and skin to the pot and simmer for another hour or so to extract all the good flavor and collagen from the carcass, adding more water as needed to keep the ingredients covered.

Discard the carcass and strain the broth into another big pot or a large bowl.

Put the broth back on the heat, taste it (don't adjust the seasoning yet; just get a baseline flavor), and simmer gently, uncovered, until it's reduced and rich, 30 to 45 minutes, depending on how much water you added.

Cook the aromatics: Heat a glug of olive oil in a large skillet over medium heat. When the oil is hot, add the carrot, celery, fennel, if using, and onion along with a pinch of salt. Cook gently until the vegetables are sweet, soft, and fragrant but not at all browned, 10 to 12 minutes.

Add the aromatic vegetables to the finished chicken broth. Taste and adjust the seasoning so the flavors are balanced. This is your chicken soup platform. You can add just shredded chicken and noodles and have a beautiful soup, or you can add seasonal vegetables and more aromatics of your choice to make an event out of it. You can also freeze the broth at this point; use within 3 to 4 months for the best flavor. Freeze the chicken meat separately, well wrapped.

Assemble and serve: Bring to a simmer as much broth as you plan to serve. A good guideline is 2 cups (480 ml) of broth per person for a full-meal portion of soup with some added vegetables and aromatics.

If you are using seasonal vegetables, add them to the broth and simmer until they are tender.

Meanwhile, fill a large pot (at least 6 quarts/L) with 1 gallon (4 L) of water; add 4 tablespoons (40 g) kosher salt, cover the pot, and add the noodles. Set your timer for 2 minutes less than the shortest suggested cooking time on the package of pasta. Stir the noodles several times during the first 2 minutes of cooking to prevent them from sticking to the bottom of the pot or otherwise clumping together.

When the timer goes off, start tasting the noodles. When they seem like they are almost a perfect al dente (see page 22), drain well and transfer them to your soup bowls.

Midsummer

Late summer

Arrange the add-ins of your choice (herbs, radishes, lettuce, et cetera) on trays or little plates in your serving area or at the table.

Add some shredded or chopped chicken meat to the broth and simmer for just a couple of minutes to reheat it.

Ladle the broth and chicken into each noodle-loaded soup bowl and serve hot, inviting diners to customize their soup as they like with any or all of the add-ins.

MORE WAYS

The vegetables listed below fall in the order in which you'd add them to the broth to cook, from longest-cooking to shortest-cooking. There's no need to use all the vegetables in the same pot of soup, as things might get a bit crowded, but use what looks most delicious.

Spring (my favorite seasonal variation for this soup): New potatoes (halved if large), nettles (stems removed, leaves left whole; see page 182), ramps (bulbs and stems sliced, leaves left whole), peas, sugar snaps (sliced), asparagus (sliced), fresh or jarred artichoke hearts (halved or quartered).

Early summer: Potatoes (halved if large), yellow beets (cut into chunks), turnips (sliced), and whatever is still around from the spring vegetable lineup.

Midsummer: Cauliflower (florets and chopped stem), broccoli (florets and chopped stalk), summer squash (small chunks), string beans (cut into pieces or in julienne).

Late summer: Fresh shell beans, sweet peppers (diced), corn kernels, tomatoes (in chunks, or halved cherry tomatoes). Eggplant is also wonderful; I roast it whole and then scoop out the flesh and swirl it into the soup.

Fall: Brussels sprouts (halved or quartered), collards (cut into ribbons), kale (leaves torn into pieces), mushrooms (chunks or slices).

Winter: Cabbage (sliced), parsnips (diced), sweet potatoes (sliced), turnips (diced). In addition, I'll add a celery root puree along with diced celery root, or winter squash puree and diced winter squash.

Fall (top)

Winter (bottom)

Spring

Artichokes with Tomato and Mint

I always emphasize the importance of using fresh seasonal produce, but with artichokes, you can cheat and use canned artichoke hearts. Trimming a whole fresh artichoke to use just the heart (the succulent base and a few tender interior leaves surrounding it) is a ton of work and wasteful; plus, artichokes can be expensive. If you'd like to use fresh, however, please do; be sure to steam them until tender before using in the recipe.

Serves 2

Kosher salt (preferably Diamond Crystal; see page 17)

Extra-virgin olive oil

3 or 4 garlic cloves, smashed

1½ cups (200 g) artichoke hearts (canned is fine), halved or quartered if large

½ teaspoon dried chile flakes, plus more to taste

1 tablespoon tomato paste

1 cup (250 g) canned whole peeled tomatoes, crushed by hand (see page 44), with their juices

Small handful of fresh mint leaves

8 ounces (225 g) spaghetti alla chitarra, spaghetti, or linguine

⅓ cup (40 g) 50/50 cheese (half Parmigiano-Reggiano, half Pecorino Romano, grated in a food processor; see page 39), plus more for serving

Finishing-quality extra-virgin olive oil, for serving (optional)

Fill a large pot (at least 6 quarts/L) with 1 gallon (4 L) of water; add 4 tablespoons (40 g) kosher salt, cover the pot, and bring the water to a boil while you make your sauce. If the water begins to boil before your sauce is ready, turn down the heat, but don't let the volume of the pasta water reduce by boiling off.

Heat a glug of olive oil in a large skillet over medium heat. When the oil is hot, add the garlic and cook gently, breaking it up a bit with your spatula, until it is soft, nicely toasted (but not too brown), and fragrant, 3 to 4 minutes.

If you're using fresh artichoke hearts, steam them until tender. If using canned artichoke hearts, blot them to remove excess liquid. Add the artichoke hearts to the skillet and cook until they are starting to get a bit brown around the edges, 5 to 7 minutes; they will start to fall apart, which is fine.

Add the chile flakes, then add the tomato paste and cook, stirring and spreading the tomato paste thinly on the pan so it toasts and darkens a bit, about 30 seconds. Add the crushed tomatoes and their juices and about half the mint (tear the leaves into a few pieces) and continue cooking, stirring frequently, until the sauce has reduced by half, 4 to 5 minutes. Slide the skillet off the heat.

Bring the pasta water (back) to a boil, add the noodles, and set your timer for 2 minutes less than the shortest suggested cooking time on the package of pasta; this will ideally be 2 minutes before the pasta is al dente. Stir the noodles several times during the first 2 minutes of cooking to prevent them from sticking to the bottom of the pot or otherwise clumping together.

When the timer goes off, start tasting the noodles. When they seem like they are 1½ to 2 minutes away from a perfect al dente (see page 22), drain and transfer them to the sauce

in the skillet using your preferred method (see page 21), making sure to reserve at least 1 cup (240 ml) of the pasta water.

Slide the skillet back onto medium heat and finish cooking the noodles, tossing and adding plenty of splashes of pasta water until the noodles are perfectly al dente and the sauce is nicely juicy. If the sauce seems watery, simmer for another few seconds to tighten it up, bearing in mind that the cheese will thicken it.

Reduce the heat to very low. Add the grated cheese and toss to emulsify it with the other sauce ingredients, adding splashes of pasta water (or plain hot water, if things are getting too salty) if needed to keep the consistency creamy and prevent the cheese from clumping. Add the rest of the mint. Taste and add more salt or chile flakes if you like.

Divide the pasta between two warm bowls, drizzle with a nice thread of good artichoke-y olive oil if you have it, and serve right away, with more cheese to add at the table.

The Flavors of Olive Oil

A bowl of pasta is a perfect destination for a drizzle of high-quality extra-virgin olive oil, or what is known as a "finishing oil." The choice of finishing oils is vast and the flavor profiles vary according to the variety of olive, the growing region, and the farming and processing methods. While all good olive oils taste and smell like olives in some way, most have notes and nuances of many other flavors, including other fruits and vegetables.

Some olive oils have strong notes of artichoke, especially those made from Frantoio olives, often produced in the Tuscany, Umbria, or Lazio regions of Italy, and those made from the Sicilian olive variety Biancolilla. If you can find one of these, finish your artichoke-centric pasta dishes with a generous drizzle to boost the artichoke flavor and fragrance.

Artichokes with Chicken and Lemon Ricotta

This dish—loaded with chicken and artichokes and finished with generous amounts of fresh herbs, arugula, and a creamy dose of lemony whipped ricotta—makes a hearty meal, yet the flavors remain light and spring-y. If you don't have Whipped Lemon Ricotta, use Whipped Plain Ricotta (page 34) and increase the amount of lemon zest in the dish to 1½ tablespoons.

Serves 2 or 3

- Kosher salt (preferably Diamond Crystal; see page 17)
- 8 ounces (225 g) boneless, skinless chicken breast or chicken tenders
- Freshly ground black pepper
- All-purpose flour
- Extra-virgin olive oil
- 3 tablespoons unsalted butter
- ½ cup (65 g) chopped red onion
- 4 or 5 garlic cloves, finely chopped
- ¼ teaspoon dried chile flakes
- 1½ cups (200 g) artichoke hearts (canned is fine), halved or quartered if large
- 1 cup (240 ml) homemade (page 143) or low-sodium store-bought chicken broth or water
- 1 tablespoon finely grated lemon zest
- 8 ounces (225 g) radiatore, rotini, or campanelle
- Small handful of fresh mint leaves
- Small handful of fresh flat-leaf parsley leaves
- ¼ cup (30 g) 50/50 cheese (half Parmigiano-Reggiano, half Pecorino Romano, grated in a food processor; see page 39), plus more for serving
- 2 tablespoons fresh lemon juice, plus more to taste
- Large handful of arugula
- 2 to 4 spoonfuls Whipped Lemon Ricotta (page 35)
- Lemon Agrumato (lemony extra-virgin olive oil; see page 41; optional)

Fill a large pot (at least 6 quarts/L) with 1 gallon (4 L) of water; add 4 tablespoons (40 g) kosher salt, cover the pot, and bring the water to a boil while you make your sauce. If the water begins to boil before your sauce is ready, turn down the heat, but don't let the volume of the pasta water reduce by boiling off.

Cut the chicken into pieces about 2 inches (5 cm) long and 1 inch (2.5 cm) wide. The exact size doesn't matter, but you want all the pieces to be similar in size so they cook at the same rate. Season generously with salt and pepper.

Put a pile of flour in a large bowl, add the chicken, and toss so all the pieces are evenly coated. Shake off any excess flour and set aside.

Heat a small glug of olive oil in a large skillet over medium heat. When the oil is hot, add about half the butter, and when the butter has melted and stopped bubbling, add the chicken. Cook until it is fully cooked, meaning golden brown on all sides and no longer pink in the center, 4 to 6 minutes, adjusting the heat as needed so you don't burn the butter. Transfer the chicken to a plate and set aside.

Add another small glug of oil to the skillet, then add the onion, garlic, and chile flakes. Cook until the onion has softened slightly and the garlic is fragrant, about 3 minutes.

If you're using fresh artichoke hearts, steam them until tender. If using canned, blot them lightly with paper towels to remove any liquid.

Add the artichokes, broth, and lemon zest and cook, breaking up the artichokes a bit so that some of the leaves are free-floating, until the broth has reduced by about half, 4 to 5 minutes. Add a splash of water from the pasta pot, then slide the skillet off the heat.

Bring the pasta water (back) to a boil, add the noodles, and set your timer for 2 minutes less than the shortest suggested cooking time

on the package of pasta; this will ideally be 2 minutes before the pasta is al dente. Stir the noodles several times during the first 2 minutes of cooking to prevent them from sticking to the bottom of the pot or otherwise clumping together.

When the timer goes off, start tasting the noodles. When they seem like they are 1½ to 2 minutes away from a perfect al dente (see page 22), drain and transfer them to the sauce in the skillet using your preferred method (see page 21), making sure to reserve at least 1 cup (240 ml) of the pasta water.

Slide the skillet back onto medium heat and finish cooking the noodles, tossing and adding splashes of pasta water until the noodles are perfectly al dente and the sauce is nicely juicy; you may not need to add much water because of the broth. If the sauce does seem watery, simmer for another few seconds to tighten it up, bearing in mind that you're going to return the chicken to the skillet, and that the cheese will thicken the sauce.

Reduce the heat to very low. Return the chicken and any accumulated juices to the pan, then add the remaining butter and the mint and parsley, tearing the leaves into a few pieces. Toss to incorporate.

Add the grated cheese and toss to emulsify it with the other sauce ingredients, adding splashes of pasta water (or plain hot water, if things are getting too salty) if needed to keep the consistency creamy and prevent the cheese from clumping. Add the lemon juice and toss to incorporate. Taste and add more salt, chile flakes, or lemon juice if you like.

Finally, add the arugula and toss just once to incorporate; you don't want the arugula to start wilting.

Divide the pasta between two or three warm bowls, top with the whipped lemon ricotta and a thin drizzle of Agrumato, if using, and serve right away, with more grated cheese to add at the table, though diners probably won't need it because of the ricotta.

Artichokes with Chicken Ragu Bianco

If you have a batch of Chicken Ragu Bianco already made, you are in luck, as this dish is as easy as reheating the ragu and opening a can of artichoke hearts. If you aren't already stocked with the ragu, this dish should be a good motivation to make it. Its pure flavors are so nice with two of my favorite springtime flavor icons—artichoke and mint.

Serves 2

Kosher salt (preferably Diamond Crystal; see page 17)

1 cup (5 ounces/140 g) artichoke hearts (canned is fine), halved or quartered lengthwise

1 cup (250 g) Chicken Ragu Bianco (page 72)

¼ teaspoon dried chile flakes, plus more to taste

8 ounces (225 g) radiatore, rotini, or campanelle

Small handful of fresh mint leaves

⅓ cup (40 g) grated Pecorino Romano, plus more for serving

Fill a large pot (at least 6 quarts/L) with 1 gallon (4 L) of water; add 4 tablespoons (40 g) kosher salt, cover the pot, and bring the water to a boil while you make your sauce. If the water begins to boil before your sauce is ready, turn down the heat, but don't let the volume of the pasta water reduce by boiling off.

If you're using fresh artichoke hearts, steam them until tender. If using canned, blot them lightly with paper towels to remove any liquid.

Place a large skillet over medium heat. Add the chicken ragu and a big splash of water from the pasta pot and bring to a gentle simmer. Add the artichokes and chile flakes, then slide the skillet off the heat.

Bring the pasta water (back) to a boil, add the noodles, and set your timer for 2 minutes less than the shortest suggested cooking time on the package of pasta; this will ideally be 2 minutes before the pasta is al dente. Stir the noodles several times during the first 2 minutes of cooking to prevent them from sticking to the bottom of the pot or otherwise clumping together.

When the timer goes off, start tasting the noodles. When they seem like they are 1½ to 2 minutes away from a perfect al dente (see page 22), drain and transfer them to the sauce in the skillet using your preferred method (see page 21), making sure to reserve at least 1 cup (240 ml) of the pasta water.

Slide the skillet back onto medium heat and finish cooking the noodles, tossing and adding plenty of splashes of pasta water until the noodles are perfectly al dente, the artichokes are tender, and the sauce is nicely juicy. If the sauce seems watery, simmer for another few seconds to tighten it up, bearing in mind that the cheese will thicken it.

Reduce the heat to very low. Add the mint, tearing the leaves into a few pieces, and the pecorino and toss to emulsify the cheese with the other sauce ingredients, adding splashes of pasta water if needed to keep the consistency creamy and prevent the cheese from clumping. Taste and add more salt or chile flakes if you like.

Divide the pasta between two warm bowls and serve right away, with more cheese to add at the table.

Artichokes, Peas, Favas, and Asparagus

This is my take on the classic Italian vignarola, a vegetable stew that assumes many forms but always features the first vegetables of spring. If you can't find all the vegetables, just increase the quantities of those you do have.

Serves 2

1 pound (450 g) fava beans in their pods

1½ cups (200 g) artichoke hearts (canned is fine), halved or quartered if large

Kosher salt (preferably Diamond Crystal; see page 17)

Extra-virgin olive oil

3 or 4 garlic cloves, smashed

Pinch of dried chile flakes, plus more to taste

⅔ cup (100 g) shelled peas (frozen is fine)

1 cup (85 g) chopped asparagus (cut into 1-inch/2.5 cm pieces)

1 tablespoon finely grated lemon zest

8 ounces (225 g) orechiette, rotelle, or rigatoni

Small handful of fresh mint leaves

½ cup (60 g) 50/50 cheese (half Parmigiano-Reggiano, half Pecorino Romano, grated in a food processor; see page 39), plus more for serving

Prepare the fava beans using the method described on page 158. Set aside.

If you're using fresh artichoke hearts, steam them until tender. Set aside.

Fill a large pot (at least 6 quarts/L) with 1 gallon (4 L) of water; add 4 tablespoons (40 g) kosher salt, cover the pot, and bring the water to a boil while you make your sauce. If the water begins to boil before your sauce is ready, turn down the heat, but don't let the volume of the pasta water reduce by boiling off.

Heat a glug of olive oil in a large skillet over medium heat. When the oil is hot, add the garlic and cook gently, breaking it up a bit with your spatula, until it is soft, lightly toasted (but not too brown), and fragrant, 3 to 4 minutes.

Add the chile flakes, then add the fava beans, artichoke hearts, peas, and asparagus. Scoop out about 1 cup (240 ml) of water from the pasta pot and add it to the skillet. Simmer, uncovered, until the vegetables are just tender, 2 to 3 minutes (the asparagus will probably take the longest, unless you're using fresh artichokes). Add the lemon zest, then slide the skillet off the heat.

Bring the pasta water (back) to a boil, add the noodles, and set your timer for 2 minutes less than the shortest suggested cooking time on the package of pasta; this will ideally be 2 minutes before the pasta is al dente. Stir the noodles several times during the first 2 minutes of cooking to prevent them from sticking to the bottom of the pot or otherwise clumping together.

When the timer goes off, start tasting the noodles. When they seem like they are 1½ to 2 minutes away from a perfect al dente (see page 22), drain and transfer them to the sauce in the skillet using your preferred method (see page 21), making sure to reserve at least 1 cup (240 ml) of the pasta water.

Slide the skillet back onto medium heat and finish cooking the noodles, tossing and adding plenty of splashes of pasta water until the noodles are perfectly al dente and the sauce is nicely juicy. If the sauce seems watery, simmer for another few seconds to tighten it up, bearing in mind that the cheese will thicken it.

Reduce the heat to very low. Add the mint, tearing the leaves into a few pieces, and the grated cheese and toss to emulsify the cheese with the other sauce ingredients, adding

splashes of pasta water (or plain hot water, if things are getting too salty) if needed to keep the consistency creamy and prevent the cheese from clumping. Taste and add more salt or chile flakes if you like.

Divide the pasta between two warm bowls and serve right away, with more cheese to add at the table.

MORE WAYS

For richness and a hint of tang, add a spoonful of Pickled Ramp Butter (page 29) when you add the mint.

For a bit of meatiness, add crisped pancetta or crumbled sausage.

How to Prepare Fava Beans

Fresh fava beans are one of spring's true delectables, made more so by the fact that they are truly seasonal; unlike so many vegetables that are grown commercially almost year-round, favas show up in stores and at farmers' markets only in spring. Also called broad beans, favas do require a bit of prep.

You'll buy favas in their pods, and they look like overgrown, puffy green beans. Inside the pods are individual beans (four or five to a pod), each of which is encased in a tough membrane that needs to be removed. The final prize is a very tender, bright-green bean that splits into two halves. You'll need about 2 pounds (900 g) of pods to yield 1 cup (140 g) of peeled beans. Note that some cuisines use dried fava beans, which are not a substitute for fresh.

To prepare fresh fava beans: Bring a medium pot of water to a boil. Split open the fava pods and pop out the beans. Add the beans to the boiling water, cook for about 30 seconds, and then drain immediately. Rinse well with cold water to stop the cooking. Cut a small slit in the whitish membrane of each bean with the tip of a paring knife or your thumbnail, then gently squeeze out the two halves of the bright-green fava.

Pasta Salad with Roasted Artichokes and Salmon

When I was growing up, my father would make a baked chicken-and-artichoke casserole that used a Newman's Own bottled salad dressing; the recipe itself came from a Paul Newman cookbook. I loved it then, and I now have fun tinkering with my own variation, which includes salmon more often than chicken and a from-scratch "Italian" salad dressing that mimics the flavors of the Paul Newman one; it's killer, and I use it for all sorts of salads.

Serves 4

1 pound (450 g) salmon fillet, preferably wild-caught (if your salmon is skin-on, make sure it has been scaled; if not, scale it or cut off the skin)

One 14-ounce (400 g) can artichoke hearts, drained

Extra-virgin olive oil

Kosher salt (preferably Diamond Crystal; see page 17)

Freshly ground black pepper

½ cup (120 ml) Italian Salad Dressing (recipe follows), plus more to taste

8 ounces (225 g) cavatappi, fusilli, or elbow macaroni

Big handful of fresh basil leaves

⅓ cup (40 g) 50/50 cheese (half Parmigiano-Reggiano, half Pecorino Romano, grated in a food processor; see page 39)

⅓ cup (15 g) Dried Breadcrumbs (page 36)

Heat the oven to 425°F (220°C).

Cut the salmon into 2-inch (5 cm) chunks and cut the artichoke hearts into halves or quarters if they're large. Pile them into a baking dish, drizzle with olive oil, season generously with salt and pepper, and toss to coat evenly with the seasonings. Spread the ingredients into an even layer.

Roast until the salmon is just cooked through and the artichoke leaves are getting crisp around the edges, 11 to 14 minutes. Cool for a few minutes, then transfer the salmon and artichokes to a large bowl (this can be the serving bowl if it's large enough to allow some tossing) and drizzle with a few tablespoons of the Italian dressing.

Meanwhile, fill a large pot (at least 6 quarts/L) with 1 gallon (4 L) of water; add 4 tablespoons (40 g) kosher salt, cover the pot, and bring the water to a boil. Add the noodles and set your timer for 2 minutes less than the shortest suggested cooking time on the package of pasta; this will ideally be 2 minutes before the pasta is al dente. Stir the noodles several times during the first 2 minutes of cooking to prevent them from sticking to the bottom of the pot or otherwise clumping together.

When the timer goes off, start tasting the noodles. When they seem like they are a perfect al dente (see page 22), drain them in a colander. Quickly rinse the noodles with warm water and shake off any excess moisture; you want them to be as dry as possible. Transfer the noodles to the bowl with the salmon.

While the noodles are still warm, sprinkle on another tablespoon of the Italian dressing and toss thoroughly so the noodles absorb it evenly; it's okay if the salmon breaks up a bit. Cool completely.

Add the basil, tearing the leaves into a few pieces, and the cheese. Drizzle on another few tablespoons of Italian dressing and toss gently to combine and moisten the ingredients. Taste a few pieces of the salad and add more dressing, salt, or pepper as needed.

When you're ready to serve, tidy up the edges of the bowl or transfer the salad to a serving bowl or platter. Distribute the breadcrumbs over the salad and serve right away at cool room temperature.

MORE WAYS

Add roughly chopped smashed green and black olives, giardiniera (pickled vegetables), and/or diced cooked new potatoes. Fold these ingredients into the salad after you add the cheese.

Italian Salad Dressing

The key to this versatile dressing, which is modeled on the bottled dressings that were always in our refrigerator when I was growing up, is having just a touch of sweetness. I achieve the sweet note by using a slightly sweet vinegar (Katz Farm late-harvest sauvignon blanc is a good choice; see Resources, page 380); if you're using regular white wine vinegar, add about ¼ teaspoon sugar.

Makes 1¾ cups (420 ml)

¼ cup (60 ml) red wine vinegar

¼ cup (60 ml) late-harvest sauvignon blanc vinegar or another slightly sweet vinegar, such as white balsamic

1 tablespoon ground fennel seed

1½ teaspoons dry mustard powder

½ teaspoon dried basil

½ teaspoon dried oregano

½ teaspoon kosher salt (preferably Diamond Crystal; see page 17)

⅛ teaspoon freshly ground black pepper

¾ cup (180 ml) extra-virgin olive oil

½ cup (120 ml) grapeseed oil

Combine the two vinegars, ground fennel, mustard powder, basil, oregano, salt, and pepper in a blender or food processor and whiz to blend. With the machine running, drizzle in the olive oil and grapeseed oil. Taste and adjust the seasoning as desired. Store in an airtight container in the refrigerator for up to 1 month.

Asparagus with Tuna

Asparagus and tuna are a tasty pairing, especially when the tuna is high quality. I often use tuna from Oregon-based supplier Sacred Sea (see Resources, page 380). A big handful of spicy arugula folded in at the last second is a great way to up the green quotient of this easy dish, or finish the dish in a hot oven, to make a grown-up version of mac and cheese.

Serves 2

- **Kosher salt (preferably Diamond Crystal; see page 17)**
- **Extra-virgin olive oil**
- **3 garlic cloves, smashed**
- **½ teaspoon freshly ground black pepper, plus more to taste**
- **One 5- or 6-ounce (142 or 170 g) can tuna, drained**
- **1½ cups (115 g) chopped asparagus (cut into ½-inch/1.25 cm pieces)**
- **8 ounces (225 g) ditalini, elbow macaroni, or penne**
- **2 tablespoons unsalted butter**
- **½ cup (60 g) 50/50 cheese (half Parmigiano-Reggiano, half Pecorino Romano, grated in a food processor; see page 39), plus more for baking and/or serving**
- **Finishing-quality extra-virgin olive oil, for serving**

Fill a large pot (at least 6 quarts/L) with 1 gallon (4 L) of water; add 4 tablespoons (40 g) kosher salt, cover the pot, and bring the water to a boil while you make your sauce. If the water begins to boil before your sauce is ready, turn down the heat, but don't let the volume of the pasta water reduce by boiling off.

Heat a glug of olive oil in a large skillet or Dutch oven over medium heat. When the oil is hot, add the garlic and cook, smashing it up a bit more with a spoon, until it's soft and nicely toasted but not too brown, about 3 minutes. Add the pepper and let it cook for a few minutes to infuse the oil. Stop the cooking process by adding about ¼ cup (60 ml) of water from the pasta pot.

Add the tuna, breaking up any large chunks with a spoon, then slide the skillet off the heat.

Bring the pasta water (back) to a boil, add the asparagus, and cook until it turns bright green and loses just a bit of crunch, 1 to 2 minutes. Scoop it out with a slotted spoon, spider, or small strainer, letting the excess water drip off, then add the asparagus to the skillet.

Add the noodles to the boiling water and set your timer for 2 minutes less than the shortest suggested cooking time on the package of pasta; this will ideally be 2 minutes before the pasta is al dente. Stir the noodles several times during the first 2 minutes of cooking to prevent them from sticking to the bottom of the pot or otherwise clumping together.

When the timer goes off, start tasting the noodles. When they seem like they are 1½ to 2 minutes away from a perfect al dente (see page 22), drain and transfer them to the sauce using your preferred method (see page 21), making sure to reserve 1 cup (240 ml) of the pasta water.

Slide the skillet back onto medium heat and finish cooking the noodles, tossing and adding plenty of pasta water until the noodles are al dente, the asparagus is crisp-tender, and the sauce is nicely juicy. If the sauce seems watery, simmer for a few seconds to tighten it up, bearing in mind that the cheese will thicken it.

Reduce the heat to very low. Add the butter and cheese and toss to emulsify with the other sauce ingredients, adding splashes of pasta water if needed to keep the consistency creamy and prevent the cheese from clumping. Taste and add more salt or pepper if you like.

Divide the pasta between two warm bowls. Give each portion a drizzle of good olive oil and another sprinkle of cheese and serve right away, with more cheese to add at the table.

To make the baked version, heat the oven to 450°F (230°C), spread the finished pasta evenly in the skillet, top generously with grated cheese, and bake until bubbling and browned, about 12 minutes.

Asparagus with Crab, Brown Butter, and Lemon

Crab and asparagus are a dynamite duo, especially when they meet in a pool of nutty brown butter. It's important to use good-quality fresh crabmeat, which is not always easy to find. I live in the Pacific Northwest, so I can find Dungeness crab for much of the year. What you don't want to use, however, is pasteurized crab in a can. That's okay for crab dip but not here.

I like to cut the asparagus pieces to match the size and shape of the noodle I'm using. If I'm using a long noodle, for example, I'll shave the asparagus into long strips. If I'm using a shorter noodle, I'll chop the spears into pieces roughly the same length.

Serves 2

Kosher salt (preferably Diamond Crystal; see page 17)

4 tablespoons (60 g) unsalted butter

2 teaspoons finely grated lemon zest

5 ounces (140 g) asparagus (about 12 trimmed medium spears), cut to match the size of your noodles

8 ounces (225 g) fusilli col buco, bucatini, or fusilli

1 cup (5 ounces/140 g) fresh crabmeat, picked through to remove any bits of shell

2 tablespoons fresh lemon juice, plus more to taste

Fill a large pot (at least 6 quarts/L) with 1 gallon (4 L) of water; add 4 tablespoons (40 g) kosher salt, cover the pot, and bring the water to a boil while you make your sauce. If the water begins to boil before your sauce is ready, turn down the heat, but don't let the volume of the pasta water reduce by boiling off.

Heat 3 tablespoons of the butter in a large skillet over medium heat until melted, then cook until browned and nutty-smelling, and the milk solids at the bottom of the pan are golden but not at all burnt. When the butter is perfectly golden brown and nutty, add about ½ cup (120 ml) of water from the pasta pot to stop the cooking. Slide the skillet off the heat. Add the lemon zest and the remaining 1 tablespoon butter.

Bring the pasta water (back) to a boil, add the asparagus, and cook just until crisp-tender, 30 seconds to 3 minutes, depending on how you've cut your asparagus. Scoop out the asparagus with a slotted spoon or tongs and transfer it to the skillet with the sauce.

Add the noodles to the boiling water and set your timer for 2 minutes less than the shortest suggested cooking time on the package of pasta; this will ideally be 2 minutes before the pasta is al dente. Stir the noodles several times during the first 2 minutes of cooking to prevent them from sticking to the pot or otherwise clumping together.

When the timer goes off, start tasting the noodles. When they seem like they are 1½ to 2 minutes away from a perfect al dente (see page 22), drain and transfer them to the sauce in the skillet using your preferred method (see page 21), making sure to reserve at least 1 cup (240 ml) of the pasta water.

Slide the skillet back onto medium heat and finish cooking the noodles, tossing and adding plenty of splashes of pasta water until the noodles are perfectly al dente, the asparagus is crisp-tender, and the sauce is nicely juicy. (Note that you won't be adding cheese, so you don't need to add quite as much liquid as you would in a dish that uses cheese.)

Add the crab and cook for a few seconds to warm it through, then take the skillet off the heat and add the lemon juice. Taste and add more salt or lemon juice if you like.

Divide the pasta between two warm bowls and serve right away.

Springtime Pasta Salad

Here's a different type of green salad—no lettuce, but rather a celebration of all the green things that signal spring. No worries if you don't have every vegetable in the ingredients list; just use what you can find. And here you can use canned artichoke hearts rather than trimming fresh ones, if you like. If using fresh, steam them until tender before adding to the salad.

Serves 4 to 6

- **8 ounces (225 g) small new potatoes or other small potatoes**
- **Kosher salt (preferably Diamond Crystal; see page 17)**
- **1 pound (450 g) fava beans in their pods**
- **⅔ cup (100 g) shelled peas (thawed frozen is fine)**
- **1 cup (110 g) sliced snap peas (cut at an angle into ¼-inch/6 mm pieces)**
- **6 ounces (170 g) asparagus (about 7 large spears), trimmed and cut into 1-inch (2.5 cm) pieces**
- **8 to 9 ounces (225 to 250 g) fusilli, rotelle, or rigatoni**
- **1 tablespoon fresh lemon juice, plus more to taste**
- **Extra-virgin olive oil**
- **1½ cups (200 g) artichoke hearts (canned is fine), halved or quartered if large**
- **3 or 4 scallions, white and light green parts only, sliced**
- **1 tablespoon finely grated lemon zest**
- **Freshly ground black pepper**
- **½ cup (120 ml) Pancetta Vinaigrette (recipe follows), plus more to taste**
- **Small handful of fresh mint leaves**
- **Small handful of fresh flat-leaf parsley leaves**

Put the potatoes in a medium saucepan, cover with water by 2 inches (5 cm), and add 1 tablespoon salt. Bring to a boil and cook until tender, 18 to 20 minutes. Scoop out the potatoes; don't discard the water. Cool the potatoes, then cut into bite-size pieces; set aside.

Prepare the fava beans following the method on page 158. You can use the potato-cooking water, if you like. Set aside.

Return the potato water to a boil (add more water if the level is getting low). Add the peas, snap peas, and asparagus and cook until crisp-tender, 3 to 5 minutes. Drain and rinse well with cold water to stop the cooking; set aside.

Fill a large pot (at least 6 quarts/L) with 1 gallon (4 L) of water; add 4 tablespoons (40 g) kosher salt, cover the pot, and bring the water to a boil.

Add the noodles and set your timer for 2 minutes less than the shortest suggested cooking time on the package of pasta; this will ideally be 2 minutes before the pasta is al dente. Stir the noodles several times during the first 2 minutes of cooking to prevent them from sticking to the pot or otherwise clumping together.

When the timer goes off, start tasting the noodles. When they seem like they are a perfect al dente (see page 22), drain them in a colander. Quickly rinse the noodles with warm water and shake off any excess moisture; you want them to be as dry as possible. Transfer the noodles to a large bowl (this can be the serving bowl if it's large enough to allow some tossing).

While the noodles are still warm, sprinkle on the lemon juice and toss thoroughly so the noodles absorb it evenly. Drizzle on about 1 tablespoon olive oil and toss again to evenly coat the noodles and prevent them from sticking together.

Add the potatoes, favas, peas, snap peas, asparagus, artichokes, scallions, lemon zest, ½ teaspoon salt, and several twists of black pepper. Toss to incorporate the ingredients, then add the vinaigrette and toss again.

Tear the mint and parsley leaves, add them to the bowl, and toss again. Taste and adjust the seasoning with more vinaigrette, lemon juice, salt, or black pepper if you like. Toss and give the salad one more taste-and-adjust.

Tidy up the edges of the bowl or transfer the salad to a serving bowl or platter and serve at cool room temperature.

Pancetta Vinaigrette

Note that the fat will solidify on top, so let the vinaigrette sit at room temperature until the fat melts, then stir to blend the ingredients before using.

Makes about 1 cup

Extra-virgin olive oil

3 ounces (85 g) pancetta, finely chopped

3 scallions, white and light green parts only, thinly sliced

2 garlic cloves, minced

¼ cup (60 ml) red wine vinegar

Kosher salt (preferably Diamond Crystal; see page 17)

Freshly ground black pepper

Heat a small glug of olive oil in a small skillet over medium heat. When the oil is hot, add the pancetta and cook slowly, stirring often, until the fat has rendered and the pancetta is barely crisp, 7 to 9 minutes.

Take the pan off the heat, and when the oil stops sizzling, add the scallions and garlic. Stir for a few minutes to soften the scallions and tame the raw garlic.

Whisk in the vinegar, season with salt and pepper, and then whisk in ¼ cup (60 ml) olive oil. Taste and add more oil, salt, or pepper as desired.

Store in an airtight container in the refrigerator for up to a few weeks.

Favas with Prosciutto, Cream, and Black Pepper

Pasta is an elegant platform for one of the season's most revered vegetables (at least in my world): the fava bean. Favas do require a two-step prep, but the process is easy and the beans are so beautiful and green that the task is a pleasure.

Prosciutto brings a hit of hammy goodness to the mix, but it can also be salty, so taste the developing sauce as you're finishing the noodles and use some plain water in place of the already-salted pasta water if things are getting salty.

Serves 2

1 pound (450 g) fava beans in their pods

Kosher salt (preferably Diamond Crystal; see page 17)

Extra-virgin olive oil

3 ounces (85 g) thinly sliced prosciutto, cut into strips

Freshly ground black pepper

½ cup (120 ml) heavy or whipping cream

8 ounces (225 g) tagliatelle, fettucine, or pappardelle

1 tablespoon finely grated lemon zest

1 tablespoon unsalted butter

Small handful of fresh mint leaves

⅓ cup (40 g) 50/50 cheese (half Parmigiano-Reggiano, half Pecorino Romano, grated in a food processor; see page 39), plus more for serving

Prepare the fava beans following the method on page 158. Set aside.

Fill a large pot (at least 6 quarts/L) with 1 gallon (4 L) of water; add 4 tablespoons (40 g) kosher salt, cover the pot, and bring the water to a boil while you make your sauce. If the water begins to boil before your sauce is ready, turn down the heat, but don't let the volume of the pasta water reduce by boiling off.

Heat a glug of olive oil in a large skillet over medium heat. When the oil is hot, add the prosciutto and cook gently to render the fat and crisp up the meat, 2 to 3 minutes. Season the prosciutto with several twists of black pepper.

Add the favas, cream, and ½ cup (120 ml) of water from the pasta pot to the skillet, reduce the heat to low, and gently simmer until the creamy mixture has reduced by about one-third, 3 to 4 minutes. Taste and add more salt and black pepper if you like. Slide the skillet off the heat.

Bring the pasta water (back) to a boil, add the noodles, and set your timer for 2 minutes less than the shortest suggested cooking time on the package of pasta; this will ideally be 2 minutes before the pasta is al dente. Stir the noodles several times during the first 2 minutes of cooking to prevent them from sticking to the pot or otherwise clumping together.

When the timer goes off, start tasting the noodles. When they seem like they are almost a perfect al dente (see page 22), drain and transfer them to the sauce using your preferred method (see page 21), making sure to reserve 1 cup (240 ml) of the pasta water.

Slide the skillet back onto medium heat and finish cooking the noodles, tossing and adding plenty of splashes of pasta water until the noodles are perfectly al dente and the sauce is nicely juicy. If the sauce seems watery, simmer for another few seconds to tighten it up, bearing in mind that the cheese will thicken it.

Take the skillet off the heat and add the lemon zest and butter. Tear the mint leaves into a few pieces and add them.

Add the grated cheese and toss to emulsify it with the other sauce ingredients, adding splashes of pasta water (or plain hot water, if things are getting too salty) if needed to prevent the cheese from clumping.

Divide the pasta between two warm bowls and serve, with more cheese to add at the table.

Fava and Almond Pesto

The pesto here is an à la minute one, to be used as soon as you make it. Keep the texture chunky as you pulse the ingredients in the food processor; unlike with a typical pesto, you want to be able to distinguish the bits in the pasta. If you can't find whole blanched almonds, you can use slivered almonds (but not sliced almonds).

Serves 2

1 pound (450 g) fava beans in their pods

Kosher salt (preferably Diamond Crystal; see page 17)

⅓ cup (40 g) whole blanched almonds, toasted and roughly chopped

⅓ cup (40 g) 50/50 cheese (half Parmigiano-Reggiano, half Pecorino Romano, grated in a food processor; see page 39), plus more for serving

Small handful of fresh mint leaves, very roughly chopped

Big pinch of dried chile flakes, plus more to taste

Freshly ground black pepper

Extra-virgin olive oil

8 ounces (225 g) spaghetti, linguine, or corzetti

1 tablespoon fresh lemon juice, plus more to taste

Chile Crisp (page 37), for serving (optional)

Prepare the fava beans following the method on page 158. Set aside.

Fill a large pot (at least 6 quarts/L) with 1 gallon (4 L) of water; add 4 tablespoons (40 g) kosher salt, cover the pot, and bring the water to a boil while you make your sauce. If the water begins to boil before your sauce is ready, turn down the heat, but don't let the volume of the pasta water reduce by boiling off.

Reserve a tablespoon each of the favas and almonds, then put the rest of the favas and almonds in a food processor along with the cheese, mint, chile flakes, many twists of black pepper, and ¼ teaspoon salt.

Pulse the mixture a couple of times, then add about ¼ cup (60 ml) olive oil and pulse a few more times until you have quite a chunky pesto, with bits of varying sizes, adding more oil if needed. Taste and add more salt or chile flakes if you like.

Set a large skillet over medium heat, add a bit of water from the pasta pot, and scrape the pesto from the food processor into the pan. Add the reserved favas and almonds and slide the skillet off the heat.

Bring the pasta water (back) to a boil, add the noodles, and set your timer for 2 minutes less than the shortest suggested cooking time on the package of pasta; this will ideally be 2 minutes before the pasta is al dente. Stir the noodles several times during the first 2 minutes of cooking to prevent them from sticking to the bottom of the pot or otherwise clumping together.

When the timer goes off, start tasting the noodles. When they seem like they are almost a perfect al dente (see page 22), drain and transfer them to the sauce in the skillet using your preferred method (see page 21), making sure to reserve at least 1 cup (240 ml) of the pasta water.

Slide the skillet back onto low heat and finish cooking the noodles and gently warming the pesto, tossing and adding splashes of pasta water until the noodles are perfectly al dente and the sauce is nicely creamy.

Add the lemon juice and toss once more. Taste and add more salt, chile flakes, or lemon juice if you like.

Divide the pasta between two warm bowls, spoon on some chile crisp, if using, and serve right away, with more cheese to add at the table.

Melted Leeks with Sausage, Olives, and Oregano

Take your time cooking the leeks, so that they don't brown at all but become very soft—"melted"—and sweet. Be sure to wash the leeks thoroughly before using, because dirt tends to hide between the layers of green leaves. Start by cutting off the hairy root plus ¼ inch (6 mm) or so and trimming back the dark green top to the lighter section, which will be more tender (use the tough top section in a vegetable stock . . . or compost it). Then you can split the leek lengthwise and fan open each leaf under cool running water to chase out the dirt, or you can slice the leek, soak the slices in cool water for a few minutes, then drain and rinse in a colander. With either method, dry the leeks before adding them to the skillet, though a bit of moisture is fine and will kick-start the melting.

Serves 2 or 3

Kosher salt (preferably Diamond Crystal; see page 17)

6 ounces (170 g) bulk Italian sausage, sweet or hot

Extra-virgin olive oil

3 cups (200 g) thinly sliced leeks, cleaned well, (white and light green parts only)

2 teaspoons fresh oregano, or 1 teaspoon dried

Big pinch of dried chile flakes, plus more to taste

1 cup (250 g) canned whole peeled tomatoes, crushed by hand (see page 44), with their juices

8 ounces (225 g) fusilli, capricci, or strozzapreti

½ cup (60 g) pitted large green olives, smashed

1 to 2 tablespoons unsalted butter

⅓ cup (40 g) 50/50 cheese (half Parmigiano-Reggiano, half Pecorino Romano, grated in a food processor; see page 39), plus more for serving

1 ball fresh mozzarella (optional)

Fill a large pot (at least 6 quarts/L) with 1 gallon (4 L) of water; add 4 tablespoons (40 g) kosher salt, cover the pot, and bring the water to a boil while you make your sauce. If the water begins to boil before your sauce is ready, turn down the heat, but don't let the volume of the pasta water reduce by boiling off.

Shape the sausage into 2 patties. Heat a glug of olive oil in a large skillet over medium-high heat. When the oil is hot, add the sausage and sear, smashing the patties down from time to time with your spatula; don't move them until a nice crust forms on the bottom, about 5 minutes.

Reduce the heat to medium, flip the patties, add the leeks, and season with salt. If the pan seems dryish, add more oil. Continue to cook until the leeks become very tender and sweet, stirring frequently and reducing the heat to make sure the leeks don't brown, another 5 minutes or so.

Add the oregano and chile flakes, cook for a few seconds, then add the crushed tomatoes and their juices. Simmer, breaking the sausage into bits with a spatula, until the tomato has reduced and concentrated in flavor, 4 to 5 minutes. Slide the skillet off the heat.

Bring the pasta water (back) to a boil, add the noodles, and set your timer for 2 minutes less than the shortest suggested cooking time on the package of pasta; this will ideally be 2 minutes before the pasta is al dente. Stir the noodles several times during the first 2 minutes of cooking to prevent them from sticking to the pot or otherwise clumping together.

When the timer goes off, start tasting the noodles. When they seem like they are 1½ to 2 minutes away from a perfect al dente (see page 22), drain and transfer them to the sauce in the skillet using your preferred method (see page 21), making sure to reserve at least 1 cup (240 ml) of the pasta water.

Slide the skillet back onto medium heat and finish cooking the noodles, tossing and adding plenty of splashes of pasta water until the noodles are perfectly al dente and the sauce is nicely juicy. If the sauce seems watery, simmer for another few seconds to tighten it up, bearing in mind that the cheese will thicken it.

Reduce the heat to very low. Add the olives, butter, and grated cheese and toss to incorporate and emulsify, adding splashes of pasta water (or plain hot water, if things are getting too salty) if needed to keep the consistency creamy and prevent the cheese from clumping. Taste and add more salt or chile flakes if you like.

Divide the pasta between two or three warm bowls. If using mozzarella, tear it into large shreds and distribute it over the pasta. Serve right away, with more grated cheese to add at the table.

MORE WAYS

Turn this dish into a baked pasta, using the tips on page 358. And don't be shy with the mozzarella.

Leek Alfredo with Shrimp

Slow, gentle cooking is the key to this dish, which features tender shrimp, a light lemon cream sauce, and leeks cut into long ribbons to mimic the long strands of spaghetti. Note that the leeks tend to clump together in the sauce, so as you're preparing to plate the final dish, be sure to tease them apart and disperse them among the noodles.

And yes, here you'll add cheese to a seafood dish, to the chagrin of Italian traditionalists, I'm sure, but rules are for breaking as long as the results are delicious.

Serves 2

Kosher salt (preferably Diamond Crystal; see page 17)

6 ounces (180 g) leeks (about 1 large), white and light green parts only, cleaned well and thinly sliced lengthwise to create long skinny ribbons

3 or 4 garlic cloves, smashed

2 teaspoons finely grated lemon zest

1½ cups (360 ml) heavy or whipping cream

8 ounces (225 g) raw shrimp, any size, preferably wild, peeled and deveined

8 ounces (225 g) spaghetti, linguine, or pappardelle

⅓ cup (40 g) 50/50 cheese (half Parmigiano-Reggiano, half Pecorino Romano, grated in a food processor; see page 39), plus more for serving

3 tablespoons fresh lemon juice, plus more to taste

Lemon wedges, for serving

Fill a large pot (at least 6 quarts/L) with 1 gallon (4 L) of water; add 4 tablespoons (40 g) kosher salt, cover the pot, and bring the water to a boil while you make your sauce. If the water begins to boil before your sauce is ready, turn down the heat, but don't let the volume of the pasta water reduce by boiling off.

Note that unlike in other recipes, you'll start with a cold skillet. Put the leeks, garlic, lemon zest, and cream in a large skillet and set over low heat. Cook gently (you want the mixture to be just below a simmer) until the leeks and garlic are meltingly tender and the cream has reduced slightly, but not a lot, about 15 minutes.

With a spoon or spatula, mash the garlic so it blends into the cream (or, if you want a less garlicky dish, scoop it out and discard). Taste the cream sauce and season with salt.

Add the shrimp and gently poach them in the sauce, still over low heat. If the shrimp are large and don't seem to be cooking after 5 or 6 minutes, increase the heat a bit, but don't let the sauce boil hard, as it will toughen the shrimp and reduce the cream too much. When the shrimp are done, slide the skillet off the heat.

Bring the pasta water (back) to a boil, add the noodles, and set your timer for 2 minutes less than the shortest suggested cooking time on the package of pasta; this will ideally be 2 minutes before the pasta is al dente. Stir the noodles several times during the first 2 minutes of cooking to prevent them from sticking to the bottom of the pot or otherwise clumping together.

When the timer goes off, start tasting the noodles. When they seem like they are almost a perfect al dente (see page 22), drain and transfer them to the sauce in the skillet using your preferred method (see page 21), making sure to reserve at least 1 cup (240 ml) of the pasta water.

Slide the skillet back onto medium heat and finish cooking the noodles, tossing and adding plenty of splashes of pasta water until the noodles are perfectly al dente and the sauce is nicely juicy. You may not need much or any water because of the cream. If the sauce seems watery, simmer for another few seconds to tighten it up, bearing in mind that the cheese will thicken it.

recipe continues →

Reduce the heat to very low. Add the grated cheese and toss to emulsify it with the other sauce ingredients, adding splashes of pasta water (or plain hot water, if things are getting too salty) if needed to keep the consistency creamy and prevent the cheese from clumping. Try to distribute the leeks throughout as well; they have a tendency to clump together.

Add the lemon juice and taste for seasoning, adding more lemon juice or a sprinkle of salt if you like.

Divide the pasta between two warm bowls, tuck a lemon wedge into each bowl, and serve right away, with more cheese to add at the table.

Nettles alla Gricia

This style of pasta dish—alla gricia—is one of what are called the four classic pastas of Rome (the others being cacio e pepe, carbonara, and amatriciana). Lore says the dish was created by shepherds, who could easily carry with them the dish's main ingredients: cured pork, noodles, and pecorino (sheep's-milk) cheese.

Here I'm adding nettles, which an enterprising shepherd could easily have foraged from the hillside.

Serves 2

Kosher salt (preferably Diamond Crystal; see page 17)

Extra-virgin olive oil

3 ounces (85 g) pancetta, thinly sliced

Freshly ground black pepper

1 big bunch fresh nettles (about 6 ounces/170 g), any thick stems trimmed off

8 ounces (225 g) spaghetti, linguine, or tagliatelle

⅓ cup (40 g) 50/50 cheese (half Parmigiano-Reggiano, half Pecorino Romano, grated in a food processor; see page 39), plus more for serving

Note: **Remember to wear gloves or otherwise avoid touching the nettles until they have been cooked.**

Fill a large pot (at least 6 quarts/L) with 1 gallon (4 L) of water; add 4 tablespoons (40 g) kosher salt, cover the pot, and bring the water to a boil while you make your sauce. If the water begins to boil before your sauce is ready, turn down the heat, but don't let the volume of the pasta water reduce by boiling off.

Heat a generous glug of olive oil in a large skillet over medium heat. When the oil is hot, add the pancetta and cook gently until the fat has rendered and the pancetta is crisp, 4 to 6 minutes. Remove the pancetta from the skillet and set aside.

Season the rendered fat in the pan with several nice twists of black pepper, add the nettles, and toss with tongs just until they are wilted, 3 to 4 minutes. Add a big splash of water from the pasta pot and slide the skillet off the heat.

Bring the pasta water (back) to a boil, add the noodles, and set your timer for 2 minutes less than the shortest suggested cooking time on the package of pasta; this will ideally be 2 minutes before the pasta is al dente. Stir the noodles several times during the first 2 minutes of cooking to prevent them from sticking to the bottom of the pot or otherwise clumping together.

When the timer goes off, start tasting the noodles. When they seem like they are 1½ to 2 minutes away from a perfect al dente (see page 22), drain and transfer them to the sauce in the skillet using your preferred method (see page 21), making sure to reserve at least 1 cup (240 ml) of the pasta water.

Slide the skillet back onto medium heat and finish cooking the noodles, tossing and adding plenty of splashes of pasta water until the noodles are perfectly al dente, the nettles are tender, and the sauce is nicely juicy. If the sauce seems watery, simmer for another few seconds to tighten it up, bearing in mind that the cheese will thicken it.

Reduce the heat to very low. Add the grated cheese and toss to emulsify it with the other sauce ingredients, adding splashes of pasta water (or plain hot water, if things are getting too salty) if needed to keep the consistency creamy and prevent the cheese from clumping. Add the cooked pancetta and toss again to integrate it.

Divide the pasta between two warm bowls and serve right away, with more cheese to add at the table.

What Are Nettles?

Nettles are herbaceous shrubs that grow wild in forests, along riverbanks, at the edges of fields, and in other areas with fairly moist, nitrogen-rich soil. The leafy greens have been consumed by humans for ages, both medicinally—they're thought to treat ailments ranging from hay fever to gout—and as something good to eat. Nettles are sometimes called stinging nettles, and for good reason.

Touching (or eating) them raw will produce a true stinging sensation and a bit of a rash due to the tiny needle-like hairs coating the leaves, but once cooked, nettles are as harmless as spinach, and more delicious, if you ask me. Their flavor is green and grassy with just a hint of spice, like arugula. Handle them using the bag from the farmers' market or wearing gloves; if you're foraging your own, you probably already know how to wrangle a nettle.

Nettles with Whipped Lemon Ricotta and Chile Crisp

I love this simple combination of springtime ingredients, but you can use any of the flavored butters (pages 27–30) and whipped ricottas (pages 34–35) in the same manner. If you'd like to add a seasonal vegetable, cook it until crisp-tender in the boiling water and then bring it to perfect doneness as you finish the noodles in the buttery sauce.

Serves 2

Kosher salt (preferably Diamond Crystal; see page 17)

8 ounces (225 g) strozzapreti, gemelli, or tagliatelle

4 tablespoons (60 g) Nettle Butter (page 29)

¼ cup (30 g) 50/50 cheese (half Parmigiano-Reggiano, half Pecorino Romano, grated in a food processor; see page 39), plus more for serving

2 spoonfuls Whipped Lemon Ricotta (page 35)

2 spoonfuls Chile Crisp (page 37)

2 tablespoons Dried Breadcrumbs (page 36)

Fill a large pot (at least 6 quarts/L) with 1 gallon (4 L) of water; add 4 tablespoons (40 g) kosher salt, cover the pot, and bring the water to a boil. Add the noodles and set your timer for 2 minutes less than the shortest suggested cooking time on the package of pasta; this will ideally be 2 minutes before the pasta is al dente. Stir the noodles several times during the first 2 minutes of cooking to prevent them from sticking to the bottom of the pot or otherwise clumping together.

While the noodles are cooking, combine the nettle butter and about ½ cup (120 ml) of the pasta water in a large skillet over low heat. Swirl the pan to emulsify the butter and water, creating a creamy sauce; don't let anything boil, which can break the emulsion. Slide the skillet off the heat.

When the timer goes off, start tasting the noodles. When they seem like they are almost a perfect al dente (see page 22), drain and transfer them to the sauce in the skillet using your preferred method (see page 21), making sure to reserve at least 1 cup (240 ml) of the pasta water.

Slide the skillet back onto medium heat and finish cooking the noodles, tossing and adding splashes of pasta water until the noodles are perfectly al dente and the sauce is nicely juicy, bearing in mind that the cheese will thicken it.

Reduce the heat to very low. Add the grated cheese and toss to emulsify it with the other sauce ingredients, adding a few splashes of pasta water if needed to keep the consistency creamy and prevent the cheese from clumping. Taste and add more salt if you like.

Divide the pasta between two warm bowls and top each serving with a spoonful of whipped lemon ricotta. Drizzle the chile crisp over the ricotta and sprinkle the breadcrumbs on top. Serve right away, with more cheese to add at the table.

MORE WAYS

Use Green Garlic Herb Butter (page 29) instead of Nettle Butter.

Add thinly sliced asparagus to the boiling water when you add the noodles.

Peas with Pancetta, Onion, and Tomato

You'll sometimes see scallions or green onions referred to as spring onions, but a true spring onion is a different creature. A spring onion, which looks like a scallion with an extra-large bulb and slightly fuller greens, is basically a baby onion, whether a sweet variety such as Vidalia or Walla Walla or a regular white, yellow, or red onion. Spring onions are harvested early in spring so they can be used while they are mild and tender, without the papery outer layers and without the strong sulfur compounds that develop with maturity. Use the bulb as well as most or all of the greens. If you can't find genuine spring onions, scallions are the best substitute.

Serves 2 or 3

Kosher salt (preferably Diamond Crystal; see page 17)

Extra-virgin olive oil

3 ounces (85 g) pancetta, cut into small strips or diced

¾ cup (70 g) sliced spring onion (cut into ¼-inch-thick/6 mm rounds)

½ teaspoon dried chile flakes, plus more to taste

1 tablespoon tomato paste

1 cup (250 g) canned whole peeled tomatoes, crushed by hand (see page 44), with their juices

1½ cups (200 g) shelled peas (thawed frozen is fine)

Small handful of fresh mint leaves

8 ounces (225 g) conchiglie, lumache, or rigatoni

⅓ cup (40 g) 50/50 cheese (half Parmigiano-Reggiano, half Pecorino Romano, grated in a food processor; see page 39), plus more for serving

Finishing-quality extra-virgin olive oil, for serving (optional)

Fill a large pot (at least 6 quarts/L) with 1 gallon (4 L) of water; add 4 tablespoons (40 g) kosher salt, cover the pot, and bring the water to a boil while you make your sauce. If the water begins to boil before your sauce is ready, turn down the heat, but don't let the volume of the pasta water reduce by boiling off.

Heat a glug of olive oil in a large skillet over medium heat. When the oil is hot, add the pancetta and cook until the fat starts to run and everything is sizzling nicely, about 2 minutes. Add the spring onion and cook until the pancetta is getting crisp and the onion is softening and lightly browning, another 5 minutes or so.

Add the chile flakes, then add the tomato paste and cook, stirring and spreading the tomato paste thinly on the pan so it toasts and darkens a bit, about 30 seconds. Add the crushed tomatoes and their juices, the peas, and about half the mint, tearing the leaves into a few pieces, and continue cooking, stirring sort of constantly, until the sauce has reduced by half and the peas are tender, 4 to 5 minutes. At this point you should have a really nice pork-flavored spicy tomato sauce. Slide the skillet off the heat.

Bring the pasta water (back) to a boil, add the noodles, and set your timer for 2 minutes less than the shortest suggested cooking time on the package of pasta; this will ideally be 2 minutes before the pasta is al dente. Stir the noodles several times during the first 2 minutes of cooking to prevent them from sticking to the bottom of the pot or otherwise clumping together.

When the timer goes off, start tasting the noodles. When they seem like they are 1½ to 2 minutes away from a perfect al dente (see page 22), drain and transfer them to the sauce in the skillet using your preferred method (see page 21), making sure to reserve at least 1 cup (240 ml) of the pasta water.

recipe continues →

Slide the skillet back onto medium heat and finish cooking the noodles, tossing and adding plenty of splashes of pasta water until the noodles are perfectly al dente and the sauce is nicely juicy. If the sauce seems watery, simmer for another few seconds to tighten it up, bearing in mind that the cheese will thicken it.

Reduce the heat to very low. Tear the remaining mint leaves into pieces and add them to the skillet along with the grated cheese. Toss to emulsify the cheese with the other sauce ingredients, adding splashes of pasta water (or plain hot water, if things are getting too salty) if needed to keep the consistency creamy and prevent the cheese from clumping. Taste and add more salt or chile flakes if you like.

Divide the pasta between two or three warm bowls, drizzle with good olive oil, and serve right away, with more cheese to add at the table.

Peas with Pistachio, Olives, and Mint

The sauce for this dish is almost like a chunky springtime pesto, though it's built in the skillet, not pureed in a food processor (or mortar and pestle, if that's more your style). Spring onions, green garlic, or ramps are my preferred "oniony" ingredient here, but regular scallions work just fine. Choose a mild green olive so you can really taste the olive flesh rather than an aggressive brine.

Serves 2 or 3

Kosher salt (preferably Diamond Crystal; see page 17)

5 tablespoons (75 g) unsalted butter

1 cup (100 g) thinly sliced spring onions, green garlic, ramps, scallions, or other tender springtime onions, or a mix

1 cup (150 g) shelled peas (thawed frozen is okay)

½ cup (70 g) roughly chopped toasted pistachios

½ cup (60 g) roughly chopped smashed pitted green olives, such as Castelvetrano, Cerignola, or Picholine

8 ounces (225 g) trecce, cavatappi, or rotini

¼ teaspoon dried chile flakes, plus more to taste

Small handful of fresh mint leaves

⅓ cup (40 g) 50/50 cheese (half Parmigiano-Reggiano, half Pecorino Romano, grated in a food processor; see page 39), plus more for serving

1 tablespoon fresh lemon juice

Lemon Agrumato (lemony extra-virgin olive oil; see page 41), for serving (optional)

Fill a large pot (at least 6 quarts/L) with 1 gallon (4 L) of water; add 4 tablespoons (40 g) kosher salt, cover the pot, and bring the water to a boil while you make your sauce. If the water begins to boil before your sauce is ready, turn down the heat, but don't let the volume of the pasta water reduce by boiling off.

Set a large skillet over medium-low heat and add 4 tablespoons (60 g) of the butter and the spring onions. Let the butter melt and then cook the onions gently, stirring occasionally and definitely not letting them actually brown, until they're very soft and sweet, 12 to 20 minutes.

Add the peas, pistachios, and olives and a splash of water from the pasta pot. Toss or stir the ingredients to emulsify the butter and pasta water and make the mixture a bit more creamy, then slide the skillet off the heat.

Bring the pasta water (back) to a boil, add the noodles, and set your timer for 2 minutes less than the shortest suggested cooking time on the package of pasta; this will ideally be 2 minutes before the pasta is al dente. Stir the noodles several times during the first 2 minutes of cooking to prevent them from sticking to the bottom of the pot or otherwise clumping together.

When the timer goes off, start tasting the noodles. When they seem like they are about 30 seconds away from a perfect al dente (see page 22), drain and transfer them to the sauce in the skillet using your preferred method (see page 21), making sure to reserve at least 1 cup (240 ml) of the pasta water.

Slide the skillet back onto medium heat, add the chile flakes and the mint, tearing the leaves into a few pieces, and finish cooking the noodles, tossing and adding plenty of splashes of pasta water until the noodles are perfectly al dente and the sauce is nicely juicy. If the sauce seems watery, simmer for another few seconds to

tighten it up, bearing in mind that the cheese will thicken it.

Reduce the heat to very low. Add the grated cheese and remaining 1 tablespoon butter and toss to emulsify them with the other sauce ingredients, adding splashes of pasta water if needed to keep the consistency creamy and prevent the cheese from clumping. Add the lemon juice and toss again; taste and add more salt or chile flakes if you like.

Divide the pasta between two or three warm bowls, drizzle with the Agrumato, if using, and serve right away, with more cheese to add at the table.

MORE WAYS

Toss in sliced or torn tender lettuce when you add the lemon juice.

Garnish the dish with chive blossoms.

Peas with Squid, Tomato, and Parsley

Cooking peas and squid together for a long time doesn't produce a glamorous-looking pasta, but it sure makes a delicious one. There's something about the combination of these two ingredients that is just perfect. If you're not familiar with cooking squid, just know that to create a tender texture, you either cook it very fast—as in flash-in-the-pan fast—or you cook it for a long time. Anything in between produces a chewy result.

Serves 2

10 ounces (280 g) cleaned squid bodies and tentacles (see page 194)

Extra-virgin olive oil

4 or 5 garlic cloves, smashed

Big pinch of dried chile flakes, plus more to taste

2 tablespoons tomato paste

1 cup (240 ml) dry white wine

¾ cup (180 g) canned whole peeled tomatoes, crushed by hand (see page 44), with their juices

¾ cup (100 g) shelled peas (thawed frozen is fine)

Kosher salt (preferably Diamond Crystal; see page 17)

8 ounces (225 g) paccheri, rigatoni, or rotelle

Small handful of mixed fresh mint and flat-leaf parsley leaves

Finishing-quality extra-virgin olive oil, for serving (optional)

Cut the squid tentacle clusters in half lengthwise and cut the bodies into ½-inch-thick (1.25 cm) slices.

Heat a generous glug of olive oil in a large skillet over medium heat. When the oil is hot, add the garlic and cook gently, breaking it up a bit with your spatula, until it is nicely toasted and fragrant but not too brown, 3 to 4 minutes.

Increase the heat to medium-high, add all the squid, in a single layer if possible, and cook without moving it for about 1 minute to try to get some browning on the squid and in the pan (scoot the garlic around to avoid burning it).

Flip the squid pieces and add the chile flakes and tomato paste. Continue cooking, stirring frequently and spreading the tomato paste thinly on the surface of the pan so it toasts and darkens a bit, another 30 seconds to 1 minute.

Reduce the heat to medium, add the wine, and simmer until it has reduced by three-quarters, 6 to 8 minutes. Add the crushed tomatoes and their juices, reduce the heat to low, and simmer gently for about 20 minutes.

Add the peas and keep simmering until the squid is very tender and the peas are on their way to mushy, 40 to 50 minutes. (If you want some textural contrast, hold back one-third of the peas and add them closer to the time when the squid will be done.) Slide the skillet off the heat while you cook the pasta.

When the sauce is getting close to done, fill a large pot (at least 6 quarts/L) with 1 gallon (4 L) of water; add 4 tablespoons (40 g) kosher salt, cover the pot, and bring the water to a boil. If the water begins to boil before your sauce is ready, turn down the heat, but don't let the volume of the pasta water reduce by boiling off.

When the sauce is done and off the heat, bring the pasta water (back) to a boil, add the noodles, and set your timer for 2 minutes less than the shortest suggested cooking time on the package of pasta; this will ideally be 2 minutes before the pasta is al dente. Stir the noodles several times during the first 2 minutes of cooking to prevent them from sticking to the bottom of the pot or otherwise clumping together.

When the timer goes off, start tasting the noodles. When they seem like they are 1½ to 2 minutes away from a perfect al dente (see page 22), drain and transfer them to the sauce

in the skillet using your preferred method (see page 21), making sure to reserve at least 1 cup (240 ml) of the pasta water.

Slide the skillet back onto medium heat and finish cooking the noodles, tossing and adding plenty of splashes of pasta water until the noodles are perfectly al dente and the sauce is nicely juicy. If the sauce seems watery, simmer for another few seconds to tighten it up.

Add the mint and parsley, tearing the leaves into a few pieces. Taste the sauce and add more salt or chile flakes if you like.

Divide the pasta between two warm bowls, drizzle with good olive oil if you like, and serve right away.

How to Clean Squid

If your squid is frozen, thaw it overnight in the fridge. Most frozen squid is already cleaned, but you'll need to rinse it and inspect it for stray bits.

If your squid hasn't yet been cleaned, here's how to do it—it's easy. There are two parts to squid—the tubular piece, which is the body, and the part that looks like a tiny octopus, which is actually the head and guts, plus the tentacles.

First, pull apart the body and the head; set the body aside. Separate the edible tentacles from the inedible head/guts by cutting just underneath the eyes. Now open out the tentacles and locate the bit of hard cartilage in the center. Squeeze or pop it out with the tip of your knife and discard.

Reach into the body to locate the long piece of clear cartilage (it almost looks like plastic). This is the cuttlebone. Slide it out and discard. Now remove the thin purplish membrane that covers the outside of the body by simply sliding it off. Rinse the inside and outside of the body.

You're now ready to cut the tentacles and body according to your recipe.

Ramps with Clams, Tomatoes, and Pancetta

The underlying structure for this dish is pasta amatriciana (page 103), but here ramps play the role of the red onion, and pancetta is used in place of guanciale. Manila clams are small, sweet, meaty, and available widely.

Serves 2

Kosher salt (preferably Diamond Crystal; see page 17)

Extra-virgin olive oil

3 ounces (85 g) pancetta, cut into small strips or diced

About 6 ounces (170 g) ramps, bulbs and stems sliced crosswise, leaves left whole

½ teaspoon dried chile flakes, plus more to taste

1 tablespoon tomato paste

1 cup (250 g) canned whole peeled tomatoes, crushed by hand (see page 44), with their juices

2 pounds (900 g) Manila or other small littleneck clams, rinsed well

8 ounces (225 g) linguine, fettucine, or spaghetti

Fill a large pot (at least 6 quarts/L) with 1 gallon (4 L) of water; add 4 tablespoons (40 g) kosher salt, cover the pot, and bring the water to a boil while you make your sauce. If the water begins to boil before your sauce is ready, turn down the heat, but don't let the volume of the pasta water reduce by boiling off.

Arrange your pasta bowls near the stove and tear off a piece of foil that will loosely cover both bowls (to keep the clams warm as you finish the dish).

Heat a glug of olive oil in a large skillet with a lid over medium-high heat. When the oil is hot, add the pancetta and cook until the fat starts to run and everything is sizzling nicely, about 2 minutes. Add the ramp bulbs and stems and cook until the pancetta is getting crisp and the ramps are frying, softening, and lightly browning, another 8 minutes or so.

Add the chile flakes, then add the tomato paste and cook, stirring and spreading the tomato paste thinly on the pan so it toasts and darkens a bit, 30 seconds to 1 minute. Add the crushed tomatoes and their juices and continue cooking, stirring sort of constantly, until the sauce has reduced by half, 4 to 5 minutes.

Add the clams, immediately pop on the lid, and cook, shaking the pan a bit, until the clamshells have opened, about 3 minutes. With a slotted spoon or tongs, pluck out all the open clams, draining their juices back into the skillet, transfer them to the pasta bowls, and cover loosely with the foil. Cook any unopened clams for another minute or so, then add the newly opened ones to the pasta bowls and cover again with the foil. If any stubbornly unopened clams remain, discard them.

Continue cooking the tomato sauce until the clam juices have integrated and the sauce is nicely reduced and tasty, another 2 minutes or so. Add the ramp leaves to the sauce and slide the skillet off the heat.

Bring the pasta water (back) to a boil, add the noodles, and set your timer for 2 minutes less than the shortest suggested cooking time on the package of pasta; this will ideally be 2 minutes before the pasta is al dente. Stir the noodles several times during the first 2 minutes of cooking to prevent them from sticking to the bottom of the pot or otherwise clumping together.

When the timer goes off, start tasting the noodles. When they seem like they are 1½ to 2 minutes away from a perfect al dente (see page 22), drain and transfer them to the sauce in the skillet using your preferred method (see

page 21), making sure to reserve at least 1 cup (240 ml) of the pasta water.

Slide the skillet back onto medium heat and finish cooking the noodles, tossing and adding plenty of splashes of pasta water (or plain hot water, if the sauce is getting salty from the clams and pancetta) until the noodles are perfectly al dente and the sauce is nicely juicy. If the sauce seems watery, simmer for another few seconds to tighten it up. Taste and add more salt or chile flakes if you like.

Divide the noodles and sauce between the two pasta bowls, piling everything right on top of the clams so that they warm up. Serve right away, encouraging diners to pick up the clams with their fingers and eat the meat from the shells. Be sure to set out another bowl in which diners can discard their shells.

What Are Ramps?

Ramps are a member of the allium family—think onion and garlic—that grow wild in wooded areas of the Northeast, South, and Midwest of the United States. Called spring ephemerals, ramps emerge in April and last only through May, making them a precious ingredient. Formerly eaten only locally by the people who were lucky enough to be able to forage them for themselves, ramps are now popular with chefs (including me) and home cooks across the country, so overforaging is becoming an issue. Responsible foragers always leave some of the patch intact so that the slow-growing plants can repopulate.

Ramps look a bit like stubby scallions, with white bulbs tinged with purple and full green leaves; both parts are edible. To cook ramps, trim off the root end, rinse the bulbs and leaves well, and chop; now you're ready to sauté them in any tasty fat (see Ramps with Extra-Virgin Olive Oil, page 199), though bacon fat would be traditional in Appalachia, where ramps are celebrated as part of traditional food culture. You can also pickle ramp bulbs (page 30).

Ramps with Extra-Virgin Olive Oil

I love everything about this pasta dish: the simplicity, the fragrance, the flavor, and especially the fact that ramps signal the beginning of spring. Ramps, a wild member of the allium family (kin to onions, garlic, and leeks), are native to certain forest environments in the eastern half of North America, and they are one of the earliest edibles to emerge from the cold winter months.

Serves 2

Kosher salt (preferably Diamond Crystal; see page 17)

Extra-virgin olive oil

About 6 ounces (170 g) ramps, bulbs and stems sliced crosswise, leaves left whole

Pinch of dried chile flakes, plus more to taste

8 ounces (225 g) bucatini, spaghetti, or linguine

1 tablespoon unsalted butter

Fill a large pot (at least 6 quarts/liters) with 1 gallon (4 L) of water; add 4 tablespoons (40 g) kosher salt, cover the pot, and bring the water to a boil while you make your sauce. If the water begins to boil before your sauce is ready, turn down the heat, but don't let the volume of the pasta water reduce by boiling off.

Heat an extra-hefty glug of olive oil in a large skillet over low heat. When the oil is warm, add the ramp bulbs and stems and the chile flakes and cook slowly until the ramps are very tender and almost melted into the oil, 3 to 4 minutes. You do not want the ramps to brown at all. Add about half the ramp leaves and a big splash of water from the pasta pot to stop the cooking and slide the skillet off the heat.

Bring the pasta water (back) to a boil, add the noodles, and set your timer for 2 minutes before the shortest suggested cooking time on the package of pasta; this will ideally be 2 minutes before the pasta is al dente. Stir the noodles several times during the first 2 minutes of cooking to prevent them from sticking to the bottom of the pot or otherwise clumping together.

When the timer goes off, start tasting the noodles. When they seem like they are almost a perfect al dente (see page 22), drain and transfer them to the sauce in the skillet using your preferred method (see page 21), making sure to reserve at least 1 cup (240 ml) of the pasta water.

Slide the skillet back onto medium heat and finish cooking the noodles, tossing and adding pasta water as needed until the noodles are perfectly al dente.

Add the remaining ramp leaves and the butter and toss again to incorporate the butter and slightly wilt the ramp leaves. Taste and add more salt or chile flakes if you like.

Divide the pasta between two warm bowls and serve right away.

Turnips and Turnip Greens with Anchovies and Garlic Butter

This recipe calls for Garlic Butter, which I hope you keep in your fridge or freezer so you are ready to make Garlic Bread (page 47) in an instant. It also incorporates Hakurei turnips, which are different from the larger, storage-type turnips. With crisp, juicy, tender flesh and delicate tops, they resemble radishes more than turnips, and in fact radishes are a good substitute for them.

Serves 2

Kosher salt (preferably Diamond Crystal; see page 17)

Extra-virgin olive oil

3 to 10 oil-packed anchovy fillets, roughly chopped

8 ounces (225 g) Hakurei turnips (also called Tokyo turnips), trimmed and sliced into thin rounds

3 tablespoons Garlic Butter (page 27)

8 ounces (225 g) pappardelle, fettucine, or pappardelle rigate

Greens from 1 bunch Hakurei turnips, washed well and roughly chopped

¼ cup (30 g) 50/50 cheese (half Parmigiano-Reggiano, half Pecorino Romano, grated in a food processor; see page 39), plus more for serving

1 tablespoon fresh lemon juice, plus more to taste

Fill a large pot (at least 6 quarts/L) with 1 gallon (4 L) of water; add 4 tablespoons (40 g) kosher salt, cover the pot, and bring the water to a boil while you make your sauce. If the water begins to boil before your sauce is ready, turn down the heat, but don't let the volume of the pasta water reduce by boiling off.

Heat a generous glug of olive oil in a large skillet over medium heat. When the oil is hot, add the anchovies and cook gently until they disintegrate and melt into the oil. Then add the sliced turnips and cook gently for a minute or two.

Add about ½ cup (120 ml) water from the pasta pot and simmer the turnips until they are crisp-tender, 3 to 4 minutes. Add the garlic butter and swirl the pan to emulsify the butter and water, creating a sauce that coats the turnips creamily; don't let anything boil, which can break the emulsion. Slide the skillet off the heat.

Bring the pasta water (back) to a boil, add the noodles, and set your timer for 2 minutes less than the shortest suggested cooking time on the package of pasta; this will ideally be 2 minutes before the pasta is al dente. Stir the noodles several times during the first 2 minutes of cooking to prevent them from sticking to the bottom of the pot or otherwise clumping together.

When the timer goes off, start tasting the noodles. When they seem like they are almost a perfect al dente (see page 22), drain and transfer them to the sauce in the skillet using your preferred method (see page 21), making sure to reserve at least 1 cup (240 ml) of the pasta water.

Slide the skillet back onto medium heat, add the turnip greens, and finish cooking the noodles, tossing and adding splashes of pasta water until the noodles are perfectly al dente, the turnips are tender, the turnips greens are wilted, and the sauce is nicely juicy.

Reduce the heat to very low. Add the grated cheese and toss to emulsify it with the other sauce ingredients, adding splashes of pasta water (or plain hot water, if things are getting too salty) if needed to keep the consistency creamy and prevent the cheese from clumping. Add the lemon juice, toss again, and taste; add more salt or lemon juice if you like.

Divide the pasta between two warm bowls and serve right away, with more cheese to add at the table.

MORE WAYS

Instead of Garlic Butter, use Brown-Butter Butter (page 30) for nutty richness.

Turnips with Lemon Ricotta and Hazelnuts

Here's a pasta dish that's creamy, crunchy, and just the slightest bit spicy from the turnips and their green tops. Be sure to rinse the tops well, because sand and grit love to hide in the ruffled leaves.

Serves 2

Kosher salt (preferably Diamond Crystal; see page 17)

Extra-virgin olive oil

2 or 3 garlic cloves, smashed

8 ounces (225 g) Hakurei turnips (also called Tokyo turnips), trimmed and cut into slim wedges

Pinch of dried chile flakes, plus more if needed

¾ cup (180 g) Whipped Lemon Ricotta (page 35)

8 ounces (225 g) rigatoni, lumache, or conchiglie

Greens from 1 bunch Hakurei turnips, washed well and roughly chopped

¼ cup (30 g) 50/50 cheese (half Parmigiano-Reggiano, half Pecorino Romano, grated in a food processor; see page 39), plus more for serving

⅓ cup (40 g) chopped toasted hazelnuts (I love Freddy Guys)

Lemon Agrumato (lemony extra-virgin olive oil; see page 41; optional)

Fill a large pot (at least 6 quarts/L) with 1 gallon (4 L) of water; add 4 tablespoons (40 g) kosher salt, cover the pot, and bring the water to a boil while you make your sauce. If the water begins to boil before your sauce is ready, turn down the heat, but don't let the volume of the pasta water reduce by boiling off.

Heat a generous glug of olive oil in a large skillet over medium heat. When the oil is hot, add the garlic and the turnip wedges and cook gently, breaking up the garlic a bit with your spatula, until the garlic is lightly toasted and fragrant and the turnips have started to brown lightly, 3 to 4 minutes; try not to brown the garlic too much.

Add the chile flakes, about ½ cup (120 ml) water from the pasta pot, and the whipped lemon ricotta. Swirl the pan to emulsify the ricotta and water, creating a sauce that coats the turnips creamily; don't let anything boil. Slide the skillet off the heat.

Bring the pasta water (back) to a boil, add the noodles, and set your timer for 2 minutes less than the shortest suggested cooking time on the package of pasta; this will ideally be 2 minutes before the pasta is al dente. Stir the noodles several times during the first 2 minutes of cooking to prevent them from sticking to the bottom of the pot or otherwise clumping together.

When the timer goes off, start tasting the noodles. When they seem like they are almost a perfect al dente (see page 22), drain and transfer them to the sauce in the skillet using your preferred method (see page 21), making sure to reserve at least 1 cup (240 ml) of the pasta water.

Slide the skillet back onto medium heat, add the turnip greens, and finish cooking the noodles, tossing and adding splashes of pasta water until the noodles are perfectly al dente, the turnips are tender, the turnips greens are wilted, and the sauce is nicely juicy.

Reduce the heat to very low. Add the grated cheese and toss to emulsify it with the other sauce ingredients, adding splashes of pasta water (or plain hot water, if things are getting too salty) if needed to keep the consistency creamy and prevent the cheese from clumping. Add the hazelnuts, toss again, and taste; add more salt or chile flakes if you like.

Divide the pasta between two warm bowls, drizzle with Agrumato, if using, and serve right away, with more cheese to add at the table.

Early Summer

Beets with Brown Butter and Poppy Seeds

The color of this dish is an eye-popping magenta, and the flavors are just as unexpected and delightful. Shredding the beets ensures that they get tender, and brown butter balances their earthiness, so take your time as you melt and brown the butter. If your beets have their greens attached (and they look pristine), slice up a few and toss them into the dish when you add your noodles to the sauce.

Serves 2

- Kosher salt (preferably Diamond Crystal; see page 17)
- Extra-virgin olive oil
- 2 cups (200 g) shredded red beets (use the large holes on a box grater or shredding disc)
- 5 tablespoons (75 g) unsalted butter
- 2 tablespoons poppy seeds, plus more for serving
- 4 to 6 fresh sage leaves
- 8 ounces (225 g) gemelli, strozzapreti, or busiate
- ⅓ cup (40 g) 50/50 cheese (half Parmigiano-Reggiano, half Pecorino Romano, grated in a food processor; see page 39)
- 2 spoonfuls Whipped Plain Ricotta (page 34; optional)

Fill a large pot (at least 6 quarts/L) with 1 gallon (4 L) of water; add 4 tablespoons (40 g) kosher salt, cover the pot, and bring the water to a boil while you make your sauce. If the water begins to boil before your sauce is ready, turn down the heat, but don't let the volume of the pasta water reduce by boiling off.

Heat a generous glug of olive oil in a large skillet over medium-high heat. When the oil is hot, add the beets and spread them into an even layer. Cook without stirring for about 5 minutes; this will help develop a varied texture.

Stir the beets and add 4 tablespoons (60 g) of the butter (keep the last tablespoon cold), the poppy seeds, and the sage leaves. Let the butter melt and, keeping your eye on it (though it may be hard to see, given the colorful beets), cook until it becomes nutty-smelling and toasty brown, 3 to 4 minutes; take your time with this so it doesn't go all the way to burnt butter. When the butter is at the perfect stage, stop the cooking with a ladleful of water from the pasta pot and slide the skillet off the heat.

Bring the pasta water (back) to a boil, add the noodles, and set your timer for 2 minutes less than the shortest suggested cooking time on the package of pasta; this will ideally be 2 minutes before the pasta is al dente. Stir the noodles several times during the first 2 minutes of cooking to prevent them from sticking to the pot or otherwise clumping together.

When the timer goes off, start tasting the noodles. When they seem like they are 1½ to 2 minutes away from a perfect al dente (see page 22), drain and transfer them to the sauce in the skillet using your preferred method (see page 21), making sure to reserve at least 1 cup (240 ml) of the pasta water.

Slide the skillet back onto medium heat and finish cooking the noodles, tossing and adding plenty of splashes of pasta water until the noodles are perfectly al dente, the beets are tender, and the sauce is nicely juicy. If the sauce seems watery, simmer for another few seconds to tighten it up, bearing in mind that the cheese will thicken it.

Reduce the heat to very low. Add the grated cheese and toss to emulsify it with the other sauce ingredients, adding splashes of pasta water if needed to keep the consistency creamy and prevent the cheese from clumping. As you are tossing, drop in the final cold tablespoon of butter, which will help everything come together creamily rather than greasily. Taste and add more salt if you like.

Divide the pasta between two warm bowls. Top each serving with a big spoonful of whipped ricotta, sprinkle with a few more poppy seeds, and serve immediately.

Golden Beets with Golden Raisins, Pine Nuts, and Sausage

Golden beets are generally milder than their deep-red cousins, but fortunately they still are sweet and earthy, the two flavor characteristics that make beets so compelling. Golden beets also have a beautiful color, which you'll play on here by using golden raisins as well. You can definitely make this recipe with regular red beets or candy-striped Chioggia beets; just know that the color palette will be a bit different.

Serves 2

⅓ cup (50 g) golden raisins

Kosher salt (preferably Diamond Crystal; see page 17)

6 ounces (170 g) bulk Italian sausage, sweet or hot

Extra-virgin olive oil

2 or 3 garlic cloves, smashed

2 cups (200 g) shredded golden beets (use the large holes on a box grater or shredding disc) or very slim wedges

¼ teaspoon dried chile flakes, plus more to taste

¼ cup (35 g) pine nuts, lightly toasted

8 ounces (225 g) radiatore, fusilli, or rotini

1 tablespoon unsalted butter

⅓ cup (40 g) 50/50 cheese (half Parmigiano-Reggiano, half Pecorino Romano, grated in a food processor; see page 39), plus more for serving

Shaved ricotta salata, for serving (optional)

Put the raisins in a small bowl and cover with hot water. Soak until plumped and tender, then drain off the water. Set aside.

Fill a large pot (at least 6 quarts/L) with 1 gallon (4 L) of water; add 4 tablespoons (40 g) kosher salt, cover the pot, and bring the water to a boil while you make your sauce. If the water begins to boil before your sauce is ready, turn down the heat, but don't let the volume of the pasta water reduce by boiling off.

Shape the sausage into 2 patties. Heat a glug of olive oil in a large skillet over medium-high heat. When the oil is hot, add the sausage and sear, smashing the patties down from time to time with your spatula to create a nicely browned crust on the bottom, about 5 minutes.

Flip the sausage, add the garlic, and continue cooking until the sausage has browned and the garlic is nicely toasted and softened (but not too dark), another 3 to 4 minutes.

Add the beets (along with another glug of olive oil if the pan seems dry) and chile flakes and cook, stirring and breaking up the sausage a bit, until the beets start to soften, about 2 minutes (a few minutes longer if using wedges).

Add the drained raisins, the pine nuts, and a splash of water from the pasta pot and continue cooking until the beets are mostly but not quite fully tender. Slide the skillet off the heat.

Bring the pasta water (back) to a boil, add the noodles, and set your timer for 2 minutes less than the shortest suggested cooking time on the package of pasta; this will ideally be 2 minutes before the pasta is al dente. Stir the noodles several times during the first 2 minutes of cooking to prevent them from sticking to the bottom of the pot or otherwise clumping together.

recipe continues →

When the timer goes off, start tasting the noodles. When they seem like they are 1½ to 2 minutes away from a perfect al dente (see page 22), drain and transfer them to the sauce in the skillet using your preferred method (see page 21), making sure to reserve at least 1 cup (240 ml) of the pasta water.

Slide the skillet back onto medium heat and finish cooking the noodles, tossing and adding plenty of splashes of pasta water until the noodles are perfectly al dente, the beets are fully tender, and the sauce is nicely juicy. If the sauce seems watery, simmer for another few seconds to tighten it up, bearing in mind that the cheese will thicken it.

Reduce the heat to very low. Add the butter and 50/50 cheese and toss to emulsify them with the other sauce ingredients, adding splashes of pasta water (or plain hot water, if things are getting too salty) if needed to keep the consistency creamy and prevent the cheese from clumping. Taste and add more salt or chile flakes if you like.

Divide the pasta between two warm bowls, top with some shavings of ricotta salata, if using, and serve right away, with more 50/50 cheese to add at the table.

Carrots with Basil Pesto

This sunny-looking pasta is simple to make, especially if you have some basil pesto in the freezer. But pesto takes only a moment to whiz up in a food processor, so this dish is an easy weeknight choice, even if you don't.

The goal with herb pestos is to keep them emulsified with some pasta water so that they are creamy rather than separated and oily. Your sauce will probably fall in and out of emulsification a few times during cooking, but it's easy to pull it back into shape at the last minute by tossing and stirring as you add a bit more pasta water. Just keep the heat gentle, which also preserves the delicate perfume of the fresh basil.

I like to cut the carrots to match the length of the pasta, but the most important thing is to cook the carrots until they are fully tender—no crunch, please.

Serves 2 or 3

Kosher salt (preferably Diamond Crystal; see page 17)

3 cups (300 g) carrot "batons," cut to match the size of the noodle

Extra-virgin olive oil

2 or 3 garlic cloves, smashed

¾ cup (180 g) Basil Pesto (page 33)

8 ounces (225 g) strozzapreti, penne, or ziti

Small handful of fresh basil leaves

¼ cup (30 g) 50/50 cheese (half Parmigiano-Reggiano, half Pecorino Romano, grated in a food processor; see page 39), plus more for serving

1 tablespoon fresh lemon juice, plus more to taste

2 tablespoons Dried Breadcrumbs (page 36)

Fill a large pot (at least 6 quarts/L) with 1 gallon (4 L) of water; add 4 tablespoons (40 g) kosher salt, cover the pot, and bring the water to a boil. Add the carrots and boil until tender (you're not looking for crisp-tender for this dish), 4 to 6 minutes. Scoop out the carrots and set aside. Keep the pot of water warm on the stove; you'll use it to cook the pasta.

Heat a glug of olive oil in a large skillet over medium heat. When the oil is hot, add the garlic and cook gently, breaking it up a bit with your spatula, until it is softened and lightly toasted but not browned, 3 to 4 minutes.

Reduce the heat to low and add the carrots, a splash of water from the pasta pot, and the pesto; toss to blend. Heat gently until the pesto has loosened up, tossing so the pesto emulsifies with the water, then slide the skillet off the heat.

Bring the pasta water (back) to a boil, add the noodles, and set your timer for 2 minutes less than the shortest suggested cooking time on the package of pasta; this will ideally be 2 minutes before the pasta is al dente. Stir the noodles several times during the first 2 minutes of cooking to prevent them from sticking to the bottom of the pot or otherwise clumping together.

When the timer goes off, start tasting the noodles. When they seem like they are almost a perfect al dente (see page 22), drain and transfer them to the sauce in the skillet using your preferred method (see page 21), making sure to reserve at least 1 cup (240 ml) of the pasta water.

Slide the skillet back onto medium heat and finish cooking the noodles, tossing for a few seconds and adding pasta water if needed until the noodles are perfectly al dente, the carrots are tender, and the sauce is nicely creamy.

recipe continues →

Reduce the heat to very low. Add the basil, tearing the leaves into a few pieces, and the grated cheese and toss to emulsify the cheese with the other sauce ingredients, adding splashes of pasta water if needed to keep the consistency creamy and prevent the cheese from clumping.

Stir in the lemon juice; taste and add more if you like.

Divide the pasta between two or three warm bowls, garnish each bowl with the breadcrumbs, and serve right away, with more cheese to add at the table.

MORE WAYS

If you have pristine carrot tops, especially if you've grown them yourself, use some in your pesto; try 2 parts basil to 1 part carrot tops.

Hawaii-Inspired Pasta Salad

This is my version of the macaroni salad that's served with a Hawaiian plate lunch. I emphasize the grated carrots, soaking them in lemon juice first, which cuts through the generous amount of mayonnaise that's key to the dish. Best Foods/ Hellmann's is the brand to use, and the dressing gets some extra tang from a splash of white wine vinegar (I like the sweet late-harvest sauvignon blanc vinegar from Katz Farm; see Resources, page 380).

Serves 6 to 8

Kosher salt (preferably Diamond Crystal; see page 17)

8 ounces (225 g) anelli, elbow macaroni, or ditalini

1 tablespoon slightly sweet white wine vinegar, plus more to taste

Extra-virgin olive oil

2 cups (200 g) grated carrots (use the large holes of a box grater or shredding disc)

¼ cup (60 ml) fresh lemon juice, plus more to taste

2 cups (160 g) sliced celery

As many celery leaves as are on your bunch, chopped

½ cup (75 g) finely chopped red onion

4 or 5 scallions, white and light green parts only, thinly sliced

Freshly ground black pepper

½ cup (115 g) mayonnaise, plus more to taste

2 hard-cooked eggs, peeled and roughly chopped

Fill a large pot (at least 6 quarts/L) with 1 gallon (4 L) of water; add 4 tablespoons (40 g) kosher salt, cover the pot, and bring the water to a boil. Add the noodles and set your timer for 2 minutes less than the shortest suggested cooking time on the package of pasta; this will ideally be 2 minutes before the pasta is al dente. Stir the noodles several times during the first 2 minutes of cooking to prevent them from sticking to the bottom of the pot or otherwise clumping together.

When the timer goes off, start tasting the noodles. When they seem like they are a perfect al dente (see page 22), drain them in a colander. Quickly rinse the noodles with warm water and shake off any excess moisture; you want them as dry as possible. Transfer the noodles to a large bowl (this can be the serving bowl if it's large enough to allow some tossing).

While noodles are still warm, sprinkle on the vinegar and toss thoroughly so they absorb it evenly. Drizzle on about 1 tablespoon olive oil and toss again to evenly coat the noodles and prevent them from sticking together. Set aside.

Put the carrots in a small bowl, add the lemon juice and a generous pinch of salt, and toss to combine. Let sit for 10 to 15 minutes so the carrots can absorb some lemon juice.

Add the carrots and the lemon juice to the bowl with the pasta. Add the celery, celery leaves, red onion, and scallions. Season lightly with black pepper. Toss to combine. Add the mayonnaise and toss again, making sure the mayonnaise thoroughly coats all the noodles. Taste and adjust the seasoning with more salt, pepper, vinegar, or mayonnaise if you like.

Add the eggs and give the salad one final toss, allowing the eggs to break up a bit but not turn into total mush.

Tidy up the bowl or transfer the salad to a serving bowl or platter. Serve at cool room temperature.

MORE WAYS

Add ½ cup (120 g) chopped peperoncini, a drizzle of the peperoncini brine from the jar, and a big spoonful of mustard (go with something American, such as French's) when you add the mayonnaise.

Pasta Salad with Celery, Provolone, Salami, Olives, and Peperoncini

A little bit like an Italian hoagie, this salad is zesty and flavorful enough to stand as a meal on its own, but it would be lovely as a side dish to anything grilled.

Serves 4 to 6

Kosher salt (preferably Diamond Crystal; see page 17)

8 ounces (225 g) casarecce, gemelli, or strozzapreti

½ cup (120 ml) Italian Salad Dressing (page 162), plus more to taste

2 cups (250 g) sliced celery (in pieces about ½ inch/1.25 cm thick)

1 cup (115 g) shredded provolone cheese

¾ cup (60 g) loosely packed thin salami strips

¼ cup (60 g) roughly chopped cored pickled peppers, such as peperoncini

½ cup (70 g) smashed pitted olives

Large handful of arugula

Small handful of fresh basil leaves

Small handful of fresh mint leaves

Small handful of fresh flat-leaf parsley leaves

3 tablespoons Dried Breadcrumbs (page 36), for serving

Fill a large pot (at least 6 quarts/L) with 1 gallon (4 L) of water; add 4 tablespoons (40 g) kosher salt, cover the pot, and bring the water to a boil. Add the noodles and set your timer for 2 minutes less than the shortest suggested cooking time on the package of pasta; this will ideally be 2 minutes before the pasta is al dente. Stir the noodles several times during the first 2 minutes of cooking to prevent them from sticking to the bottom of the pot or otherwise clumping together.

When the timer goes off, start tasting the noodles. When they seem like they are a perfect al dente (see page 22), drain them in a colander. Quickly rinse the noodles with warm water and shake off any excess moisture; you want them to be as dry as possible. Transfer the noodles to a large bowl (this can be the serving bowl if it's large enough to allow some tossing).

While the noodles are still warm, drizzle on 2 tablespoons of the Italian dressing and toss thoroughly so they absorb it evenly.

Add the celery, provolone, salami, peperoncini, olives, arugula, and half the herb leaves (tear them into a few pieces). Pour on the remaining Italian dressing and toss to incorporate thoroughly. Taste, and if you think the salad needs it, add more dressing. Add the remaining herb leaves (again tearing them into pieces) and toss once more. Finish by showering the salad with the breadcrumbs.

Tidy up the edges of the bowl or transfer to another serving bowl or platter. Serve at cool room temperature.

Celery with Shrimp, Jalapeño, and Walnuts

Celery usually makes its appearance in pasta dishes only as a role player in a soffritto, but in this recipe, it's the lead. Paired with other light, delicate ingredients and cooked until still a little crisp but mostly tender, the celery is surprisingly right. If your celery still has tender leaves, definitely add them along with the mint and parsley.

Serves 2

Kosher salt (preferably Diamond Crystal; see page 17)

Extra-virgin olive oil

2 or 3 garlic cloves, smashed

1 small jalapeño, sliced into rings, core and seeds removed

½ cup (45 g) roughly chopped walnuts

8 ounces (225 g) raw shrimp, any size, preferably wild, peeled and deveined

1 tablespoon unsalted butter

⅓ cup (40 g) sliced scallions (white and light green parts only)

Small handful of fresh mint leaves

Small handful of fresh flat-leaf parsley leaves

1 tablespoon finely grated lemon zest

2 cups (160 g) sliced celery

8 ounces (225 g) spaghetti, spaghetti alla chitarra, or fettucine

¼ cup (30 g) 50/50 cheese (half Parmigiano-Reggiano, half Pecorino Romano, grated in a food processor; see page 39; optional)

2 tablespoons fresh lemon juice

Lemon Agrumato (lemony extra-virgin olive oil; see page 41; optional)

Chunk of Parmigiano, for grating at the table

Fill a large pot (at least 6 quarts/L) with 1 gallon (4 L) of water; add 4 tablespoons (40 g) kosher salt, cover the pot, and bring the water to a boil while you make your sauce. If the water begins to boil before your sauce is ready, turn down the heat, but don't let the volume of the pasta water reduce by boiling off.

Heat a glug of olive oil in a large skillet over medium heat. When the oil is hot, add the garlic and jalapeño and cook gently, breaking it up a bit with your spatula as it cooks, until the garlic is lightly toasted and fragrant and the chile is soft and a bit golden, 2 to 3 minutes.

Add the walnuts and continue cooking until they are lightly toasted, scooting the ingredients around in the pan so they cook evenly, another 3 minutes or so.

Add the shrimp and cook on one side for about 45 seconds, then add the butter, scallions, and half the mint and parsley, tearing the leaves into a few pieces. Cook, tossing the ingredients, until the scallions are starting to soften and the shrimp has taken on a bit more color, another 2 to 3 minutes (or longer if your shrimp are very large). You don't want to fully cook the shrimp yet, as it will cook further once you add the noodles.

Add the lemon zest and slide the skillet off the heat.

Bring the pasta water (back) to a boil and add the celery. Boil for about 30 seconds, then scoop out the celery with a slotted spoon or spider and add it to the skillet with the sauce. Don't worry if you miss a few celery slices; they'll ride along with the noodles later.

Add the noodles to the boiling water and set your timer for 2 minutes less than the shortest suggested cooking time on the package of pasta; this will ideally be 2 minutes before the pasta is al dente. Stir the noodles several times during the first 2 minutes of cooking to prevent

them from sticking to the bottom of the pot or otherwise clumping together.

When the timer goes off, start tasting the noodles. When they seem like they are almost a perfect al dente (see page 22), drain and transfer them to the sauce in the skillet using your preferred method (see page 21), making sure to reserve at least 1 cup (240 ml) of the pasta water.

Slide the skillet back onto medium heat and finish cooking the noodles, tossing and adding pasta water as needed until the noodles are perfectly al dente, the shrimp is fully cooked, and the sauce is nicely juicy. If the sauce seems watery, simmer for another few seconds to tighten it up, bearing in mind that the cheese, if you're using it, will thicken it.

Reduce the heat to very low. Add the 50/50 cheese, if using, and toss to emulsify it with the other sauce ingredients, adding splashes of pasta water if needed to keep the consistency creamy and prevent the cheese from clumping. Taste and add more salt if you like.

Take the skillet off the heat, add the remaining mint and parsley, the lemon juice, and a nice drizzle of Agrumato, if using, and toss to mix.

Divide the pasta between two warm bowls, grate some Parmigiano on top, and serve right away.

MORE WAYS

Add chopped peperoncini to give the dish a "shrimp salad" quality, which is a good thing.

Fennel with Mascarpone and Arugula

Creamy but not too rich, this pasta is all about the mellow, anise-scented fennel. Some fennel can be quite fibrous, especially the outer layers. If your bulb looks at all stringy or tough, you can shave off the surface layer using a vegetable peeler, rendering it more tender and able to cook evenly with the inner layers.

Serves 2 or 3

1 large fennel bulb (about 10 ounces/ 280 g after trimming off the stalks and fronds)

Kosher salt (preferably Diamond Crystal; see page 17)

Extra-virgin olive oil

½ cup (60 g) diced pancetta

2 or 3 garlic cloves, smashed

¼ teaspoon dried chile flakes, plus more to taste

1 cup (240 ml) dry white wine

¾ cup (185 g) mascarpone

8 ounces (225 g) fettucine, tagliatelle, or pappardelle

⅓ cup (40 g) 50/50 cheese (half Parmigiano-Reggiano, half Pecorino Romano, grated in a food processor; see page 39), plus more for serving

2 big handfuls of arugula (about 2 ounces/60 g)

Cut the fennel bulb in half lengthwise and cut out the core. Cut the halves into ½-inch-thick (1.25 cm) slices; it's fine if the layers fall apart. Set aside.

Fill a large pot (at least 6 quarts/L) with 1 gallon (4 L) of water; add 4 tablespoons (40 g) kosher salt, cover the pot, and bring the water to a boil while you make your sauce. If the water begins to boil before your sauce is ready, turn down the heat, but don't let the volume of the pasta water reduce by boiling off.

Heat a generous glug of olive oil in a large skillet over medium heat. When the oil is hot, add the fennel slices, pancetta, garlic, and chile flakes. Cook, stirring frequently, until the fennel is crisp-tender (it will continue to cook in subsequent steps), 10 to 12 minutes. You may want to add a splash or two of water from the pasta pot to help the fennel get tender.

Add the wine, increase the heat to medium-high, and cook at a lively simmer until the wine has reduced by about half, 4 to 5 minutes.

Add the mascarpone, reduce the heat to medium, and simmer gently until the sauce has thickened slightly, 2 to 3 minutes. (If the sauce looks like it will separate, whisk in a few drops of cold water.) Slide the skillet off the heat.

Bring the pasta water (back) to a boil, add the noodles, and set your timer for 2 minutes less than the shortest suggested cooking time on the package of pasta; this will ideally be 2 minutes before the pasta is al dente. Stir the noodles several times during the first 2 minutes of cooking to prevent them from sticking to the bottom of the pot or otherwise clumping together.

When the timer goes off, start tasting the noodles. When they seem like they are 1½ to 2 minutes away from a perfect al dente (see page 22), drain and transfer them to the sauce in the skillet using your preferred method (see

page 21), making sure to reserve at least 1 cup (240 ml) of the pasta water.

Slide the skillet back onto medium heat and finish cooking the noodles, tossing and adding plenty of splashes of pasta water until the noodles are perfectly al dente, the fennel is tender, and the mascarpone sauce is nicely juicy, bearing in mind that the cheese will thicken it.

Reduce the heat to very low. Add the grated cheese and toss to emulsify it with the other sauce ingredients, adding splashes of pasta water if needed to keep the consistency creamy and prevent the cheese from clumping. Taste and add more salt or chile flakes if you like.

Add the arugula and toss once or twice just to incorporate the greens but not so much that you start to cook them.

Divide the pasta between two or three warm bowls and serve right away, with more cheese to add at the table.

Fennel with Salami, Tomato, and Mussels

Try using fennel salami (finocchiona) to double down on the fennel flavor. If you can't find it, any Genoa-type salami works well, or you can go for something spicier, as the other ingredients can stand up to some assertive spice.

Serves 2

Kosher salt (preferably Diamond Crystal; see page 17)

Extra-virgin olive oil

3 or 4 garlic cloves, smashed

¼ teaspoon dried chile flakes

¼ cup (30 g) thinly sliced fresh chile, such as jalapeño (core and seed it before slicing; optional)

⅓ cup (40 g) thin strips of salami (start with sliced salami, then cut each slice into ¼-inch-wide/ 6 mm strips)

1½ cups (120 g) lightly packed thinly sliced fennel bulb (core the bulb, then slice it crosswise)

2 tablespoons tomato paste

1 cup (250 g) canned whole peeled tomatoes, crushed by hand (see page 44), with their juices

12 ounces (340 g) fresh mussels in the shell, scrubbed and debearded if necessary

8 ounces (225 g) bucatini, spaghetti, or trenette

2 tablespoons unsalted butter

Fill a large pot (at least 6 quarts/L) with 1 gallon (4 L) of water; add 4 tablespoons (40 g) kosher salt, cover the pot, and bring the water to a boil while you make your sauce. If the water begins to boil before your sauce is ready, turn down the heat, but don't let the volume of the pasta water reduce by boiling off.

Arrange your pasta bowls near the stove and tear off a piece of foil that will loosely cover both bowls (to keep the mussels warm as you finish the dish).

Heat a generous glug of olive oil in a large skillet with a lid over medium heat. When the oil is hot, add the garlic and cook gently, smashing the cloves a bit to break them up, until the garlic is fragrant, tender, and very lightly toasted but not browned, 3 to 4 minutes.

Add the chile flakes and cook for another 30 seconds so they can bloom. If using the fresh chile, add it and cook until slightly softened, another 1 minute.

Toss in the salami and cook, stirring a bit, until some of the fat starts to render and the salami strips start to crisp around the edges, 1 to 2 minutes. Add the fennel and cook, stirring, until the fennel slices are just tender and translucent, 5 to 6 minutes.

Scoot some of the ingredients to one side of the skillet to make a space and add the tomato paste. Cook, spreading it on the surface of the skillet, until slightly darkened and toasted, 30 seconds to 1 minute.

Add the crushed tomatoes and their juices, adjust the heat to maintain a very lively simmer, and cook until the sauce has reduced and thickened slightly, about 2 minutes.

Add the mussels and cover the skillet with a lid. Cook, shaking the pan a bit, until the mussel shells have opened, about 3 minutes. With a slotted spoon or tongs, pluck out all the open mussels, draining their juices back into the skillet, transfer them to the pasta bowls, and cover loosely with the foil. Cook any unopened mussels for another minute or so, then add the newly opened ones to the pasta bowls and cover again with the foil. If any stubbornly unopened mussels remain, discard them.

Continue cooking the tomato sauce until the mussel juices have integrated and the sauce is nicely reduced and tasty, another 2 minutes or so. Slide the skillet off the heat.

recipe continues →

Bring the pasta water (back) to a boil, add the noodles, and set your timer for 2 minutes less than the shortest suggested cooking time on the package of pasta; this will ideally be 2 minutes before the pasta is al dente. Stir the noodles several times during the first 2 minutes of cooking to prevent them from sticking to the bottom of the pot or otherwise clumping together.

When the timer goes off, start tasting the noodles. When they seem like they are 1½ to 2 minutes away from a perfect al dente (see page 22), drain and transfer them to the sauce in the skillet using your preferred method (see page 21), making sure to reserve at least 1 cup (240 ml) of the pasta water.

Slide the skillet back onto medium heat and finish cooking the noodles, tossing and adding plenty of splashes of pasta water until the noodles are perfectly al dente, the fennel is tender, and the sauce is nicely juicy. If the sauce seems watery, simmer for another few seconds to tighten it up.

Reduce the heat to very low, add the butter, and swirl or toss to incorporate and emulsify it.

Divide the noodles and sauce between the two pasta bowls, piling everything right on top of the mussels so they warm up. Serve right away, encouraging the diners to pick up the mussels with their fingers and eat the meat from the shells. Be sure to set out another bowl in which diners can discard their mussel shells.

MORE WAYS

Substitute small clams, such as Manila, for the mussels, cooking them in the same way.

Pasta Salad with Fennel, Arugula, Radish, and Ricotta Salata

This refreshing salad is all about contrasting textures—uber-crisp fennel and radishes, plump raisins, and crunchy pine nuts, all dressed in creamy whipped lemon ricotta. To ensure the fennel and radishes are as crisp as can be, I soak them in ice water.

Serves 4

1 large fennel bulb, stalks and fronds trimmed off, bulb cored and sliced as thinly as possible

1 small bunch radishes, trimmed and thinly sliced

⅓ cup (50 g) raisins

Kosher salt (preferably Diamond Crystal; see page 17)

8 ounces (225 g) elbow macaroni, cavatappi, or penne

¼ cup (60 ml) fresh lemon juice

Extra-virgin olive oil or lemon Agrumato (lemony extra-virgin olive oil; see page 41)

Large handful of arugula

Small handful of fresh mint leaves

1 or 2 spring onions, sliced, or 3 or 4 scallions, trimmed and sliced

⅓ cup (40 g) pine nuts, lightly toasted

¼ teaspoon dried chile flakes, plus more to taste

Freshly ground black pepper

¾ cup (180 g) Whipped Lemon Ricotta (page 35)

1 teaspoon grated lemon zest

½ cup (60 g) crumbled ricotta salata, for serving

Put the fennel and radish slices in a medium bowl and fill with ice water. Soak until the vegetables are nicely crisp, 30 minutes to 1 hour. Drain well.

Meanwhile, put the raisins in a small bowl, cover with warm water, and soak until they have plumped up, 15 to 30 minutes. Drain well.

Fill a large pot (at least 6 quarts/L) with 1 gallon (4 L) of water; add 4 tablespoons (40 g) kosher salt, cover the pot, and bring the water to a boil. Add the noodles and set your timer for 2 minutes less than the shortest suggested cooking time on the package of pasta; this will ideally be 2 minutes before the pasta is al dente. Stir the noodles several times during the first 2 minutes of cooking to prevent them from sticking to the bottom of the pot or otherwise clumping together.

When the timer goes off, start tasting the noodles. When they seem like they are a perfect al dente (see page 22), drain them in a colander. Quickly rinse the noodles with warm water and shake off any excess moisture; you want them to be as dry as possible. Transfer the noodles to a large bowl (this can be the serving bowl if it's large enough to allow some tossing).

While the noodles are still warm, sprinkle on 1 tablespoon of the lemon juice and toss thoroughly so they absorb it evenly. Drizzle on about 1 tablespoon olive oil and toss again to evenly coat the noodles and prevent them from sticking together.

Add the fennel and radishes, raisins, arugula, mint leaves (tear them into a few pieces), spring onions, and pine nuts to the noodles. Sprinkle on ½ teaspoon salt, the chile flakes, and several twists of black pepper. Toss to combine.

In a small bowl, whisk together the remaining 3 tablespoons lemon juice, the whipped lemon ricotta, and the lemon zest. Pour the mixture over the salad and toss to thoroughly combine. Taste and adjust the seasoning with more salt, black pepper, or chile flakes if needed.

Drizzle on about 2 tablespoons olive oil or Agrumato and toss once again. Tidy up the edges of the bowl or transfer the salad to a serving bowl or platter. Distribute the ricotta salata over the salad and serve right away at cool room temperature.

AGRUMATO

Snap Peas with 'Nduja and Spring Onion

True spring onions are a seasonal treat. They're essentially baby onions that are still sweet and tender, with bright, grassy notes. Some have bulbs that are quite large and round, while others are slender, looking like plump scallions. Scallions are an acceptable substitute.

Serves 2

Kosher salt (preferably Diamond Crystal; see page 17)

Extra-virgin olive oil

½ cup (75 g) thinly sliced spring onion (white bulb and some green stalk)

3½ ounces (100 g) 'nduja

1 tablespoon tomato paste

1 cup (250 g) canned whole peeled tomatoes, crushed by hand (see page 44), with their juices

1 cup (120 g) sliced snap peas (cut at an angle into ¼-inch/6 mm pieces)

8 ounces (225 g) casarecce, pici, or trenette

½ cup (60 g) 50/50 cheese (half Parmigiano-Reggiano, half Pecorino Romano, grated in a food processor; see page 39), plus more for serving

1 tablespoon unsalted butter

Small handful of fresh tender herbs, such as chervil, chives, mint, and/or parsley, roughly chopped or torn

A few chive blossoms (optional)

Fill a large pot (at least 6 quarts/L) with 1 gallon (4 L) of water; add 4 tablespoons (40 g) kosher salt, cover the pot, and bring the water to a boil while you make your sauce. If the water begins to boil before your sauce is ready, turn down the heat, but don't let the volume of the pasta water reduce by boiling off.

Heat a generous glug of olive oil in a large skillet over medium heat. When the oil is hot, add the spring onion and cook gently until soft and sweet but not browned, about 5 minutes.

Add the 'nduja to the skillet and smash it down a bit, then cook until it starts to get slightly browned and the oil separates out, about 4 minutes.

Add the tomato paste and cook, stirring and smearing the tomato paste onto the surface of the pan, until it has darkened slightly, 30 seconds to 1 minute.

Add the crushed tomatoes and their juices and simmer, stirring frequently, until they have reduced by about half, another 5 minutes or so. Toss in the snap peas and slide the skillet off the heat.

Add the noodles to the boiling water and set your timer for 2 minutes less than the shortest suggested cooking time on the package of pasta; this will ideally be 2 minutes before the pasta is al dente. Stir the noodles several times during the first 2 minutes of cooking to prevent them from sticking to the bottom of the pot or otherwise clumping together.

When the timer goes off, start tasting the noodles. When they seem like they are 1½ to 2 minutes away from a perfect al dente (see page 22), drain and transfer them to the skillet using your preferred method (see page 21), reserving at least 1 cup (240 ml) of the pasta water.

Slide the skillet back onto medium heat and finish cooking the noodles, tossing and adding plenty of splashes of pasta water until the noodles are perfectly al dente, and the sauce is nicely juicy. If the sauce seems watery, simmer for another few seconds to tighten it up, bearing in mind that the cheese will thicken it.

Reduce the heat to very low. Add the grated cheese and toss to emulsify it with the other sauce ingredients, adding splashes of pasta water (or plain hot water, if things are getting too salty) if needed to keep the consistency creamy and prevent the cheese from clumping. Add the butter and toss to blend. Add the herbs and toss once more to distribute them.

Divide the pasta between two warm bowls, garnish with the chive blossoms, if using, and serve right away, with more cheese to add at the table.

Snap Peas with Lamb Ragu and Fiore Sardo

This lamb ragu is slightly rich, so thinly sliced yet still crunchy snap peas are a great contrast. The peas need only a few minutes of cooking because you want them crisp-tender, so you'll add them to the pasta water at the last minute and then finish them along with the noodles in the sauce. Fiore Sardo is a lightly smoked sheep's-milk cheese from Sardinia. It might take some hunting to find, but it will be worth your while.

Serves 2

Kosher salt (preferably Diamond Crystal; see page 17)

1 cup (250 g) Lamb Ragu (page 77)

⅛ teaspoon dried chile flakes, plus more to taste

8 ounces (225 g) fusilli col buco, bucatini, or fusilli

1½ cups (170 g) sliced snap peas (cut at an angle into ¼-inch/6 mm pieces)

1 tablespoon unsalted butter

⅔ cup (60 g) finely grated Fiore Sardo, plus more for serving

Fill a large pot (at least 6 quarts/L) with 1 gallon (4 L) of water; add 4 tablespoons (40 g) kosher salt, cover the pot, and bring the water to a boil while you make your sauce. If the water begins to boil before your sauce is ready, turn down the heat, but don't let the volume of the pasta water reduce by boiling off.

Put a splash of the pasta water into a large skillet over medium heat, add the lamb ragu and the chile flakes, and cook gently until the ragu is loosened and heated through; slide the skillet off the heat.

Bring the pasta water (back) to a boil, add the noodles, and set your timer for 2 minutes less than the shortest suggested cooking time on the package of pasta; this will ideally be 2 minutes before the pasta is al dente. Stir the noodles several times during the first 2 minutes of cooking to prevent them from sticking to the bottom of the pot or otherwise clumping together.

When the timer goes off, start tasting the noodles. When they seem like they are 1½ to 2 minutes away from a perfect al dente (see page 22), add the sliced snap peas. Drain and transfer the noodles and snap peas to the sauce in the skillet using your preferred method (see page 21), making sure to reserve at least 1 cup (240 ml) of the pasta water.

Slide the skillet back onto medium heat and finish cooking the noodles, tossing and adding plenty of splashes of pasta water until the noodles are perfectly al dente, the snap peas are tender, and the sauce is nicely juicy. If the sauce seems watery, simmer for another few seconds to tighten it up, bearing in mind that the cheese will thicken it.

Reduce the heat to very low. Add the butter and grated Fiore Sardo and toss to emulsify them with the other sauce ingredients, adding splashes of pasta water if needed to keep the consistency creamy and prevent the cheese from clumping. Taste and add more salt or chile flakes if you like.

Divide the pasta between two warm bowls and serve right away, with more cheese to add at the table.

Midsummer

Broccoli Fra Diavolo with Jalapeño

Fresh hot chile and a copious quantity of dried chile flakes create layers of heat in this rather zesty broccoli and tomato dish. You can cut back on the quantities if you don't like things too spicy, but this dish really is all about the heat, so maybe take a chance? The final dollop of whipped ricotta will cool things down.

Serves 2

- Kosher salt (preferably Diamond Crystal; see page 17)
- Extra-virgin olive oil
- 4 garlic cloves, smashed
- ½ cup (75 g) finely chopped onion
- 1 medium (or large, if you like spicy) jalapeño, cored, seeded, and finely chopped
- 2 cups (200 g) ½-inch (1.25 cm) broccoli florets and stems
- 1 teaspoon dried chile flakes, plus more as desired
- 1 tablespoon tomato paste
- 2 cups (500 g) canned whole peeled tomatoes, crushed by hand (see page 44), with their juices
- 8 ounces (225 g) tagliatelle, fettucine, or linguine
- ⅓ cup (40 g) 50/50 cheese (half Parmigiano-Reggiano, half Pecorino Romano, grated in a food processor; see page 39), plus more for serving
- Small handful of fresh basil leaves
- 2 spoonfuls Whipped Plain Ricotta (page 34; optional)

Fill a large pot (at least 6 quarts/L) with 1 gallon (4 L) of water; add 4 tablespoons (40 g) kosher salt, cover the pot, and bring the water to a boil while you make your sauce. If the water begins to boil before your sauce is ready, turn down the heat, but don't let the volume of the pasta water reduce by boiling off.

Heat a generous glug of olive oil in a large skillet over medium heat. When the oil is hot, add the garlic and cook gently until it begins to soften, 3 to 4 minutes, smashing it a bit so it breaks up. Add the chopped onion and jalapeño and continue cooking until the onion is soft and fragrant, another 2 to 3 minutes. Increase the heat to medium-high, add the broccoli, and cook until the florets are starting to brown a bit, 3 to 4 minutes, stirring and scraping everything so the garlic and onions don't burn.

Add the chile flakes and cook for a few seconds so they wake up a bit. Then add the tomato paste and cook, smearing it into a thin layer on the surface of the pan, until slightly toasted, 30 seconds to 1 minute.

Add the crushed tomatoes and their juices. Give everything a big stir and adjust the heat to maintain a lively simmer. Simmer until the tomato sauce has reduced a bit, the broccoli is not quite tender, and all the flavors are concentrated, 4 to 5 minutes. Slide the skillet off the heat.

Bring the pasta water (back) to a boil, add the noodles, and set your timer for 2 minutes less than the shortest suggested cooking time on the package of pasta; this will ideally be 2 minutes before the pasta is al dente. Stir the noodles several times during the first 2 minutes of cooking to prevent them from sticking to the bottom of the pot or otherwise clumping together.

When the timer goes off, start tasting the noodles. When they seem like they are 1½ to 2 minutes away from a perfect al dente (see page 22), drain and transfer them to the sauce in the skillet using your preferred method (see page 21), making sure to reserve at least 1 cup (240 ml) of the pasta water.

Slide the skillet back onto medium heat and finish cooking the noodles, tossing and adding plenty of splashes of pasta water until the noodles are perfectly al dente, the broccoli is tender, and the sauce is nicely juicy. If the sauce seems watery, simmer for another few seconds to tighten it up, bearing in mind that the cheese will thicken it.

Reduce the heat to very low. Add the 50/50 cheese and toss to emulsify it with the other sauce ingredients, adding splashes of pasta water if needed to keep the consistency creamy and prevent the cheese from clumping. Add the basil leaves, tearing them into a few pieces, and toss again. Taste and add more salt or, if you dare, more chile flakes.

Divide the pasta between two warm bowls. If you're serving with the whipped ricotta, dollop each bowl with a spoonful, then serve right away, with more 50/50 cheese to add at the table.

Broccoli with Pancetta, Black Pepper, and Pecorino

The broccoli in this dish gets pulverized in a food processor until it's crumble-size. The crumbles get cooked in two phases, resulting in an almost ragu-like texture, which I love for its ability to cling to pasta. The whole dish is earthy and savory; the pancetta and pecorino are both salty ingredients, so go easy on the salted pasta water as you cook the noodles.

Serves 2

10 ounces (280 g) broccoli (both florets and a good bit of the stalk)

Kosher salt (preferably Diamond Crystal; see page 17)

Extra-virgin olive oil

3 ounces (85 g) pancetta, very finely chopped

½ teaspoon freshly ground black pepper, plus more to taste

8 ounces (225 g) cavatappi, fusilli, or rotini

⅓ cup (40 g) grated Pecorino Romano, plus more for serving

Cut the broccoli florets into smaller pieces and cut the stalk into small chunks; aim for nothing bigger than 1 inch (2.5 cm).

Put the stalk pieces in a food processor and pulse a few times until they are chopped into pea-size pieces. Add the florets and pulse until all the broccoli is fairly fine, about the size of grains of rice. Take care that you don't go so far that you end up with a puree. You should have about 3 cups (280 g) of broccoli crumbles.

Fill a large pot (at least 6 quarts/L) with 1 gallon (4 L) of water; add 4 tablespoons (40 g) kosher salt, cover the pot, and bring the water to a boil while you make your sauce. If the water begins to boil before your sauce is ready, turn down the heat, but don't let the volume of the pasta water reduce by boiling off.

Heat a generous glug of olive oil in a large skillet over medium heat. When the oil is hot, add the pancetta and cook until the fat has rendered and the pancetta is starting to get crisp, 5 to 7 minutes.

Increase the heat to medium-high, add half the broccoli crumbles, and cook, without stirring, for 2 minutes to develop some deep browning on the bottom.

Cook for another minute, stirring and scraping the bottom of the pan, then add the remaining broccoli. Cook until the first batch of broccoli is starting to disintegrate and get a bit mushy, another 2 to 3 minutes.

Add the black pepper, then add a big splash of water from the pasta pot to stop the cooking; slide the skillet off the heat.

Bring the pasta water (back) to a boil, add the noodles, and set your timer for 2 minutes less than the shortest suggested cooking time on the package of pasta; this will ideally be 2 minutes before the pasta is al dente. Stir the noodles several times during the first 2 minutes of cooking to prevent them from sticking to the bottom of the pot or otherwise clumping together.

When the timer goes off, start tasting the noodles. When they seem like they are 1½ to 2 minutes away from a perfect al dente (see page 22), drain and transfer them to the sauce in the skillet using your preferred method (see page 21), making sure to reserve at least 1 cup (240 ml) of the pasta water.

Slide the skillet back onto medium heat and finish cooking the noodles, tossing and adding plenty of splashes of water (alternate between pasta water and plain water so things don't get too salty) until the noodles are perfectly al dente, the broccoli is tender, and the sauce is nicely juicy. If the sauce seems watery, simmer for another few seconds to tighten it up, bearing in mind that the cheese will thicken it.

Reduce the heat to very low. Add the grated cheese and toss to emulsify it with the other sauce ingredients, adding splashes of pasta water if needed to keep the consistency creamy and prevent the cheese from clumping. Taste and add more salt or pepper if you like.

Divide the pasta between two warm bowls and serve right away, with more cheese to add at the table.

Broccoli and Sausage

This dish is my interpretation of an Italian classic that uses broccoli rabe and orecchiette, a fairly dense and chewy cup-shaped noodle. While I love broccoli rabe, I've swapped it out for regular broccoli, which is easy to prep, cooks quickly, and gives you the opportunity to play around with textures. You'll cook part of the broccoli in the skillet with the other sauce ingredients and boil the other half in the pasta water until it is quite tender and almost falling apart.

Serves 2

Kosher salt (preferably Diamond Crystal; see page 17)

6 ounces (180 g) bulk Italian sausage, sweet or hot

Extra-virgin olive oil

3 or 4 garlic cloves, smashed

2 cups (200 g) broccoli florets and roughly chopped stalk

Pinch of dried chile flakes, plus more to taste

Freshly ground black pepper

8 ounces (225 g) paccheri, orecchiette, or rigatoni

2 tablespoons unsalted butter

⅓ cup (40 g) 50/50 cheese (half Parmigiano-Reggiano, half Pecorino Romano, grated in a food processor; see page 39), plus more for serving

Finishing-quality extra-virgin olive oil, for serving (optional)

Fill a large pot (at least 6 quarts/L) with 1 gallon (4 L) of water; add 4 tablespoons (40 g) kosher salt, cover the pot, and bring the water to a boil while you make your sauce. If the water begins to boil before your sauce is ready, turn down the heat, but don't let the volume of the pasta water reduce by boiling off.

Shape the sausage into 2 patties. Heat a glug of olive oil in a large skillet over medium-high heat. When the oil is hot, add the sausage and sear, smashing the patties down from time to time; don't move them until a nice crust forms on the bottom, about 5 minutes.

Flip the patties, then add the garlic and half the broccoli. Cook until the garlic is soft and nicely toasted but not browned and the sausage is almost cooked through, another 4 to 5 minutes. With the back of a spoon, smash the garlic into the oil and break up the sausage patties into smaller bits.

Add the chile flakes and many twists of black pepper and cook for a few seconds to infuse the oil with the spices.

Add about ½ cup (120 ml) water from the pasta pot and then slide the skillet off the heat, but keep everything warm.

Bring the pasta water (back) to a boil, add the rest of the broccoli, and boil until tender but still bright green, 3 to 4 minutes. Scoop out the broccoli with a slotted spoon and add it to the skillet with the sauce; it's fine if some broccoli bits remain in the pasta water.

Add the noodles to the boiling water and set your timer for 2 minutes less than the shortest suggested cooking time on the package of pasta; this will ideally be 2 minutes before the pasta is al dente. Stir the noodles several times during the first 2 minutes of cooking to prevent them from sticking to the bottom of the pot or otherwise clumping together.

When the timer goes off, start tasting the noodles. When they seem like they are 1½ to 2 minutes away from a perfect al dente (see page 22), drain and transfer them to the sauce in the skillet using your preferred method (see page 21), making sure to reserve at least 1 cup (240 ml) of the pasta water.

Slide the skillet back onto medium heat and finish cooking the noodles, tossing and adding plenty of splashes of pasta water until the noodles are perfectly al dente, the broccoli is tender, and the sauce is nicely juicy. If the sauce

seems watery, simmer for another few seconds to tighten it up, bearing in mind that the cheese will thicken it.

Reduce the heat to very low. Add the butter and the grated cheese and toss to emulsify them with the other sauce ingredients, adding splashes of pasta water (or plain hot water, if things are getting too salty) if needed to keep the consistency creamy and prevent the cheese from clumping. Taste and add more salt, pepper, or chile flakes if you like.

Divide the pasta between two warm bowls, drizzle on a bit of good olive oil, if you like, and serve right away, with more cheese to add at the table.

Broccoli with Halibut and Lemon

This is an elegant and (despite the butter) light pasta dish that is also a good way to stretch a modest amount of fish. The timing is a bit tricky, however, and will depend on the thickness of your fish. You should count on 10 minutes of cooking time for every 1 inch (2.5 cm) of thickness in the fish (measuring by the thickest part of your fillet). I've written the recipe for a ½-inch-thick (1.25 cm) fillet; if you have a thicker one, you'll start your fish sooner, and vice versa for a very flat fillet.

Serves 2

Kosher salt (preferably Diamond Crystal; see page 17)

6 ounces (170 g) broccoli (both florets and a good bit of the stalk)

8 ounces (225 g) skinless fillet of halibut or another white-fleshed fish, such as sole, flounder, or cod

All-purpose flour

Extra-virgin olive oil

2 or 3 garlic cloves, thinly sliced

⅛ teaspoon dried chile flakes, plus more to taste

2 tablespoons drained brined capers

4 tablespoons (60 g) unsalted butter

1 tablespoon finely grated lemon zest

8 ounces (225 g) orecchiette, conchiglie, or lumache

2 to 3 tablespoons fresh lemon juice

¼ cup (8 g) roughly chopped fresh flat-leaf parsley, mint, cilantro, or basil leaves, or a mix of any of these

Fill a large pot (at least 6 quarts/L) with 1 gallon (4 L) of water; add 4 tablespoons (40 g) kosher salt, cover the pot, and bring the water to a boil while you prepare the broccoli. If the water begins to boil before the broccoli is ready, turn down the heat, but don't let the volume of the pasta water reduce by boiling off.

Cut the florets off the broccoli stalk, and cut any larger florets into smaller pieces—you don't want them larger than about 1 inch (2.5 cm) at the widest point. Trim off the dried end of the stalk and then peel off the outer layer using a vegetable peeler or sharp paring knife; don't go too deep, because you want to remove just the fibrous outer layer. Cut the stalk into coins just a bit skinnier than ¼ inch (6 mm).

Bring the pasta water (back) to a boil, add the broccoli, and boil just until tender, 4 to 6 minutes. Scoop out the broccoli with a slotted spoon and transfer it to a bowl or plate; set aside and keep warmish. Don't worry about retrieving all the broccoli bits; anything remaining will ride along with the noodles. Keep the pasta water warm to use for the noodles.

Season both sides of the fish with salt, dredge in the flour, and shake off any excess. Heat a glug of olive oil in a large skillet over medium heat. When the oil is hot, add the fish. Cook the fish without moving it for 1 minute; this will let it develop a crust and make it easier to move without sticking.

Add the garlic and cook alongside the fish for another minute, scooting the bits around so they soften but don't get dark. Add the chile flakes, capers, and 3 tablespoons of the butter.

Flip the fish and continue cooking another 2 to 3 minutes (don't worry if the fish falls apart a bit, as you will flake it up at the end anyway). Then increase the heat to medium-high and cook until the butter begins to brown and smell nutty, another minute or so. Take care not to burn the garlic or any browned bits left by the floured fish.

As soon as the fish is fully cooked and the butter is golden brown, add a big splash of water from the pasta pot to stop the cooking. Add the broccoli to the skillet, then slide it off the heat and add the lemon zest.

Bring the pasta water (back) to a boil, add the noodles, and set your timer for 2 minutes less than the shortest suggested cooking time on the package of pasta; this will ideally be 2 minutes before the pasta is al dente. Stir the noodles several times during the first 2 minutes of cooking to prevent them from sticking to the bottom of the pot or otherwise clumping together.

When the timer goes off, start tasting the noodles. When they seem like they are a perfect al dente (see page 22), drain and transfer them to the sauce in the skillet using your preferred method (see page 21), making sure to reserve at least 1 cup (240 ml) of the pasta water.

Slide the skillet back onto medium heat. Add the remaining 1 tablespoon butter and the lemon juice, along with a few small splashes of pasta water to emulsify with the butter and make everything lovely and juicy. Toss everything together gently. Taste and add more salt or chile flakes if you like.

Add the herbs, toss once more, and then divide the pasta between two warm bowls and serve right away.

Cauliflower "Alfredo" with Shrimp, Parsley, and Lemon

Making an Alfredo sauce without any cream is quite a trick, but cauliflower is up to the challenge. The magic happens by simmering the cauliflower until it is tender, along with gently sautéed onion and garlic, then pureeing it all until velvety.

Serves 2

Extra-virgin olive oil

3 garlic cloves, smashed

½ cup (75 g) chopped onion

2 cups (200 g) cauliflower florets and stems (chop large stems into ½-inch/1.25 cm pieces)

Kosher salt (preferably Diamond Crystal; see page 17)

Pinch of dried chile flakes, plus more to taste

½ cup (15 g) chopped fresh flat-leaf parsley leaves

6 ounces (170 g) raw shrimp, any size, preferably wild, peeled and deveined

2 teaspoons finely grated lemon zest

8 ounces (225 g) mafaldine, pappardelle, or fettucine

¼ cup (30 g) 50/50 cheese (half Parmigiano-Reggiano, half Pecorino Romano, grated in a food processor; see page 39), plus more for serving (optional)

1 to 2 tablespoons fresh lemon juice, plus more to taste

Heat a glug of olive oil in a medium skillet or sauté pan over medium heat. When the oil is hot, add 1 clove of the garlic and cook until it's just beginning to soften, 1 to 2 minutes. Add the onion and continue cooking until both the onion and garlic are soft and fragrant but not at all browned, another 4 to 5 minutes.

Add the cauliflower, ⅔ cup (160 ml) water, and ¼ teaspoon kosher salt. Bring to a simmer and cook until the cauliflower is completely tender and starting to fall apart, 10 to 13 minutes. Remove from the heat.

Let the cauliflower mixture cool a bit, then puree in a blender until completely smooth. Add 1 tablespoon olive oil and pulse another few times to blend. Measure out 1 cup (240 g) and set aside.

Fill a large pot (at least 6 quarts/L) with 1 gallon (4 L) of water; add 4 tablespoons (40 g) kosher salt, cover the pot, and bring the water to a boil while you make your sauce. If the water begins to boil before your sauce is ready, turn down the heat, but don't let the volume of the pasta water reduce by boiling off.

Heat a glug of olive oil in a large skillet over medium heat. When the oil is hot, add the remaining 2 cloves garlic and cook gently, smashing the cloves with your spoon to break them up a bit, until they have softened and are lightly toasted but not too brown, 2 to 4 minutes. Add the chile flakes and half the chopped parsley and cook for another few seconds to allow the flavors to bloom.

Increase the heat to medium-high, add the shrimp, and cook until they are just cooked through (no longer opaque), but not any longer (they'll cook more as you finish the noodles). Splash in a bit of water from the pasta pot to stop the cooking, add the lemon zest and cauliflower puree, and then slide the skillet off the heat.

Bring the pasta water (back) to a boil, add the noodles, and set your timer for 2 minutes less than the shortest suggested cooking time on the package of pasta; this will ideally be 2 minutes before the pasta is al dente. Stir the noodles several times during the first 2 minutes of cooking to prevent them from sticking to the bottom of the pot or otherwise clumping together.

recipe continues →

When the timer goes off, start tasting the noodles. When they seem like they are 1½ to 2 minutes away from a perfect al dente (see page 22), drain and transfer them to the sauce in the skillet using your preferred method (see page 21), making sure to reserve at least 1 cup (240 ml) of the pasta water.

Slide the skillet back onto medium heat and finish cooking the noodles, tossing and adding plenty of splashes of pasta water until the noodles are perfectly al dente, the shrimp are fully cooked, and the sauce is nicely juicy. If the sauce seems watery, simmer for another few seconds to tighten it up, bearing in mind that the cheese (if you're using it) will thicken it.

If you're using cheese, reduce the heat to very low. Add the grated cheese and toss to emulsify it with the other sauce ingredients, adding splashes of pasta water (or plain hot water, if things are getting too salty) if needed to keep the consistency creamy and prevent the cheese from clumping.

When the noodles are ready, stir in the lemon juice and the remaining parsley. Taste and add more salt, chile flakes, or lemon juice if you like.

Divide the pasta between two warm bowls and serve right away, with more cheese, if using, to add at the table.

MORE WAYS

Make this dish vegetarian by omitting the shrimp, or vegan by omitting the shrimp and the cheese; it will still be delicious.

Cauliflower with Olives and Tomato

Cauliflower is a bit of a chameleon. On its own, its flavor is mild and mellow, but when it encounters more assertive flavors, as in this recipe, cauliflower takes them on, becoming downright zesty. Look for a new variety of cauliflower called caulilini, which is slightly spindly and quite sweet. Adding the olives as the last step ensures that their flavor and texture stay distinct, rather than becoming muddy, as they would with longer cooking.

Serves 2

- Kosher salt (preferably Diamond Crystal; see page 17)
- Extra-virgin olive oil
- 4 or 5 garlic cloves, smashed
- ¼ teaspoon dried chile flakes, plus more to taste
- 2½ cups (250 g) small cauliflower florets or caulilini
- 1 tablespoon tomato paste
- 1 teaspoon dried oregano
- One 15-ounce (425 g) can whole peeled tomatoes, crushed by hand (see page 44), with their juices
- 8 ounces (225 g) papiri, strozzapreti, or garganelli
- ½ cup (70 g) roughly chopped pitted mixed olives
- ¼ cup (30 g) 50/50 cheese (half Parmigiano-Reggiano, half Pecorino Romano, grated in a food processor; see page 39), for serving (optional)
- Finishing-quality extra-virgin olive oil, for serving

Fill a large pot (at least 6 quarts/L) with 1 gallon (4 L) of water; add 4 tablespoons (40 g) kosher salt, cover the pot, and bring the water to a boil while you make your sauce. If the water begins to boil before your sauce is ready, turn down the heat, but don't let the volume of the pasta water reduce by boiling off.

Heat a generous glug of olive oil in a large skillet over medium heat. When the oil is hot, add the garlic and cook gently, smashing the cloves with your spoon to break them up a bit, until they have softened and are lightly toasted but not too brown, 3 to 4 minutes.

Add the chile flakes and the cauliflower and cook until the cauliflower has browned a bit, 3 to 4 minutes (take care not to burn the garlic).

Add the tomato paste and cook, spreading it on the surface of the pan, until it darkens a bit, 30 seconds to 1 minute. Add the oregano and crushed tomatoes and their juices, increase the heat to medium-high, and cook until the tomatoes have reduced by half, 3 to 4 minutes.

Add ½ cup (120 ml) water from the pasta pot and stir to blend. Slide the skillet off the heat.

Bring the pasta water (back) to a boil, add the noodles, and set your timer for 2 minutes less than the shortest suggested cooking time on the package of pasta; this will ideally be 2 minutes before the pasta is al dente. Stir the noodles several times during the first 2 minutes of cooking to prevent them from sticking to the pot or otherwise clumping together.

When the timer goes off, start tasting the noodles. When they seem like they are 1½ to 2 minutes away from a perfect al dente (see page 22), drain and transfer them to the sauce in the skillet using your preferred method (see page 21), making sure to reserve at least 1 cup (240 ml) of the pasta water.

Cook, tossing the pasta and adding splashes of pasta water as needed, until the noodles are perfectly al dente, another 2 minutes or so.

Fold in the olives. Taste and add more salt or chile flakes if you like.

Divide the pasta between two warm bowls, shower with the cheese, if using, drizzle with some excellent olive oil, and serve right away.

MORE WAYS

If you can find nepitella, an herb that's common in Italy but not so common in the United States, add it just before you add the olives; its flavor is a heady mash-up of mint, oregano, and basil, and it's perfect for this dish.

Sweet-and-Sour Cauliflower with Tomato, Raisins, and Pine Nuts

The flavors in this dish could come straight from Sicily—tomato, raisins, pine nuts, capers, anchovies . . . but here, the anchovies come via Southeast Asia, in the form of fish sauce. Fish sauce is made from fermented anchovies and delivers the same super-savory hit of umami that anchovies do, in an easier-to-use form. Be sure to buy a good, authentic brand, such as Red Boat (see Resources, page 380), for the cleanest sweet-salty flavor. Note that on its own, fish sauce smells and tastes very strong, but it integrates beautifully and subtly with the other ingredients in the dish.

Serves 2

⅓ cup (50 g) raisins (any color)

3 tablespoons good-quality vinegar (red wine, sherry, or white wine), plus more to taste

2 tablespoons fish sauce, plus more to taste

Kosher salt (preferably Diamond Crystal; see page 17)

Extra-virgin olive oil

2 cups (200 g) cauliflower (cut into small florets, stems cut into ½-inch/ 1.25 cm pieces)

¼ cup (30 g) pine nuts

3 garlic cloves, sliced

½ teaspoon dried chile flakes, plus more to taste

2 tablespoons tomato paste

1 cup (250 g) canned whole peeled tomatoes, crushed by hand (see page 44), with their juices

8 ounces (225 g) fusilli col buco, bucatini, or spaghetti

½ cup (15 g) roughly chopped fresh flat-leaf parsley

¼ cup (30 g) drained brined capers

⅓ cup (40 g) 50/50 cheese (half Parmigiano-Reggiano, half Pecorino Romano, grated in a food processor; see page 39), plus more for serving (optional)

Combine the raisins, vinegar, and fish sauce in a small bowl and set aside so the raisins can plump up.

Fill a large pot (at least 6 quarts/L) with 1 gallon (4 L) of water; add 4 tablespoons (40 g) kosher salt, cover the pot, and bring the water to a boil while you make your sauce. If the water begins to boil before your sauce is ready, turn down the heat, but don't let the volume of the pasta water reduce by boiling off.

Heat a generous glug of olive oil in a large skillet over medium-high heat. When the oil is hot, add the cauliflower, spreading it into a single layer. Cook, undisturbed, until the cauliflower has developed some nice browning on the bottom, 4 to 5 minutes. Shake the pan so the cauliflower flips (or just stir things around) and continue cooking to get more browning, another 3 to 4 minutes. (The cauliflower will be only partially cooked at this point; you will fully cook it later in the process.)

Reduce the heat to medium and scoot the cauliflower to one side of the skillet. Add another drizzle of olive oil if the pan seems dry and then add the pine nuts, garlic, and chile flakes. Cook gently until the garlic is soft and light golden and the pine nuts are golden to golden brown, 3 to 4 minutes; if things are browning too fast, reduce the heat. Meanwhile, make sure the cauliflower is happy; stir it a bit so it doesn't brown too much.

Add the tomato paste and cook, spreading it on the surface of the skillet, until slightly darkened and toasted, another 30 seconds to 1 minute.

Add the crushed tomatoes and their juices, along with the raisins and their soaking liquid. Stir everything together and adjust the heat to maintain a lively simmer. Cook until the sauce has reduced a bit and is concentrated in flavor, 3 to 4 minutes. Then slide the skillet off the heat.

recipe continues →

Bring the pasta water (back) to a boil, add the noodles, and set your timer for 2 minutes less than the shortest suggested cooking time on the package of pasta; this will ideally be 2 minutes before the pasta is al dente. Stir the noodles several times during the first 2 minutes of cooking to prevent them from sticking to the bottom of the pot or otherwise clumping together.

When the timer goes off, start tasting the noodles. When they seem like they are 1½ to 2 minutes away from a perfect al dente (see page 22), drain and transfer them to the sauce in the skillet using your preferred method (see page 21), making sure to reserve at least 1 cup (240 ml) of the pasta water.

Slide the skillet back onto medium heat and finish cooking the noodles, tossing and adding plenty of splashes of pasta water until the noodles are perfectly al dente, the cauliflower is tender, and the sauce is nicely juicy. If the sauce seems watery, simmer for another few seconds to tighten it up, bearing in mind that the cheese, if using, will thicken it.

Add the parsley and capers. If you're using cheese, reduce the heat to very low. Add the grated cheese and toss to emulsify it with the other sauce ingredients, adding splashes of pasta water (or plain hot water, if things are getting too salty) if needed to keep the consistency creamy and prevent the cheese from clumping.

Taste and adjust the sweet-sour-hot balance with a few more drops of vinegar or fish sauce or a pinch of chile flakes.

Divide the pasta between two warm bowls and serve right away, with more cheese, if using, to add at the table.

Long-Cooked Green Beans with Tomato, Mint, and Breadcrumbs

When people cook green beans, they often aim toward "crisp-tender," especially when it comes to delicate, skinny haricots verts. Here, however, the goal is more "cooked to death," like what you'd find in recipes from the American South or the Middle East. When you let a green bean cook all the way to fully tender, the flavor becomes mellow, meaty, and sweet, and the texture is almost silky. Different beans have different cooking times, so you'll need to finesse the recipe a bit to suit yours. I love making this with romano beans, wide flat green beans that definitely need long cooking but are worth the wait.

Serves 2

Kosher salt (preferably Diamond Crystal; see page 17)

Extra-virgin olive oil

3 ounces (85 g) pancetta, diced

⅔ cup (85 g) sliced red onion (cut about ¼ inch/6 mm thick)

½ teaspoon dried chile flakes, plus more to taste

1 tablespoon tomato paste

2 cups (200 g) 1-inch (2.5 cm) pieces green beans or a mix of other pole beans

One 15-ounce (425 g) can whole peeled tomatoes, crushed by hand (see page 44), with their juices

Small handful of fresh mint leaves

8 ounces (225 g) gemelli, garganelli, or strozzapreti

⅓ cup (40 g) 50/50 cheese (half Parmigiano-Reggiano, half Pecorino Romano, grated in a food processor; see page 39), plus more for serving

2 tablespoons Dried Breadcrumbs (page 36), for serving (optional)

Fill a large pot (at least 6 quarts/L) with 1 gallon (4 L) of water; add 4 tablespoons (40 g) kosher salt, cover the pot, and bring the water to a boil while you make your sauce. If the water begins to boil before your sauce is ready, turn down the heat, but don't let the volume of the pasta water reduce by boiling off.

Heat a generous glug of olive oil in a large skillet over medium heat. When the oil is hot, add the pancetta and onion and cook until the pancetta has rendered much of its fat and is getting slightly crisp and the onion is soft and fragrant, about 5 minutes.

Add the chile flakes and cook for 30 seconds so they start to infuse the oil. Add the tomato paste and cook, spreading it on the surface of the pan, until it thickens and darkens a bit, 30 seconds to 1 minute.

Add the green beans, crushed tomatoes and their juices, and about half the mint, tearing the leaves into a few pieces. Adjust the heat so the tomato sauce simmers nicely and cook until the green beans are completely tender and silky. This can take anywhere between 15 and 45 minutes, depending on the maturity and toughness of your beans. If you have a stubborn batch, you can speed the cooking by adding a bit of water and/or covering the pan with a lid; you may need to reduce the heat a bit if using the lid to prevent the tomato sauce from scorching. You also want the tomato sauce to cook down, thicken, and get slightly jammy, so you'll need to play with time, burner temperature, and lid or no lid.

When the beans are soft and the tomato sauce has achieved a nice consistency, slide the skillet off the heat.

Bring the pasta water (back) to a boil, add the noodles, and set your timer for 2 minutes less than the shortest suggested cooking time on the package of pasta; this will ideally be 2 minutes before the pasta is al dente. Stir the noodles several times during the first 2 minutes of cooking to prevent them from sticking to the bottom of the pot or otherwise clumping together.

When the timer goes off, start tasting the noodles. When they seem like they are 1½ to 2 minutes away from a perfect al dente (see page 22), drain and transfer them to the sauce in the skillet using your preferred method (see page 21), making sure to reserve at least 1 cup (240 ml) of the pasta water.

Slide the skillet back onto medium heat and finish cooking the noodles, tossing and adding plenty of splashes of pasta water until the noodles are perfectly al dente, the green beans are silky, and the tomato sauce is nicely juicy. If the sauce seems watery, simmer for another few seconds to tighten it up, bearing in mind that the cheese will thicken it.

Reduce the heat to very low. Add the grated cheese and toss to emulsify it with the other sauce ingredients, adding splashes of pasta water (or plain hot water, if things are getting too salty) if needed to keep the consistency creamy and prevent the cheese from clumping. Add the remaining mint leaves, tearing them into pieces, and toss again. Taste and add more salt or chile flakes if you like.

Divide the pasta between two warm bowls, sprinkle with the breadcrumbs, if using, and serve right away, with more cheese to add at the table.

Green Beans with Pickled Ramp Butter and Chile Crisp

In this super-simple dish, the fun comes from using a mix of beans—green, yellow, purple—as well as more than one variety of basil, if possible. You can cook the beans right in the boiling water with the noodles to streamline your work, but if you're not sure how long they will take to become nicely tender, you can cook the beans in the boiling water first, scoop them out, and then follow with the noodles. I like to cook my beans until they're silky-tender so they integrate easily with the pasta noodles.

Serves 2

Kosher salt (preferably Diamond Crystal; see page 17)

8 ounces (225 g) green beans or other string beans, ends trimmed

4 tablespoons (60 g) Pickled Ramp Butter (page 29), plus more to taste

8 ounces (225 g) rigatoni, penne, or ziti

Small handful of fresh basil leaves

⅓ cup (40 g) 50/50 cheese (half Parmigiano-Reggiano, half Pecorino Romano, grated in a food processor; see page 39), plus more for serving

2 spoonfuls Chile Crisp (page 37), for serving

Fill a large pot (at least 6 quarts/L) with 1 gallon (4 L) of water; add 4 tablespoons (40 g) kosher salt, cover the pot, and bring the water to a boil.

Add the green beans and boil until very tender, 7 to 10 minutes. Scoop out with tongs or a slotted spoon and transfer to a large skillet over medium heat. Add a splash of water from the pasta pot and the ramp butter, and swirl the pan to emulsify the butter and water, creating a sauce that coats the beans creamily; don't let anything boil, which can break the emulsion. Slide the skillet off the heat.

Bring the pasta water (back) to a boil, add the noodles, and set your timer for 2 minutes less than the shortest suggested cooking time on the package of pasta; this will ideally be 2 minutes before the pasta is al dente. Stir the noodles several times during the first 2 minutes of cooking to prevent them from sticking to the bottom of the pot or otherwise clumping together.

When the timer goes off, start tasting the noodles. When they seem like they are almost a perfect al dente (see page 22), drain and transfer them to the sauce in the skillet using your preferred method (see page 21), making sure to reserve at least 1 cup (240 ml) of the pasta water.

Slide the skillet back onto medium heat and finish cooking the noodles, tossing and adding splashes of pasta water until the noodles are perfectly al dente, the beans are tender, and the sauce is nicely juicy; add more ramp butter if you'd like the sauce to be richer. Tear the basil into a few pieces, add to the skillet, and toss once more.

Reduce the heat to very low. Add the grated cheese and toss to emulsify it with the other sauce ingredients, adding splashes of pasta water if needed to keep the consistency creamy and prevent the cheese from clumping. Taste and add more salt if you like.

Divide the pasta between two warm bowls and top each serving with some chile crisp. Serve right away, with more cheese to add at the table.

MORE WAYS

Instead of Pickled Ramp Butter, use Green Garlic Herb Butter (page 29) or Garlic Butter (page 27), which, in tandem with Chile Crisp, will make the dish a garlic lover's dream.

Green Beans with Tuna and Mushrooms

Inspired by the classic green bean casserole (a favorite dish that my mom often made for me), this version delivers all the comfort of that dish without the can of cream of mushroom soup—and with some excellent tuna, if possible. I am a big fan and supporter of an Oregon producer, Sacred Sea (see Resources, page 380), a family fishing operation that catches albacore tuna by hook and line, processes them swiftly and well, and cans the meat in nothing but its own juices.

Serves 2

Kosher salt (preferably Diamond Crystal; see page 17)

Extra-virgin olive oil

½ cup (75 g) finely chopped onion

2 ounces (60 g) pancetta, chopped

2 cups (140 g) thinly sliced cremini mushrooms

1½ cups (150 g) 2-inch (5 cm) pieces green beans

1 cup (240 ml) heavy or whipping cream

Freshly ground black pepper

8 ounces (225 g) campanelle, lumache, or trottole

One 5- or 6-ounce (142 or 170 g) can tuna, drained

⅓ cup (40 g) 50/50 cheese (half Parmigiano-Reggiano, half Pecorino Romano, grated in a food processor; see page 39), plus more for serving

3 tablespoons Dried Breadcrumbs (page 36), for serving

Fill a large pot (at least 6 quarts/L) with 1 gallon (4 L) of water; add 4 tablespoons (40 g) kosher salt, cover the pot, and bring the water to a boil while you make your sauce. If the water begins to boil before your sauce is ready, turn down the heat, but don't let the volume of the pasta water reduce by boiling off.

Heat a glug of olive oil in a large skillet over medium heat. When the oil is hot, add the onion and pancetta and cook until the pancetta is starting to render some fat, 1 to 2 minutes. Add the mushrooms and cook, stirring frequently, until the mushrooms and onion are tender and the pancetta and mushrooms are slightly browned around the edges, 10 to 12 minutes.

Add the green beans and the cream, adjust the heat so the cream simmers, and cook until the beans are crisp-tender, 4 to 6 minutes. If the cream is reducing and getting thick, add a few splashes of pasta water to keep it slightly loose. Season with several twists of black pepper. Slide the skillet off the heat.

Bring the pasta water (back) to a boil, add the noodles, and set your timer for 2 minutes less than the shortest suggested cooking time on the package of pasta; this will ideally be 2 minutes before the pasta is al dente. Stir the noodles several times during the first 2 minutes of cooking to prevent them from sticking to the bottom of the pot or otherwise clumping together.

When the timer goes off, start tasting the noodles. When they seem like they are almost a perfect al dente (see page 22), drain and transfer them to the sauce in the skillet using your preferred method (see page 21), making sure to reserve at least 1 cup (240 ml) of the pasta water.

Slide the skillet back onto medium heat and finish cooking the noodles, tossing and adding plenty of splashes of pasta water until the noodles are perfectly al dente, the green beans are tender, and the sauce is creamy.

Reduce the heat to very low. Add the tuna and toss a bit to break it into flakes. Add the grated cheese and toss to emulsify it with the other sauce ingredients, adding splashes of pasta water (or plain hot water, if things are getting too salty) if needed to keep the consistency creamy and prevent the cheese from clumping.

Divide the pasta between two warm bowls, top with the breadcrumbs, and serve right away, with more cheese to add at the table.

Green Beans with Garlic Confit, Mussels, and Almonds

The combination of ingredients in this dish may seem unexpected, but once you taste them together, you'll understand my flavor logic. The key to the recipe is the garlic confit, which you'll need to make ahead, but it keeps nicely in the refrigerator for a couple of weeks. You can make a batch and have it on hand for this and other dishes, the simplest of which would be a piece of good bread, grilled, spread with garlic confit, and drizzled with good olive oil. The garlic confit oil on its own is a dynamite flavor builder for any number of dishes.

Serves 2

Kosher salt (preferably Diamond Crystal; see page 17)

5 or 6 cloves Garlic Confit (recipe follows), plus a glug of the garlic oil

¼ teaspoon dried chile flakes, plus more to taste

½ cup (70 g) finely chopped blanched almonds

4 tablespoons (60 g) unsalted butter

1½ cups (150 g) 2-inch (5 cm) pieces green beans (cut at an angle)

1 cup (240 ml) dry white wine

1 pound (450 g) fresh mussels in the shell, scrubbed and debearded as needed

8 ounces (225 g) fusilli col buco, linguine, or spaghetti alla chitarra

Small handful of fresh flat-leaf parsley leaves, torn into small pieces

2 teaspoons finely grated lemon zest

2 tablespoons fresh lemon juice, plus more to taste

Fill a large pot (at least 6 quarts/L) with 1 gallon (4 L) of water; add 4 tablespoons (40 g) kosher salt, cover the pot, and bring the water to a boil while you make your sauce. If the water begins to boil before your sauce is ready, turn down the heat, but don't let the volume of the pasta water reduce by boiling off.

Arrange your pasta bowls near the stove and tear off a piece of foil that will loosely cover both bowls (to keep the mussels warm as you finish the dish).

Heat a glug of the garlic oil (from the garlic confit) in a large skillet with a lid over medium heat. Add the garlic confit cloves and cook gently until they're heated. Add the chile flakes and cook for 30 seconds. Then add the almonds and cook, stirring constantly, until they are lightly toasted, about 5 minutes. Take care not to let the smaller pieces of almonds get too dark, which will make them bitter. Pay close attention to the temperature and take your time with this step.

Add 3 tablespoons of the butter and the green beans and continue cooking until the butter is melted and has turned a rich gold and the beans are slightly tender, 4 to 5 minutes, taking care not to let the butter get brown.

Add the white wine, increase the heat so the liquid is actively simmering, then add the mussels and cover the skillet with the lid. Cook, shaking the pan a bit, until the mussel shells have opened, about 3 minutes. With a slotted spoon or tongs, pluck out all the open mussels, draining their juices back into the skillet, transfer them to the pasta bowls, and cover loosely with the foil. Cook any unopened mussels for another minute or so, then add the newly opened ones to the pasta bowls and cover again with the foil. If any stubbornly unopened mussels remain, discard them.

Mash the garlic cloves so they disintegrate and blend into the liquid in the skillet, then simmer until the liquid reduces and concentrates by about one-quarter, 3 to 4 minutes. Slide the skillet off the heat.

Bring the pasta water (back) to a boil, add the noodles, and set your timer for 2 minutes less than the shortest suggested cooking time

on the package of pasta; this will ideally be 2 minutes before the pasta is al dente. Stir the noodles several times during the first 2 minutes of cooking to prevent them from sticking to the bottom of the pot or otherwise clumping together.

When the timer goes off, start tasting the noodles. When they seem like they are 1½ to 2 minutes away from a perfect al dente (see page 22), drain and transfer them to the sauce in the skillet using your preferred method (see page 21), making sure to reserve at least 1 cup (240 ml) of the pasta water.

Slide the skillet back onto medium heat and finish cooking the noodles, tossing and adding plenty of splashes of pasta water until the noodles are perfectly al dente, the green beans are tender, and the sauce is nicely juicy. If the sauce seems watery, simmer for another few seconds to tighten it up.

Take the skillet off the heat, add the remaining 1 tablespoon butter, the parsley, lemon zest, and lemon juice, and toss to emulsify the butter and lemon juice. Taste and add salt, or more chile flakes or lemon juice, if you like.

Divide the pasta and sauce between the pasta bowls with the mussels, piling the pasta on top so the mussels are warmed. Serve right away, with another bowl for the empty mussel shells, and perhaps some extra napkins.

Garlic Confit

Choose the freshest garlic you can find, ideally from a farmers' market or your own garden (garlic is fun and easy to grow!). If you end up with older garlic that has sprouted, remove the green sprouts from the cloves before making your confit.

Makes as many cloves as you like

As many garlic cloves as you like, peeled and root ends trimmed

Extra-virgin olive oil

Put the garlic cloves in a small saucepan; you want them to be huddled fairly close together so you don't need to use a large amount of oil. Pour in enough olive oil to cover the garlic by about ½ inch (1.25 cm).

Heat the oil over medium-low heat, adjusting the temperature so that you can see tiny bubbles emanating from the garlic but nothing is actually sizzling (older garlic contains less moisture, so you may not see many bubbles); the oil temperature should stay between 190° and 200°F (88° and 95°C).

Continue cooking the garlic, monitoring the temperature occasionally, until the cloves are completely tender and very light golden, 1 to 1½ hours.

Let cool completely, then transfer to a clean jar or other container with a lid; if some of the garlic pokes up above the level of the oil, add more olive oil so everything is submerged. Seal the jar or container.

Garlic confit will keep in the refrigerator for up to 2 weeks. Use a clean utensil to fish out garlic cloves as needed.

New Potatoes and Green Beans with Sun-Dried Tomato and Almond Pesto

A Ligurian pasta classic was my inspiration here, but rather than the traditional basil pesto as the partner for potatoes and green beans, I use a pesto made from sun-dried tomatoes and almonds. Try to find true new potatoes—dug from the soil when small, tender, and wrapped in still-sheer papery skin—but any medium- to low-starch small potato, such as baby Yukon Golds, will be fine.

Serves 2 or 3

Kosher salt (preferably Diamond Crystal; see page 17)

5 ounces (140 g) small new potatoes or other small potatoes, halved or quartered if large

1 cup (100 g) 2-inch (5 cm) pieces green beans (or a mix of colors)

¾ cup (180 g) Sun-Dried Tomato and Almond Pesto (page 33)

Pinch of dried chile flakes, plus more to taste

8 ounces (225 g) papiri, strozzapreti, or garganelli

Small handful of fresh basil leaves

Small handful of fresh mint leaves

⅓ cup (40 g) 50/50 cheese (half Parmigiano-Reggiano, half Pecorino Romano, grated in a food processor; see page 39), plus more for serving

Fill a large pot (at least 6 quarts/L) with 1 gallon (4 L) of cold water. Add 4 tablespoons (40 g) kosher salt. Add the potatoes, cover the pot, and bring the water to a boil. Boil until the potatoes are tender, 12 to 20 minutes.

Scoop out the potatoes and transfer them to a large skillet. Add the beans to the boiling water and boil until crisp-tender, 3 to 4 minutes. Scoop out the beans and add to the potatoes.

Add a splash or two of the boiling water to the skillet and then add the pesto. Stir everything together. Taste the pesto, season with the chile flakes, and slide the skillet off the heat.

Bring the water (back) to a boil, add the noodles, and set your timer for 2 minutes less than the shortest suggested cooking time on the package of pasta, ideally 2 minutes before the pasta is al dente. Stir the noodles several times during the first 2 minutes of cooking to prevent them from sticking to the pot or clumping together.

When the timer goes off, start tasting the noodles. When they seem like they are 1½ to 2 minutes away from a perfect al dente (see page 22), drain and transfer them to the skillet with the potatoes and beans using your preferred method (see page 21), making sure to reserve at least 1 cup (240 ml) of the pasta water.

Slide the skillet back onto medium heat and finish cooking the noodles, tossing and adding plenty of splashes of pasta water until the noodles are perfectly al dente, the potatoes and beans are fully tender, and the sauce is nicely juicy. If the sauce seems watery, simmer for another few seconds to tighten it up, bearing in mind that the cheese will thicken it.

Reduce the heat to very low. Add the basil and mint, tearing the leaves into a few pieces, then add the grated cheese and toss to emulsify it with the other sauce ingredients, adding splashes of pasta water if needed to keep the consistency creamy and prevent the cheese from clumping. Taste and add more salt or chile flakes if you like.

Divide the pasta between two or three warm bowls and serve right away, with more cheese to add at the table.

MORE WAYS

Swap in Basil Pesto (page 33) for the sun-dried tomato version. Basil pesto is delicate, so cook the noodles all the way to al dente before adding them to the sauce in order to minimize the amount of cooking the pesto experiences.

Spaghetti alla Nerano

This is my version of the pasta dish made by several restaurants in the town of Nerano on the Amalfi Coast and made famous by actor Stanley Tucci on his show about eating his way through Italy. In the version featured on the show, the zucchini is deep-fried, but I sauté mine in a bit of olive oil, adding the sliced zucchini in batches to create varying textures, and then I finish it with a swim through brown butter, letting the zucchini both drink up and infuse the butter.

Serves 2

Kosher salt (preferably Diamond Crystal; see page 17)

Extra-virgin olive oil

5 garlic cloves, smashed

2 cups (280 g) sliced summer squash (a mix of green zucchini and yellow varieties, cut into pieces ⅛ inch/3 mm thick)

4 tablespoons (60 g) unsalted butter

Big pinch of dried chile flakes, plus more to taste

Small handful of fresh mint leaves, plus more for serving (optional)

2 teaspoons finely grated lemon zest

8 ounces (225 g) spaghetti

⅓ cup (40 g) 50/50 cheese (half Parmigiano-Reggiano, half Pecorino Romano, grated in a food processor; see page 39), plus more for serving

3 tablespoons fresh lemon juice, plus more to taste

A few torn basil leaves (optional)

A few torn zucchini blossoms (optional)

Fill a large pot (at least 6 quarts/L) with 1 gallon (4 L) of water; add 4 tablespoons (40 g) kosher salt, cover the pot, and bring the water to a boil while you make your sauce. If the water begins to boil before your sauce is ready, turn down the heat, but don't let the volume of the pasta water reduce by boiling off.

Heat a small glug of olive oil in a large skillet over medium-high heat (you need only enough oil for the summer squash not to stick, as you'll be adding a lot of butter soon). When the oil is hot, add the garlic and toast gently for a few minutes, breaking it up a bit with your spatula, then add enough of the squash slices to create a single layer. Cook, undisturbed, until the undersides are browned, about 2 minutes. During this time, you want to keep the garlic toasting gently but not browning very much, so you may need to move it around or even remove it temporarily.

Flip the squash slices, brown the second side lightly, and then add another layer of squash. As the bottom layer browns and sort of melts, flip everything so the new layer comes in contact with the pan and starts to brown. Continue with the rest of the squash slices, layering and flipping the stack of slices so that you end up with squash cooked to varying degrees, which will make a nice variety of textures, all the while sort of smashing the garlic so it disintegrates into smaller bits but doesn't actually brown.

Add the butter, chile flakes, mint (tearing the leaves into a few pieces, if using), and lemon zest. Let the butter melt and bubble, cooking until it becomes lightly browned and smells nutty and the squash is infused with it, 7 to 10 minutes, depending on how much moisture your squash gives off.

Splash about ½ cup (120 ml) of water from the pasta pot into the skillet to stop the cooking. Slide the skillet off the heat.

Bring the pasta water (back) to a boil, add the noodles, and set your timer for 2 minutes less than the shortest suggested cooking time on the package of pasta; this will ideally be 2 minutes before the pasta is al dente. Stir the noodles several times during the first 2 minutes of cooking to prevent them from sticking to the bottom of the pot or otherwise clumping together.

When the timer goes off, start tasting the noodles. When they seem like they are 1½ to 2 minutes away from a perfect al dente (see

page 22), drain and transfer them to the sauce in the skillet using your preferred method (see page 21), making sure to reserve at least 1 cup (240 ml) of the pasta water.

Slide the skillet back onto medium heat and finish cooking the noodles, tossing and adding plenty of splashes of pasta water until the noodles are perfectly al dente and the sauce is nicely juicy. If the sauce seems watery, simmer for another few seconds to tighten it up, bearing in mind that the cheese will thicken it.

Reduce the heat to very low. Add the grated cheese and toss to emulsify it with the other sauce ingredients, adding splashes of pasta water (or plain hot water, if things are getting too salty) if needed to keep the consistency creamy and prevent the cheese from clumping.

Slide the skillet off the heat, add the lemon juice, and toss again. Taste and add more salt, chile flakes, or lemon juice if you like.

Add more torn mint, basil, or squash blossoms, if using. Divide the pasta between two warm bowls and serve right away, with more cheese to add at the table.

Summer Squash with Basil, Mint, and Pine Nuts

Choose a mix of yellow and green squash, if possible, to emphasize the summery feeling of this dish. Cut the summer squash to a similar size and shape as the noodle you're using—for example, small chunks for ditalini, or batons for penne. For long noodles, cut the squash in thin even rounds so they wrap around and melt into the noodles.

If you can get your hands on shiso, sometimes called perilla, an herb in the mint family, definitely use it along with the basil and mint; shiso has an intriguing flavor that will blow your mind. A torn squash blossom is a beautiful seasonal finish.

Serves 2

Kosher salt (preferably Diamond Crystal; see page 17)

Extra-virgin olive oil

3 or 4 garlic cloves, smashed

Big pinch of dried chile flakes, plus more to taste

2 cups (280 g) cut-up summer squash (a mix of green zucchini and yellow varieties), sized to match your noodles

Small handful of fresh basil leaves

Small handful of fresh mint leaves

Small handful of shiso leaves (optional)

8 ounces (225 g) bucatini, pici, or spaghetti

¼ cup (30 g) 50/50 cheese (half Parmigiano-Reggiano, half Pecorino Romano, grated in a food processor; see page 39), plus more for serving

1 tablespoon fresh lemon juice, plus more to taste

2 tablespoons roughly chopped toasted pine nuts, for serving

1 or 2 squash blossoms, for garnish (optional)

Fill a large pot (at least 6 quarts/L) with 1 gallon (4 L) of water; add 4 tablespoons (40 g) kosher salt, cover the pot, and bring the water to a boil while you make your sauce. If the water begins to boil before your sauce is ready, turn down the heat, but don't let the volume of the pasta water reduce by boiling off.

Heat a glug of olive oil in a large skillet over medium heat. When the oil is hot, add the garlic and chile flakes and cook gently, breaking up the garlic a bit with your spatula, until it is lightly toasted and fragrant but not at all brown, 3 to 4 minutes.

Add about half the squash in a single layer. Let it cook undisturbed until the underside is browned, about 2 minutes. During this time, you want to keep the garlic toasting gently but not browning very much, so you may need to move it around or even remove it temporarily.

Flip the squash pieces and add the second half. Continue cooking until the new squash is crisp-tender, about 3 minutes. (Cooking the squash in two phases creates more textural interest.)

Splash about ½ cup (120 ml) of water from the pasta pot into the skillet to stop the cooking. Add about half the basil, mint, and shiso leaves, if using, tearing them into a few pieces. Slide the skillet off the heat.

Bring the pasta water (back) to a boil, add the noodles, and set your timer for 2 minutes less than the shortest suggested cooking time on the package of pasta; this will ideally be 2 minutes before the pasta is al dente. Stir the noodles several times during the first 2 minutes of cooking to prevent them from sticking to the bottom of the pot or otherwise clumping together.

When the timer goes off, start tasting the noodles. When they seem like they are 1½ to 2 minutes away from a perfect al dente (see page 22), drain and transfer them to the sauce in the skillet using your preferred method (see

page 21), making sure to reserve at least 1 cup (240 ml) of the pasta water.

Slide the skillet back onto medium heat and finish cooking the noodles, tossing and adding plenty of splashes of pasta water until the noodles are perfectly al dente and the squash is tender, smashing some of the squash with your spatula to blend it into the sauce. If the sauce seems watery, simmer for another few seconds to tighten it up, bearing in mind that the cheese will thicken it.

Reduce the heat to very low. Add the grated cheese and toss to emulsify it with the other sauce ingredients, adding splashes of pasta water if needed to keep the consistency creamy and prevent the cheese from clumping.

Slide the skillet off the heat, add the lemon juice, and toss again. Add the remaining basil, mint, and shiso leaves, if using, tearing the leaves into pieces; toss again. Taste and add more salt, chile flakes, or lemon juice if you like.

Divide the pasta between two warm bowls and sprinkle each dish with the pine nuts. If you have a squash blossom, tear it into pieces and use them to garnish the bowls. Serve right away, with more cheese to add at the table.

Summer Squash and Cherry Tomatoes with Basil and Mint

Cherry tomatoes are generally the early ripeners of tomato season, so this dish is a nice bridge, joining midsummer squash and late-summer tomato. Part of the dish's appeal is color, so definitely use different colors of squashes and tomatoes if possible; Sun Gold tomatoes are always welcome.

Choose slender, firm squash, which will have the nuttiest flavor and best texture. Larger, more mature squash tend to have pithier, seedier interiors, which can taste bland and get floppy during cooking. Anyone who grows summer squash knows that it's easy for them to go from tiny to ginormous in what seems like hours, so if you're a gardener, stay vigilant!

Serves 2

Kosher salt (preferably Diamond Crystal; see page 17)

Extra-virgin olive oil

3 or 4 garlic cloves, smashed

6 ounces (170 g) summer squash (a mix of green zucchini and yellow varieties), quartered lengthwise and then sliced crosswise into ½-inch-thick (1.25 cm) pieces

6 ounces (about half a pint/170 g) cherry tomatoes, halved if large

Large pinch of dried chile flakes, plus more to taste

Small handful of fresh mint leaves

8 ounces (225 g) casarecce, gemelli, or strozzapreti

Large handful of fresh basil leaves

⅓ cup (40 g) 50/50 cheese (half Parmigiano-Reggiano, half Pecorino Romano, grated in a food processor; page 39), plus more for serving

1 to 2 tablespoons unsalted butter

Fill a large pot (at least 6 quarts/liters) with 1 gallon (4 L) of water; add 4 tablespoons (40 g) kosher salt, cover the pot, and bring the water to a boil while you make your sauce. If the water begins to boil before your sauce is ready, turn down the heat, but don't let the volume of the pasta water reduce by boiling off.

Heat a glug of olive oil in a large skillet over medium-high heat. When the oil is hot, add the garlic and cook gently, breaking it up a bit with your spatula, until it is nicely toasted and fragrant but not too brown, 3 to 4 minutes.

Add the summer squash, spreading it into a single layer (as best you can), and season lightly with salt. Cook, undisturbed, until the slices are nicely browned on the bottom, 2 to 3 minutes.

Flip the squash, add the tomatoes, chile flakes, and a few of the mint leaves (tear them up a bit), and continue cooking, stirring things around a bit and slightly smashing the tomatoes so they burst and release their juices (not all the tomatoes need to burst).

Add a few splashes of water from the pasta pot to the skillet and continue to cook the zucchini and tomatoes until they start getting a bit "stewy," 3 to 4 minutes. Slide the skillet off the heat.

Bring the pasta water (back) to a boil, add the noodles, and set your timer for 2 minutes less than the shortest suggested cooking time on the package of pasta; this will ideally be 2 minutes before the pasta is al dente. Stir the noodles several times during the first 2 minutes of cooking to prevent them from sticking to the bottom of the pot or otherwise clumping together.

When the timer goes off, start tasting the noodles. When they seem like they are 1½ to 2 minutes away from a perfect al dente (see page 22), drain and transfer them to the sauce in the skillet using your preferred method (see

page 21), making sure to reserve at least 1 cup (240 ml) of the pasta water.

Slide the skillet back onto medium heat and finish cooking the noodles, tossing and adding plenty of splashes of pasta water until the noodles are perfectly al dente and the sauce is nicely juicy. If the sauce seems watery, simmer for another few seconds to tighten it up, bearing in mind that the cheese will thicken it.

Reduce the heat to very low. Add the remaining mint and the basil (tear the leaves into a few pieces); toss to wilt the herbs a bit. Add the grated cheese and toss to emulsify it with the other sauce ingredients, adding a bit of pasta water to keep the consistency creamy and prevent the cheese from clumping. Add the butter and toss to blend. Taste and add more salt or chile flakes if you like.

Divide the pasta between two warm bowls and serve right away, with more cheese to add at the table.

Summer Squash with Pork and Beef Ragu with Kale and Chile

Summer squash can be a demure vegetable (meaning bland), but here I pair it with a vivacious ragu. I cut the squash into large chunks and cook it only until tender and juicy, so *bland* isn't in its vocabulary. The key to any summer squash dish is to choose slender, firm squash, whether green zucchini, yellow crookneck, UFO-shaped pattypan, or any of the colorful and shapely varieties you may encounter at a farmers' market or in your own garden.

Serves 2

Kosher salt (preferably Diamond Crystal; see page 17)

Extra-virgin olive oil

2 or 3 garlic cloves, smashed

8 ounces (225 g) summer squash (a mix of types is nice), halved lengthwise and then cut into ¾-inch-thick (2 cm) half-moons

1 cup (250 g) Pork and Beef Ragu with Kale and Chile (page 85)

8 ounces (225 g) le principesse, mafaldine, or pappardelle rigate

½ cup (50 g) sliced scallions, white and light green parts only

Small handful of fresh basil leaves

Small handful of fresh mint leaves

⅓ cup (40 g) 50/50 cheese (half Parmigiano-Reggiano, half Pecorino Romano, grated in a food processor; see page 39), plus more for serving

Fill a large pot (at least 6 quarts/L) with 1 gallon (4 L) of water; add 4 tablespoons (40 g) kosher salt, cover the pot, and bring the water to a boil while you make your sauce. If the water begins to boil before your sauce is ready, turn down the heat, but don't let the volume of the pasta water reduce by boiling off.

Heat a glug of olive oil in a large skillet over medium heat. When the oil is hot, add the garlic and cook gently, breaking it up a bit with your spatula, until softened and lightly toasted, 2 to 3 minutes.

Increase the heat to medium-high, and add the squash. Let it cook undisturbed until it is nicely browned on the bottom, 3 to 4 minutes, making sure the garlic isn't getting too brown (you can scoot it on top of some squash slices if you want to keep it out of the heat). Flip the squash and brown the other side, cooking until it is just crisp-tender but not more than that; you'll cook it further with the noodles.

Add the ragu to the skillet, splash in a bit of water from the pasta pot, and slide the skillet off the heat.

Bring the pasta water (back) to a boil, add the noodles, and set your timer for 2 minutes less than the shortest suggested cooking time on the package of pasta; this will ideally be 2 minutes before the pasta is al dente. Stir the noodles several times during the first 2 minutes of cooking to prevent them from sticking to the bottom of the pot or otherwise clumping together.

When the timer goes off, start tasting the noodles. When they seem like they are 1½ to 2 minutes away from a perfect al dente (see page 22), drain and transfer them to the sauce in the skillet using your preferred method (see page 21), making sure to reserve at least 1 cup (240 ml) of the pasta water.

recipe continues →

Slide the skillet back onto medium heat and finish cooking the noodles, tossing and adding plenty of splashes of pasta water until the noodles are perfectly al dente, the squash is tender but not mushy, and the sauce is nicely juicy. If the sauce seems watery, simmer for another few seconds to tighten it up, bearing in mind that the cheese will thicken it.

Reduce the heat to very low. Add the scallions, basil, and mint (tear the herb leaves a bit) and toss. Add the grated cheese and toss again to emulsify it with the other sauce ingredients, adding splashes of pasta water (or plain hot water, if things are getting too salty) if needed to keep the consistency creamy and prevent the cheese from clumping. Taste and add more salt if you like.

Divide the pasta between two warm bowls and serve right away, with more cheese to add at the table.

Pasta Salad with Summer Squash, Tomatoes, Almonds, and Sun-Dried Tomato and Almond Pesto

In this dish, the freshness of all the raw vegetables is contrasted by tossing them with one cooked ingredient—grilled scallions. If you don't have your outdoor grill going, you can get the same effect using a cast-iron skillet or grill pan.

Serves 4

- Kosher salt (preferably Diamond Crystal; see page 17)
- 8 ounces (225 g) casarecce, gemelli, or strozzapreti
- ¼ cup (60 ml) red wine vinegar, plus more to taste
- Extra-virgin olive oil
- 1 bunch scallions, trimmed and left whole
- Freshly ground black pepper
- 1½ cups (210 g) thinly sliced summer squash (ideally a mix of colors and types)
- ½ cup (70 g) roughly chopped toasted whole almonds
- Small handful of fresh basil leaves
- Small handful of fresh mint leaves
- Small handful of fresh flat-leaf parsley leaves
- ¾ cup (180 g) Sun-Dried Tomato and Almond Pesto (page 33)
- 1½ cups (250 g) tomato wedges, slices, or chunks or halved cherry tomatoes
- A few torn zucchini blossoms (optional)
- 1 ball fresh mozzarella or burrata (optional)

Fill a large pot (at least 6 quarts/L) with 1 gallon (4 L) of water; add 4 tablespoons (40 g) kosher salt, cover the pot, and bring the water to a boil. Add the noodles and set your timer for 2 minutes less than the shortest suggested cooking time on the package of pasta; this will ideally be 2 minutes before the pasta is al dente. Stir the noodles several times during the first 2 minutes of cooking to prevent them from sticking to the pot or otherwise clumping together.

When the timer goes off, start tasting the noodles. When they seem like they are a perfect al dente (see page 22), drain them in a colander. Quickly rinse the noodles with warm water and shake off any excess moisture; you want them to be as dry as possible. Transfer the noodles to a large bowl (this can be the serving bowl if it's large enough to allow some tossing).

While the noodles are still warm, sprinkle on 1 tablespoon of the vinegar and toss thoroughly so they absorb it evenly. Drizzle on about 1 tablespoon olive oil and toss again to evenly coat the noodles and prevent them from sticking together. Set aside.

Heat a grill pan or cast-iron skillet over high heat, or heat the broiler on high (or get your outdoor grill going). Toss the scallions with a little olive oil and season well with salt and black pepper. Cook them until they are soft and blackened in spots, turning them as needed to cook them evenly. Let them cool until you can handle them, then chop them into 2-inch (5 cm) lengths.

Add the scallions, squash, almonds, and half the basil, mint, and parsley (tear the herb leaves into a few pieces) to the noodles and toss to combine. In a small bowl, whisk the remaining 3 tablespoons vinegar with the sun-dried tomato pesto and then pour it over the salad. Toss again and then taste for seasoning, adding more vinegar, salt, or pepper as needed.

Drizzle on another tablespoon or two of olive oil, add the tomatoes, the remaining basil, mint, and parsley (again tearing up the herb leaves), and the zucchini blossoms, if using, and toss once more.

Tidy up the edges of the bowl or transfer the salad to a serving bowl or platter. If using mozzarella, tear it into large shreds and distribute over the salad. Serve right away at cool room temperature.

Late Summer

Sweet Peppers with Pancetta, Shrimp, and Oregano

Here's your chance to feature some of those sweet pepper varieties you've seen at the farmers' market or grown in your own garden. While a good ol' red bell pepper, with thick juicy flesh and mild sweet flavor, works just fine, other varieties such as Jimmy Nardello, lipstick, or pimento will add character and complexity.

Serves 2

Kosher salt (preferably Diamond Crystal; see page 17)

Extra-virgin olive oil

½ cup (60 g) chopped pancetta

1½ cups (225 g) thinly sliced bell pepper or other sweet pepper

1 teaspoon chopped fresh oregano leaves, or ½ teaspoon dried

6 ounces (170 g) raw shrimp, any size, preferably wild, peeled and deveined

8 ounces (225 g) spaghetti, linguine, or bucatini

1 tablespoon unsalted butter

⅓ cup (40 g) 50/50 cheese (half Parmigiano-Reggiano, half Pecorino Romano, grated in a food processor; see page 39), plus more for serving

Chile Crisp (page 37), for serving (optional)

Fill a large pot (at least 6 quarts/L) with 1 gallon (4 L) of water; add 4 tablespoons (40 g) kosher salt, cover the pot, and bring the water to a boil while you make your sauce. If the water begins to boil before your sauce is ready, turn down the heat, but don't let the volume of the pasta water reduce by boiling off.

Heat a generous glug of olive oil in a large skillet over medium heat. When the oil is hot, add the pancetta and cook until the fat has mostly rendered and the pancetta is starting to get crisp, 3 to 4 minutes.

Add the peppers and oregano and continue cooking until the peppers are getting soft and fragrant, another 4 to 6 minutes.

Increase the heat to medium-high and add the shrimp. Sauté until the shrimp are just barely opaque (they'll fully cook later) and the peppers are starting to brown a tiny bit, another 4 to 5 minutes. Stop the cooking with a splash of water from the pasta pot and slide the skillet off the heat.

Bring the pasta water (back) to a boil, add the noodles, and set your timer for 2 minutes less than the shortest suggested cooking time on the package of pasta; this will ideally be 2 minutes before the pasta is al dente. Stir the noodles several times during the first 2 minutes of cooking to prevent them from sticking to the bottom of the pot or otherwise clumping together.

When the timer goes off, start tasting the noodles. When they seem like they are 1½ to 2 minutes away from a perfect al dente (see page 22), drain and transfer them to the sauce in the skillet using your preferred method (see page 21), making sure to reserve at least 1 cup (240 ml) of the pasta water.

Slide the skillet back onto medium heat and finish cooking the noodles, tossing and adding plenty of splashes of pasta water until the noodles are perfectly al dente, the shrimp are fully cooked, and the sauce is nicely juicy. If the sauce seems watery, simmer for another few seconds to tighten it up, bearing in mind that the cheese will thicken it.

Reduce the heat to very low. Add the butter and the grated cheese and toss to emulsify them with the other sauce ingredients, adding splashes of pasta water (or plain hot water, if things are getting too salty) if needed to keep the consistency creamy and prevent the cheese from clumping. Taste and add more salt if you like.

Divide the pasta between two warm bowls, drizzle on some chile crisp, if using, and serve right away, with more cheese to add at the table.

Pasta Salad with Roasted Red Peppers, Salami, Mozzarella, and Croutons

A red pepper panzanella (bread salad)—one of my favorite summer salads—is the inspiration for this cold pasta dish, in which juicy roasted peppers, tender mozzarella, and good-quality vinegar moisten and mingle with all the other ingredients. I use bread in this salad, too, in the form of croutons, adding another layer of texture to the dish. If you have a batch of Italian Salad Dressing (page 162) in the fridge (and I hope you do), you can use that in place of the red wine vinegar and olive oil.

Serves 4

Kosher salt (preferably Diamond Crystal; see page 17)

8 ounces (225 g) cavatappi, busiate, or elbow macaroni

3 tablespoons red wine vinegar, plus more to taste

Extra-virgin olive oil

2 large red or orange bell peppers or other sweet, thick-fleshed peppers (about 1 pound/450 g total)

¼ small red onion, thinly sliced

1 or 2 garlic cloves, finely chopped

2 ounces (60 g) spicy or mild salami, thinly sliced

1 teaspoon dried oregano

⅛ teaspoon dried chile flakes, plus more to taste

Small handful of fresh mint leaves

Small handful of fresh flat-leaf parsley leaves

Freshly ground black pepper

1 recipe Torn Croutons (page 37)

1 ball fresh mozzarella (about 4 ounces/115 g)

Fill a large pot (at least 6 quarts/L) with 1 gallon (4 L) of water; add 4 tablespoons (40 g) kosher salt, cover the pot, and bring the water to a boil. Add the noodles and set your timer for 2 minutes less than the shortest suggested cooking time on the package of pasta; this will ideally be 2 minutes before the pasta is al dente. Stir the noodles several times during the first 2 minutes of cooking to prevent them from sticking to the bottom of the pot or otherwise clumping together.

When the timer goes off, start tasting the noodles. When they seem like they are a perfect al dente (see page 22), drain them in a colander. Quickly rinse the noodles with warm water and shake off any excess; you want them to be as dry as possible. Transfer the noodles to a large bowl (this can be the serving bowl if it's large enough to allow some tossing).

While the noodles are still warm, sprinkle on 1 tablespoon of the vinegar and toss thoroughly so the noodles absorb it evenly. Drizzle on about 1 tablespoon olive oil and toss again to evenly coat the noodles and prevent them from sticking together. Set aside.

Heat the broiler and line a small sheet pan with foil. Arrange the peppers on the prepared pan and broil them, turning them as each side blackens, until the skins are mostly blackened and blistered, 10 to 20 minutes total, depending on your broiler.

Gather up the foil around the peppers to create a little pouch and leave them to cool; this will allow the flesh to fully soften and the skins to be peeled off easily. When they're cool enough to handle, peel and seed them, then cut them into 1-inch-wide (2.5 cm) strips. Transfer to the bowl with the noodles and add the red onion, garlic, salami, oregano, chile flakes, half the mint and parsley, about ½ teaspoon salt, and many twists of black pepper and toss to combine. Sprinkle on the remaining 2 tablespoons vinegar and another

¼ cup (60 ml) olive oil and toss again. Taste and adjust the seasoning with more salt, black pepper, chile flakes, vinegar, or olive oil.

Add the croutons and, yes, toss once more. Let the salad rest for 15 to 30 minutes before serving so the croutons can soak up some juices and soften just a bit. The croutons should become moist and chewy; if not, add a bit more vinegar and olive oil and let rest for a few more minutes.

When you're ready to serve, tidy up the edges of the bowl or transfer the salad to a serving bowl or platter. Tear the mozzarella into shreds and distribute over the salad along with the remaining mint and parsley. Serve at cool room temperature.

Hot Chiles with Shrimp, Mussels, Squid, Basil, and Mint

Chock-full of seafood, fresh chiles, and handfuls of fragrant herbs, this dish is summer at the beach . . . even if you don't live anywhere near the ocean. Note that I don't use cheese in this dish, not because of the unspoken Italian no-cheese-with-seafood rule (I like to break rules), but because the clear and straightforward flavors of this dish shine on their own. A touch of butter brings them all together, and if you can drizzle the pasta with lemony Agrumato before serving, all the better.

Serves 2

Kosher salt (preferably Diamond Crystal; see page 17)

Extra-virgin olive oil

5 or 6 garlic cloves, smashed

¼ cup (30 g) sliced fresh chile, such as jalapeño or serrano (core and seed it before slicing)

½ pound (225 g) fresh mussels in the shell, scrubbed and debearded as needed

1½ cups (360 ml) dry white wine

6 ounces (170 g) raw shrimp, any size, preferably wild, peeled and deveined

4 ounces (115 g) cleaned squid (see page 194), bodies sliced into ½-inch-wide (1.25 cm) rounds, tentacles halved

8 ounces (225 g) spaghetti, bucatini, or linguine

2 tablespoons unsalted butter

Small handful of fresh basil leaves

Small handful of fresh mint leaves

2 tablespoons fresh lemon juice, plus more to taste

Big drizzle of lemon Agrumato (lemony extra-virgin olive oil; see page 41; optional)

Fill a large pot (at least 6 quarts/L) with 1 gallon (4 L) of water; add 4 tablespoons (40 g) kosher salt, cover the pot, and bring the water to a boil while you make your sauce. If the water begins to boil before your sauce is ready, turn down the heat, but don't let the volume of the pasta water reduce by boiling off.

Arrange your pasta bowls near the stove and tear off a piece of foil that will loosely cover both bowls (to keep the mussels warm as you finish the dish). Also get out a medium bowl to hold the shrimp and squid for a few minutes, and tear off a piece of foil to cover that, too.

Heat a generous glug of olive oil in a large skillet or Dutch oven with a lid over medium heat. When the oil is hot, add the garlic and chile and cook gently until the garlic is light golden and soft and the chile is becoming fragrant and soft, 3 to 4 minutes.

Increase the heat to medium-high, tumble in the mussels, pour in the white wine, and immediately cover the skillet. Cook, shaking the pan a bit, until the mussel shells have opened, about 3 minutes. With a slotted spoon or tongs, pluck out all the open mussels, draining their juices back into the skillet, transfer them to the pasta bowls, and cover loosely with the foil. Cook any unopened mussels for another minute or so; then add the newly opened ones to the pasta bowls and cover again with the foil. If any stubbornly unopened mussels remain, discard them.

Reduce the heat to medium, add the shrimp, and simmer in the winey broth until about half cooked, 2 to 4 minutes, depending on the size of your shrimp. Add the squid and simmer just until it is tender and the shrimp are almost cooked through, another 2 to 4 minutes. Scoop out the shrimp and squid with a slotted spoon and transfer to the medium bowl; cover with the foil to keep warm.

recipe continues →

Simmer the broth until it has reduced by about half and nicely concentrated in flavor (and the raw wine flavor has cooked off), 3 to 4 minutes. Slide the skillet off the heat.

Bring the pasta water (back) to a boil, add the noodles, and set your timer for 2 minutes less than the shortest suggested cooking time on the package of pasta; this will ideally be 2 minutes before the pasta is al dente. Stir the noodles several times during the first 2 minutes of cooking to prevent them from sticking to the bottom of the pot or otherwise clumping together.

When the timer goes off, start tasting the noodles. When they seem like they are 1½ to 2 minutes away from a perfect al dente (see page 22), drain and transfer them to the sauce in the skillet using your preferred method (see page 21), making sure to reserve at least 1 cup (240 ml) of the pasta water.

Slide the skillet back onto medium heat and finish cooking the noodles, tossing and adding plenty of splashes of pasta water until the noodles are perfectly al dente and the sauce is nicely juicy.

Add the butter to the skillet, along with the squid, shrimp, and the basil and mint leaves (tear them up a bit). Toss again, adding more plain water or pasta water as needed to keep everything nicely saucy, and simmer gently until the seafood is heated through and the broth is very hot. Add the lemon juice and drizzle in the Agrumato, if using. Taste and add more salt or lemon juice if you like.

Distribute the seafood and noodles evenly between the two mussel-filled pasta bowls and ladle the piping-hot broth over everything. Serve right away, with an extra bowl for the discarded mussel shells.

Hot Chiles with Fennel, Sausage, and Tomato

At my former restaurant Ava Gene's, this was one of the most popular pastas; we called it "pizza as pasta." We made it with our house-pickled chiles, so if you're into preserving, put up some chiles of your own and feature them in this dish (but store-bought is just fine, too). A tip: If you're serving spicy-averse diners, slice your chiles fairly thick so that they're easy to extract, or use a milder chile.

Serves 2 or 3

Kosher salt (preferably Diamond Crystal; see page 17)

6 ounces (170 g) bulk Italian sausage, sweet or hot

Extra-virgin olive oil

3 garlic cloves, smashed

2 cups (200 g) thinly sliced fennel (from 1 medium bulb, cored and trimmed)

Pinch of dried chile flakes

1 cup (250 g) canned whole peeled tomatoes, crushed by hand (page 44), with their juices

½ cup (60 g) thickly sliced pickled hot chiles, plus some of their pickling liquid

8 ounces (225 g) chiocciole, lumache, or conchiglie

1 teaspoon chopped fresh oregano, or ½ teaspoon dried

⅓ cup (40 g) 50/50 cheese (half Parmigiano-Reggiano, half Pecorino Romano, grated in a food processor; see page 39), plus more for serving

2 or 3 spoonfuls Whipped Plain Ricotta (page 34; optional)

Fill a large pot (at least 6 quarts/L) with 1 gallon (4 L) of water; add 4 tablespoons (40 g) kosher salt, cover the pot, and bring the water to a boil while you make your sauce. If the water begins to boil before your sauce is ready, turn down the heat, but don't let the volume of the pasta water reduce by boiling off.

Shape the sausage into 2 patties; set aside.

Heat a generous glug of olive oil in a large skillet over medium heat. When the oil is hot, add the garlic and fennel. Cook gently, breaking it up a bit with your spatula, until the garlic is nicely toasted and fragrant but not too brown and the fennel is slightly soft, 3 to 4 minutes.

Scoot the fennel and garlic to the edges of the skillet. Add the sausage patties and sear, smashing them down from time to time with your spatula to create a nicely browned crust on the bottom, 5 to 6 minutes.

Flip the patties and continue cooking until the sausage is browned, the garlic is toasted (but not too dark), and the fennel softens further, another 2 to 3 minutes (the sausage will finish cooking in the tomato sauce, so it doesn't need to be fully cooked now).

Add the chile flakes, then add the crushed tomatoes and their juices, pickled chiles, and a splash of their pickling liquid and simmer, breaking up the sausage and garlic into smaller bits, until the sauce has thickened and concentrated, another 3 to 4 minutes. Slide the skillet off the heat.

Bring the pasta water (back) to a boil, add the noodles, and set your timer for 2 minutes less than the shortest suggested cooking time on the package of pasta; this will ideally be 2 minutes before the pasta is al dente. Stir the noodles several times during the first 2 minutes of cooking to prevent them from sticking to the pot or otherwise clumping together.

When the timer goes off, start tasting the noodles. When they seem like they are 1½ to 2 minutes away from a perfect al dente (see page 22), drain and transfer them to the sauce in the skillet using your preferred method (see page 21), making sure to reserve at least 1 cup (240 ml) of the pasta water.

Slide the skillet back onto medium heat and finish cooking the noodles, tossing and adding plenty of splashes of pasta water until the noodles are perfectly al dente, the sausage is fully cooked, and the sauce is nicely juicy. If the sauce seems watery, simmer for another few seconds to tighten it up, bearing in mind that the cheese will thicken it.

Reduce the heat to very low. Add the oregano and the 50/50 cheese and toss to emulsify the cheese with the other sauce ingredients, adding splashes of pasta water (or plain hot water, if things are getting too salty) if needed to keep the consistency creamy and prevent the cheese from clumping.

Divide the pasta between two or three warm bowls, dollop each serving with a spoonful of whipped ricotta, if using, and serve right away, with more 50/50 cheese to add at the table.

Corn with Jalapeños and Brown Butter

This dish is all about the fresh corn, so don't be tempted to make it unless you can get the sweet, tender corn of the season. The jalapeños are sliced into rings so that diners who don't like a ton of heat can remove them, though some of the heat will have infused into the cream. If jalapeños aren't your thing, omit them and season the cream sauce generously with freshly ground black pepper.

Serves 2

Kosher salt (preferably Diamond Crystal; see page 17)

3 ears of corn, shucked, silk removed

Extra-virgin olive oil

3 tablespoons unsalted butter

¾ cup (180 ml) heavy or whipping cream

1 medium jalapeño or other chile, cored, seeded, and sliced into rings, or freshly ground black pepper

8 ounces (225 g) mafaldine, pappardelle, or fettucine

¼ cup (30 g) 50/50 cheese (half Parmigiano-Reggiano, half Pecorino Romano, grated in a food processor; see page 39), plus more for serving

Small handful of fresh basil leaves

Fill a large pot (at least 6 quarts/L) with 1 gallon (4 L) of water; add 4 tablespoons (40 g) kosher salt, cover the pot, and bring the water to a boil while you make your sauce. If the water begins to boil before your sauce is ready, turn down the heat, but don't let the volume of the pasta water reduce by boiling off.

Slice the corn kernels off the cobs and put them in a bowl. Scrape the cobs with the back of a knife or a soup spoon to capture all the creamy pulp that's left and add that to the kernels.

Heat a small glug of olive oil in a large skillet over medium heat. When the oil is hot, add about half the corn and sauté for about 1 minute, then add the butter. Cook gently until the butter is browned and super nutty-smelling, 3 to 4 minutes.

Add the cream and the jalapeño and bring to a simmer. (If you're not using jalapeño, season the cream generously with black pepper.) Simmer gently until the mixture has reduced by about three-quarters, smashing some of the corn against the pan to create varying textures, 5 to 7 minutes. You want a chunky corn puree.

Splash in a ladleful of water from the pasta pot and add the remaining corn kernels. Slide the skillet off the heat.

Bring the pasta water (back) to a boil, add the noodles, and set your timer for 2 minutes less than the shortest suggested cooking time on the package of pasta; this will ideally be 2 minutes before the pasta is al dente. Stir the noodles during the first 2 minutes of cooking to prevent them from sticking to the pot.

When the timer goes off, start tasting the noodles. When they seem like they are almost a perfect al dente (see page 22), drain and transfer them to the sauce in the skillet using your preferred method (see page 21), making sure to reserve at least 1 cup (240 ml) of the pasta water.

Slide the skillet back onto medium heat and continue to cook the noodles for a few seconds, adding pasta water if the sauce is getting thick, until the noodles are perfectly al dente, the corn is heated through, and the sauce is nicely creamy. If the sauce seems watery, simmer for another few seconds to tighten it up, bearing in mind that the cheese will thicken it.

Reduce the heat to very low. Add the grated cheese and toss to emulsify it with the other sauce ingredients, adding splashes of pasta water if needed to keep the consistency creamy and prevent the cheese from clumping. Add the basil, tearing the leaves into a few pieces, and toss once more. Remove the jalapeño slices if you like.

Divide the pasta between two warm bowls and serve right away, with more cheese at the table.

Pasta Salad with Corn, Walnuts, Mozzarella, and Jalapeños

When corn is in peak season and you can find it locally, eating it raw is a real treat. Taste your corn, and if you think it has been quite some time since it was picked from the field, you can either blanch it until it is tender or grill it (still on the cob, of course). Even when I have excellent corn, I sometimes grill half and use the other half raw to add complexity to this dish.

Serves 4

- **Kosher salt (preferably Diamond Crystal; see page 17)**
- **8 ounces (225 g) conchiglie, lumache, or rotelle**
- **¼ cup (60 ml) fresh lemon juice, plus more to taste**
- **Extra-virgin olive oil**
- **2 cups (300 g) corn kernels**
- **½ cup (65 g) sliced red onion**
- **½ cup (60 g) roughly chopped walnuts**
- **¼ cup (30 g) sliced jalapeño (core and seed it before slicing)**
- **1 teaspoon finely grated lemon zest**
- **¼ teaspoon dried chile flakes, plus more to taste**
- **Freshly ground black pepper**
- **Small handful of fresh basil leaves**
- **Small handful of fresh mint leaves**
- **Small handful of fresh flat-leaf parsley leaves**
- **1 ball fresh mozzarella (about 4 ounces/115 g)**
- **Lemon Agrumato (lemony extra-virgin olive oil; see page 41; optional)**

Fill a large pot (at least 6 quarts/L) with 1 gallon (4 L) of water; add 4 tablespoons (40 g) kosher salt, cover the pot, and bring the water to a boil. Add the noodles and set your timer for 2 minutes less than the shortest suggested cooking time on the package of pasta; this will ideally be 2 minutes before the pasta is al dente. Stir the noodles several times during the first 2 minutes of cooking to prevent them from sticking to the bottom of the pot or otherwise clumping together.

When the timer goes off, start tasting the noodles. When they seem like they are a perfect al dente (see page 22), drain them in a colander. Quickly rinse the noodles with warm water and shake off any excess moisture; you want them to be as dry as possible. Transfer the noodles to a large bowl (this can be the serving bowl if it's large enough to allow some tossing).

While the noodles are still warm, sprinkle on 1 tablespoon of the lemon juice and toss thoroughly so they absorb it evenly. Drizzle on about 1 tablespoon olive oil and toss again to evenly coat the noodles and prevent them from sticking together.

Add the corn, red onion, walnuts, jalapeño, lemon zest, chile flakes, ½ teaspoon salt, and several twists of black pepper. Toss to incorporate the ingredients, then add the remaining 3 tablespoons lemon juice and toss again.

Tear up about half the basil, mint, and parsley leaves, add them to the bowl, and toss again. Taste and adjust the seasoning with more lemon juice, chile flakes, salt, or black pepper.

Tear the mozzarella into shreds and add to the bowl. Drizzle on about ¼ cup (60 ml) olive oil or Agrumato, if using, and add the remaining herb leaves, also torn. Tidy up the edges of the bowl or transfer the salad to another serving bowl or platter. Toss and give the salad one more taste-and-adjust, then serve at cool room temperature.

Eggplant with Sun-Dried Tomato and Almond Pesto and Mint

Eggplant is a master at absorbing flavors, but it also absorbs oil like crazy. While you want some of that nice olive oil flavor to penetrate the cubes of eggplant, too much is, well, too much. Maintain control by starting with a generous amount of oil and a hot skillet, and then focus on browning the first side of the eggplant to hit the pan. Getting good color on one side will achieve the goal of creating a toasty flavor; browning the eggplant on all sides becomes tricky and can end up using a lot of oil and making the dish too rich and heavy.

Serves 2

9 ounces (250 g) eggplant, peeled in alternating stripes (think zebra)

Kosher salt (preferably Diamond Crystal; see page 17)

Extra-virgin olive oil

Scant 1 cup (200 g) Sun-Dried Tomato and Almond Pesto (page 33)

½ cup (60 g) sliced scallions, white and light green parts only

Small handful of fresh mint leaves

Small handful of fresh flat-leaf parsley leaves

8 ounces (225 g) linguine, tagliatelle, or spaghetti alla chitarra

⅓ cup (40 g) 50/50 cheese (half Parmigiano-Reggiano, half Pecorino Romano, grated in a food processor; see page 39), plus more for serving

A few fresh basil leaves, for serving

Cut the eggplant into 1-inch (2.5 cm) cubes. Put them in a bowl and toss with 1 teaspoon salt. Transfer the eggplant to a colander and let sit for about 30 minutes so the salt can draw out some moisture. Blot off the salt and liquid with paper towels and then press the eggplant a bit to squeeze out even more moisture (without smashing the eggplant).

Fill a large pot (at least 6 quarts/L) with 1 gallon (4 L) of water; add 4 tablespoons (40 g) kosher salt, cover the pot, and bring the water to a boil while you make your sauce. If the water begins to boil before your sauce is ready, turn down the heat, but don't let the volume of the pasta water reduce by boiling off.

Heat a very generous glug of olive oil in a large skillet over high heat (you need a lot of oil for this). When the oil is very hot, add the eggplant, keeping it in one layer if possible. Reduce the heat just a bit so the oil isn't smoking and cook without moving the eggplant until it's deeply browned, 3 to 4 minutes. Once you've got nice browning, flip the pieces and try to brown as much of the other sides as possible, but don't add more oil or the dish will get a bit heavy.

When the eggplant is nicely browned and tender, another 10 minutes or so, splash in a bit of water from the pasta pot to stop the cooking and slide the skillet off the heat. Add the sun-dried tomato pesto, the scallions, and the mint and parsley, tearing the herb leaves into a few pieces, and stir to mix.

Bring the pasta water (back) to a boil, add the noodles, and set your timer for 2 minutes less than the shortest suggested cooking time on the package of pasta; this will ideally be 2 minutes before the pasta is al dente. Stir the noodles several times during the first 2 minutes of cooking to prevent them from sticking to the bottom of the pot or otherwise clumping together.

When the timer goes off, start tasting the noodles. When they seem like they are 1½ to 2 minutes away from a perfect al dente (see page 22), drain and transfer them to the sauce in the skillet using your preferred method (see page 21), making sure to reserve at least 1 cup (240 ml) of the pasta water.

Slide the skillet back onto medium heat and finish cooking the noodles, tossing and adding plenty of splashes of pasta water until the noodles are perfectly al dente, the eggplant is fully tender (it's okay if it falls apart a bit; better overcooked than undercooked), and the sauce is nicely juicy. If the sauce seems watery, simmer for another few seconds to tighten it up, bearing in mind that the cheese will thicken it.

Reduce the heat to very low. Add the grated cheese and toss to emulsify it with the other sauce ingredients, adding splashes of pasta water (or plain hot water, if things are getting too salty) if needed to keep the consistency creamy and prevent the cheese from clumping. Taste and add more salt if you like.

Divide the pasta between two warm bowls, add the basil leaves, and serve right away, with more cheese to add at the table.

Eggplant with Garlic, Capers, Raisins, and Herbs

I haven't spent much time in Sicily, but I feel like I know it through its flavors, such as the caper-raisin-anchovy combo here, especially when paired with earthy, creamy eggplant.

Serves 2

- **⅓ cup (50 g) golden raisins**
- **1 tablespoon balsamic vinegar, plus more for finishing**
- **9 ounces (250 g) eggplant, peeled in alternating stripes (think zebra) and cut into 1-inch (2.5 cm) chunks**
- **Kosher salt (preferably Diamond Crystal; see page 17)**
- **Extra-virgin olive oil**
- **3 or 4 garlic cloves, smashed**
- **3 to as many as you want oil-packed anchovy fillets**
- **Big pinch of dried chile flakes, plus more to taste**
- **2 tablespoons roughly chopped brined capers**
- **8 ounces (225 g) mafaldine, pappardelle, or fettucine**
- **½ cup (15 g) roughly chopped fresh flat-leaf parsley leaves**
- **Small handful of fresh basil leaves, torn into pieces**
- **2 tablespoons Dried Breadcrumbs (page 36; optional)**
- **Chunk of Parmigiano, for grating at the table**

Combine the raisins and vinegar in a small bowl and set aside until the raisins are plump, 20 to 30 minutes; drain and set aside.

Put the eggplant in a bowl and toss with 1 teaspoon salt. Transfer the eggplant to a colander and let sit for about 30 minutes so the salt can draw out some moisture. Blot off the salt and liquid with paper towels and then press the eggplant a bit to squeeze out even more moisture (without smashing the eggplant).

Fill a large pot (at least 6 quarts/L) with 1 gallon (4 L) of water; add 4 tablespoons (40 g) kosher salt, cover the pot, and bring the water to a boil while you make your sauce. If the water begins to boil before your sauce is ready, turn down the heat, but don't let the volume of the pasta water reduce by boiling off.

Heat a very generous glug of olive oil in a large skillet over medium heat (you need a lot of oil for this). When the oil is hot, add the garlic and cook gently, breaking it up a bit with your spatula, until it is lightly toasted and fragrant but not at all brown, 3 to 4 minutes.

Add the eggplant, keeping it in one layer if possible, and cook without moving the eggplant until it's deeply browned, 3 to 4 minutes; keep an eye on the garlic so it doesn't burn. Once you've got nice browning, flip the pieces and try to brown as much of the other sides as possible, cooking for another 5 to 6 minutes, but don't add more oil or the whole dish will get a bit heavy. The eggplant should be mostly tender, but you'll cook it a bit more later.

Add the anchovies and chile flakes and cook for another several seconds, smashing the anchovies a bit so they break up and dissolve into the mixture. Add the capers and raisins, stir to blend everything, then splash some water from the pasta pot into the skillet to stop the cooking; slide the skillet off the heat.

Bring the pasta water (back) to a boil, add the noodles, and set your timer for 2 minutes less than the shortest suggested cooking time on the package of pasta; this will ideally be 2 minutes before the pasta is al dente. Stir the noodles several times during the first 2 minutes of cooking to prevent them from sticking to the bottom of the pot or otherwise clumping together.

When the timer goes off, start tasting the noodles. When they seem like they are 1½ to 2 minutes away from a perfect al dente (see page 22), drain and transfer them to the sauce

in the skillet using your preferred method (see page 21), making sure to reserve at least 1 cup (240 ml) of the pasta water.

Slide the skillet back onto medium heat and finish cooking the noodles, tossing and adding plenty of splashes of pasta water until the noodles are perfectly al dente, the eggplant is tender, and the sauce is nicely juicy. If the sauce seems watery, simmer for another few seconds to tighten it up.

Add the chopped parsley and torn basil leaves, drizzle with more balsamic, and toss. Taste and add more salt, chile flakes, or balsamic if you like.

Divide the pasta between two warm bowls, top with the breadcrumbs, if using, and serve right away, grating the Parmigiano at the table.

Eggplant Puttanesca with Fresh Tomatoes

This is my quicker and, I think, fresher version of a classic eggplant puttanesca. The cherry tomatoes bring a brighter sweetness than a basic marinara sauce would, and adding the olives, capers, and anchovies in the final minutes of cooking creates cleaner flavors than when you cook those ingredients into the sauce. For a changeup, use a few drops of colatura, which is like Italian fish sauce, in place of the anchovies. Be cautious, however, because a little goes a long way.

Serves 2

- 9 ounces (250 g) eggplant, peeled in alternating stripes (think zebra)
- Kosher salt (preferably Diamond Crystal; see page 17)
- Extra-virgin olive oil
- 3 or 4 garlic cloves, smashed
- 6 ounces (170 g) cherry tomatoes, halved if large
- 3 to as many as you want oil-packed anchovy fillets, chopped
- ½ cup (60 g) roughly chopped pitted green or mild black olives
- 2 tablespoons roughly chopped brined capers
- Big pinch of dried chile flakes, plus more to taste
- Small handful of fresh flat-leaf parsley leaves
- Big pinch of fresh oregano leaves
- 8 ounces (225 g) paccheri, rigatoni, or conchiglie
- Finishing-quality extra-virgin olive oil, for serving (optional)

Cut the eggplant into 1-inch (2.5 cm) cubes. Put them in a bowl and toss with 1 teaspoon salt. Transfer the eggplant to a colander and let sit for about 30 minutes so the salt can draw out some moisture. Blot off the salt and liquid with paper towels and then press the eggplant a bit to squeeze out even more moisture (without smashing the eggplant).

Fill a large pot (at least 6 quarts/L) with 1 gallon (4 L) of water; add 4 tablespoons (40 g) kosher salt, cover the pot, and bring the water to a boil while you make your sauce. If the water begins to boil before your sauce is ready, turn down the heat, but don't let the volume of the pasta water reduce by boiling off.

Heat a very generous glug of olive oil in a large skillet over medium heat (you need a lot of oil for this). When the oil is hot, add the garlic and cook gently, breaking it up a bit with your spatula, until it is lightly toasted and fragrant but not at all brown, 3 to 4 minutes.

Add the eggplant, keeping it in one layer if possible, and cook without moving the eggplant until it's deeply browned, 3 to 4 minutes; keep an eye on the garlic so it doesn't burn. Once you've got nice browning, flip the pieces and try to brown as much of the other sides as possible, cooking for another 3 to 4 minutes, but don't add more oil or the whole dish will get a bit heavy. The eggplant should be mostly tender, but you'll cook it a bit more later.

Add the cherry tomatoes and continue cooking, tossing and stirring a bit, until they have popped open and are releasing their juices, 5 to 6 minutes. You can smash a few tomatoes against the pan with the back of your spoon to encourage sauciness, but leave some whole as well.

Add the anchovies, olives, capers, and chile flakes plus a splash of water from the pasta pot and simmer the sauce for another minute or so. Slide the skillet off the heat and add about half the parsley and all of the oregano, tearing the herb leaves into a few pieces as you add them.

Bring the pasta water (back) to a boil, add the noodles, and set your timer for 2 minutes less than the shortest suggested cooking time on the package of pasta; this will ideally be 2 minutes before the pasta is al dente. Stir the noodles several times during the first 2 minutes of cooking to prevent them from sticking to the bottom of the pot or otherwise clumping together.

When the timer goes off, start tasting the noodles. When they seem like they are 1½ to 2 minutes away from a perfect al dente (see page 22), drain and transfer them to the sauce in the skillet using your preferred method (see page 21), making sure to reserve at least 1 cup (240 ml) of the pasta water.

Slide the skillet back onto medium heat and finish cooking the noodles, tossing and adding plenty of splashes of pasta water until the noodles are perfectly al dente, the eggplant is tender, and the sauce is nicely juicy. If the sauce seems watery, simmer for another few seconds to tighten it up.

Add the remaining parsley. Taste and add more salt or chile flakes if you like.

Divide the pasta between two warm bowls, drizzle generously with finishing olive oil, if using, and serve right away.

Pasta Salad with Roasted Eggplant, Tomatoes, Herbs, and Ricotta Salata

When you roast a whole eggplant until it almost collapses, the flesh becomes silky and smoky. I like to enhance the eggplant puree with vinegar, olive oil, and seasonings to create a dressing. The color can be a bit dull, but cherry tomatoes, mint, and crumbled ricotta salata brighten up the situation nicely.

Serves 4

One 12-ounce (340 g) eggplant

Red wine vinegar

¼ teaspoon dried chile flakes, plus more to taste

Kosher salt (preferably Diamond Crystal; see page 17)

Extra-virgin olive oil

8 ounces (225 g) radiatore, rotini, or campanelle

12 ounces (340 g) cherry tomatoes, halved (choose a mix of colors and shapes, if possible)

4 or 5 scallions, white and light green parts only, thinly sliced

Small handful of fresh mint leaves

½ cup (60 g) crumbled ricotta salata

Heat the oven to 450°F (230°C).

Prick the eggplant a few times to keep it from bursting as it roasts. Line a small sheet pan with foil, set the eggplant on it, and roast until totally tender and starting to collapse, 30 minutes to 1 hour, depending on the size and shape. Let the eggplant cool on the pan until it's cool enough to handle.

Cut the eggplant open and scoop the flesh into a food processor; discard the skin. Pulse a few times to make a rough puree. Add 1 teaspoon vinegar, the chile flakes, ½ teaspoon salt, and 3 tablespoons olive oil and pulse several more times, adding more olive oil if needed to create a creamy consistency. Taste (watch out for the processor blade!) and adjust the seasoning with more salt, chile flakes, or vinegar as needed.

Measure out 1 cup (250 g) of the eggplant puree and set aside (if you have any left over, you can enjoy it with some pita bread as a snack).

Fill a large pot (at least 6 quarts/L) with 1 gallon (4 L) of water; add 4 tablespoons (40 g) kosher salt, cover the pot, and bring the water to a boil. Add the noodles, and set your timer for 2 minutes less than the shortest suggested cooking time on the package of pasta; this will ideally be 2 minutes before the pasta is al dente. Stir the noodles several times during the first 2 minutes of cooking to prevent them from sticking to the pot or otherwise clumping together.

When the timer goes off, start tasting the noodles. When they seem like they are a perfect al dente (see page 22), drain them in a colander. Quickly rinse the noodles with warm water and shake off any excess; you want them to be as dry as possible. Transfer the noodles to a large bowl (this can be the serving bowl if it's large enough to allow some tossing).

While the noodles are still warm, sprinkle on 1 tablespoon vinegar and toss thoroughly so they absorb it evenly. Drizzle on about 1 tablespoon olive oil and toss again to evenly coat the noodles and prevent them from sticking together.

Add the eggplant puree to the noodles and fold together. Add the tomatoes, scallions, and mint, tearing the leaves into a few pieces. Drizzle on another 2 tablespoons vinegar, then toss the salad. Taste and add more salt or vinegar if needed, remembering that the ricotta salata will add a bit of salt.

Drizzle on another 2 tablespoons olive oil and toss again. Tidy up the edges of the bowl or transfer the salad to a serving bowl or platter. Sprinkle the ricotta salata over the top and serve at cool room temperature.

How to Invent Your Own Pasta Salad

Pasta salad is a seasonal dish for me. I make and eat different versions of it from spring through late summer, at which point my appetite changes and I crave heartier food . . . and more butter.

But you can make pasta salad any time your appetite asks you to. The following principles should be useful guidelines to help you choose ingredients that harmonize.

Ratios. Exact quantities aren't required with a salad, so use what looks right to you. A general ratio, however, is half noodles, half everything else.

Noodles. Short noodles are best for pasta salads. My favorite shapes are fusilli, cavatappi, ditalini, and orzo, but I also use rigatoni sometimes and, of course, macaroni, though a good pasta salad bears no resemblance to a grocery store deli's macaroni salad.

With short shapes, I like to cut the other ingredients to approximately the same size and shape as the noodle because I think it makes the overall texture of the dish quite pleasing.

Though short noodles are my typical choice, fusilli col buco—a long noodle with a hole through the center—can be amazing when served cold. The slightly squiggly noodle will wrap around the other ingredients and break up a bit into shorter lengths as you toss.

Whatever noodle you use, here's the way to prep it:

1. Cook in salted water all the way to al dente; no need to reserve any pasta water. You don't want mushy noodles, of course, but nothing's worse than a cold underdone noodle with a chalky center.

2. Right after draining them, rinse the noodles quickly under warm water. You want to rinse off surface starch but not fully cool the noodles. Keep them slightly warm.

3. Transfer the noodles to a large bowl and dress lightly, first with whatever acid you're using—vinegar or citrus juice—and then with a small amount of olive oil. You'll dress the salad more fully later, but this small initial amount allows the bright acid flavor to penetrate into the noodles, and the oil keeps them from sticking together. If your recipe calls for an actual vinaigrette, use a small amount of that instead of separate acid and oil.

Vegetables. Any vegetable can do well in a pasta salad, provided it tastes good raw or you've cooked and cooled it—think chunks of grilled yellow squash, grilled onions, or roasted golden beets. And don't forget salad greens, especially arugula or other spicy greens. These are best added just before serving so they don't totally wilt.

Beware of watery ingredients, however—I'm looking at you, tomato. Cucumber as well. While these summery ingredients are naturals for pasta salads, add them at the last minute so that their juices don't dilute the rest of the ingredients. Salting them and letting them drain ahead of time (and still adding them last minute) is another tactic for avoiding a soggy situation.

Meat and seafood. Always welcome, provided it tastes good cold. Seafood choices can include cooked shrimp, scallops, lobster, and any kind of hot-smoked fish like trout or salmon, though the texture of cold-smoked salmon (lox) is a bit too soft for me. Cooked salmon, whether roasted, poached, or grilled, works beautifully. Grilled or seared fresh tuna and good-quality canned tuna are made for pasta salads.

Roasted or grilled chicken is a natural, and even cooked beef, pork, or lamb can work with the right combination of ingredients, though very fatty meats can feel greasy when they're cold. I wouldn't use shredded short ribs, for example.

Cured meat, of course, such as any type of salami or prosciutto, is a perfect pasta salad ingredient. Bacon, including pancetta, is trickier, as cold congealed fat is unappealing. When I include pancetta, I make sure it's cooked until super crisp and I add at the last minute. Or I use a pancetta vinaigrette (page 169), which incorporates pancetta flavor without the flabby-fat texture.

Cheeses. While I love a heap of grated Parmigiano and/or Pecorino Romano on warm pasta dishes, this kind of cheese usually doesn't work in a salad because it dries things out (the one exception is Pasta Salad with Roasted Artichokes and Salmon, page 161).

I prefer softer, creamier cheeses such as fresh mozzarella (don't dice it—pull it apart into big shreds so the edges can soak up dressing). Ditto with burrata—just pull it apart into forkable pieces, letting the creamy interior run all over the place. Fontina can also work; grate it using the large holes of a box grater and let it integrate into the other ingredients.

I also love to use a whipped ricotta (pages 34–35) in pasta salad, which adds cheese, technically, but mostly adds creaminess. Loosen the consistency a bit with water or, if the salad isn't already too rich, a little olive oil. (Skip the whipped basil ricotta because the color can turn gray.)

Dressings. Whatever dressing you use, you're looking for a good balance of acid and fat. Think of an Italian hoagie—the reason it's so good is because of the oil and vinegar balancing the starchy bread. You've already dressed the noodles lightly, but the main dose of dressing will coat all the ingredients in the salad, lightly enough that the salad doesn't get gloppy but generously enough that you've got a full-flavored dish. Always start by adding a small amount, then toss and add more if needed. If I'm making the salad ahead of time, I'll go very light on the dressing and then refresh it with a last-minute application.

Your simplest choice is oil and vinegar. The oil should, of course, be extra-virgin, and a really good, grassy olive oil will sing in a salad. I also use lemon Agrumato (see page 41) in salads; the lemon flavor is perfect, and while it doesn't add the acid that lemon juice would, the lemony fragrance complements any actual lemon juice.

Vinegar should also be excellent quality. I'm a huge fan of Katz Farm vinegars, most of which are slightly sweet and are crafted using traditional fermentation methods. I also like Lindera Farms, which uses real-deal methods and makes an amazing array of flavors (see Resources, page 380).

You can also use fresh-squeezed citrus juice—lemon, lime, or possibly orange, depending on what else is going on in your salad.

Of course, an actual vinaigrette will combine the oil and the acid, plus bring in other seasonings, so that's always a good choice.

Herbs. Fresh herbs bring the important elements of flavor, fragrance, and freshness to a salad. Basil, mint, and parsley are my go-tos. As in my other pasta dishes, I add them by the handful, usually tearing up the bigger leaves, which also releases their perfume. Add herbs only at the last minute so they don't wilt and darken too much. And don't use tougher, more resinous herbs, such as rosemary or thyme; those are best in cooked dishes.

Other accents. I don't want you to think of a pasta salad as an anything-goes dish; you need to restrain yourself to key ingredients that make sense together. However, don't hesitate to toss in a few accents once you've worked out your main-ingredient program.

I love accents that provide a pop of salt, heat, or tang. Chopped or sliced peperoncini are brilliant at this, contributing a lifting, mild chile heat along with briny-tangy pickle flavor; use some of the liquid from the jar in your dressing. Ditto for other pickled ingredients, such as giardiniera, pickled hot chiles, or spicy Calabrian chiles in oil (drained).

Olives are natural pasta salad ingredients, as are capers; both will add more salt and brininess, so keep those flavors in balance. Grated lemon zest contributes a bright perfumed accent without actually adding any sour citrus.

Think about textural accents, too. Lightly toasted pine nuts, chopped nuts (walnuts, pistachios, hazelnuts, almonds), or dried breadcrumbs (page 36) add a crunchy contrast to tender noodles. Add these textural accents only at the very last minute, because once they get soggy, they can't do their job anymore.

Roasted Cherry Tomatoes with Green Lentil Ragu

So full of goodness, this lentil ragu is delicious on its own but loves a lift from bright accent ingredients, such as fresh basil and mint and—the featured player here—roasted cherry tomatoes.

If you are using lentil ragu that you've frozen, allow enough time for it to thaw gently, ideally in the fridge, but on the counter is fine, too. If you try to thaw it directly in the skillet, which works with other ragus, you'll end up with a mushy sauce. The flavor will be fine, but the texture will suffer. No matter how you prepare the ragu, the lentils will break down a bit, creating an earthy creaminess.

Serves 2

1 pint (12 ounces/340 g) cherry tomatoes (a mix of colors and shapes is nice), halved

Extra-virgin olive oil

Kosher salt (preferably Diamond Crystal; see page 17)

Freshly ground black pepper

1 cup (250 g) Green Lentil Ragu (page 60), thawed if previously frozen

¼ teaspoon dried chile flakes, plus more to taste

8 ounces (225 g) cascatelli, campanelle, or rotelle

Small handful of fresh basil leaves

Small handful of fresh mint leaves

⅓ cup (40 g) 50/50 cheese (half Parmigiano-Reggiano, half Pecorino Romano, grated in a food processor; see page 39), plus more for serving

Big handful of arugula

Good-quality balsamic vinegar, for serving (optional)

Heat the oven to 375°F (190°C).

Spread the tomatoes on a sheet pan (ideally one that allows for a single layer of tomatoes without too much space between them). Drizzle the tomatoes with olive oil and season generously with salt and pepper. Roast until the tomatoes are sizzling, a bit shrunken, and lightly browned around the edges, 25 to 45 minutes. Let cool on the sheet pan until ready to use (you can do this up to 3 days ahead, keeping the tomatoes refrigerated).

Fill a large pot (at least 6 quarts/L) with 1 gallon (4 L) of water; add 4 tablespoons (40 g) kosher salt, cover the pot, and bring the water to a boil while you make your sauce. If the water begins to boil before your sauce is ready, turn down the heat, but don't let the volume of the pasta water reduce by boiling off.

Splash a bit of the pasta water into a large skillet, add the lentil ragu, and gently heat the ragu over low heat without breaking up the lentils too much and making it mushy. Gently fold in the roasted tomatoes, season with the chile flakes, and slide the skillet off the heat.

Bring the pasta water (back) to a boil, add the noodles, and set your timer for 2 minutes less than the shortest suggested cooking time on the package of pasta; this will ideally be 2 minutes before the pasta is al dente. Stir the noodles several times during the first 2 minutes of cooking to prevent them from sticking to the bottom of the pot or otherwise clumping together.

When the timer goes off, start tasting the noodles. When they seem like they are almost a perfect al dente (see page 22), drain and transfer them to the sauce in the skillet using your preferred method (see page 21), making sure to reserve at least 1 cup (240 ml) of the pasta water.

recipe continues →

Slide the skillet back onto medium heat and toss the noodles with the lentils and tomatoes, adding splashes of pasta water as needed until the noodles are perfectly al dente and the sauce is nicely juicy. If the sauce seems watery, simmer for another few seconds to tighten it up, bearing in mind that the cheese will thicken it.

Reduce the heat to very low. Add the basil and mint, tearing the leaves into a few pieces, then add the grated cheese and toss to emulsify it with the other sauce ingredients, adding splashes of pasta water if needed to keep the consistency creamy and prevent the cheese from clumping. Taste and add more salt or chile flakes if you like.

Add the arugula and toss just once or twice to integrate it without completely wilting.

Divide the pasta between two warm bowls, drizzle with more olive oil and the balsamic, if using, and serve right away, with more cheese to add at the table.

MORE WAYS

Cut a sweet onion, such as Vidalia or Walla Walla, into 1-inch (5 cm) dice and roast it along with the tomatoes, adding a bit more oil to ensure that all the ingredients are lightly coated.

Sun Gold Tomatoes with Basil and Garlic

There's a moment in the summer when cherry tomato plants go crazy, producing so many tomatoes that it's hard to keep up with them. This is the pasta for that moment! I strongly suggest using Sun Gold tomatoes if you grow them or can find them at a market. Not only are they a gorgeous deep orange, their flavor is sweeter and fruitier than that of any other cherry tomato I've tasted; I'm addicted. But any variety will work in this recipe, and a mix of colors is always welcome.

Serves 2

Kosher salt (preferably Diamond Crystal; see page 17)

Extra-virgin olive oil

3 or 4 garlic cloves, smashed

1 pint (12 ounces/340 g) Sun Gold or a mix of cherry tomatoes, halved if large

Large pinch of dried chile flakes, plus more to taste

Freshly ground black pepper

Large handful of fresh basil leaves

8 ounces (225 g) bucatini, spaghetti, or linguine

⅓ cup (40 g) 50/50 cheese (half Parmigiano-Reggiano, half Pecorino Romano, grated in a food processor; see page 39), plus more for serving

1 to 2 tablespoons unsalted butter

2 tablespoons Dried Breadcrumbs (page 36; optional)

Fill a large pot (at least 6 quarts/L) with 1 gallon (4 L) of water; add 4 tablespoons (40 g) kosher salt, cover the pot, and bring the water to a boil while you make your sauce. If the water begins to boil before your sauce is ready, turn down the heat, but don't let the volume of the pasta water reduce by boiling off.

Heat a glug of olive oil in a large skillet over medium-high heat. When the oil is hot, add the garlic and cook gently, breaking it up a bit with your spatula, until it is nicely toasted and fragrant but not too brown, 3 to 4 minutes.

Add a bit more than half the tomatoes to the skillet (watch out, as they will probably spatter a bit). Cook until the tomatoes burst open and get juicy, 5 to 8 minutes; you can encourage this by piercing them with a knife. Remove the skillet from the heat and gently smash the tomatoes with the back of a spoon. Add the chile flakes and season generously with salt and black pepper.

Return the skillet to the heat, add half the basil (tear the leaves into a few pieces), and cook until you have a slightly thick sauce, another 5 minutes or so. Slide the skillet off the heat.

Bring the pasta water (back) to a boil, add the noodles, and set your timer for 2 minutes less than the shortest suggested cooking time on the package of pasta; this will ideally be 2 minutes before the pasta is al dente. Stir the noodles several times during the first 2 minutes of cooking to prevent them from sticking to the bottom of the pot or otherwise clumping together.

When the timer goes off, start tasting the noodles. When they seem like they are 1½ to 2 minutes away from a perfect al dente (see page 22), drain and transfer them to the sauce in the skillet using your preferred method (see page 21), making sure to reserve at least 1 cup (240 ml) of the pasta water.

Slide the skillet back onto medium heat and add the rest of the tomatoes. Continue cooking the noodles, tossing and adding plenty of splashes of pasta water, until they are perfectly al dente and the sauce is nicely juicy; the newly added tomatoes will keep some of their firmer texture.

recipe continues →

If the sauce seems watery, simmer for another few seconds to tighten it up, bearing in mind that the cheese will thicken it.

Reduce the heat to very low. Add the rest of the basil; toss to wilt the herbs a bit. Add the cheese and toss to emulsify it with the other sauce ingredients, adding a bit of pasta water to keep the consistency creamy and prevent the cheese from clumping. Add the butter and toss to blend. Taste and add more salt or chile flakes if you like.

Divide the pasta between two warm bowls, sprinkle with the breadcrumbs, if using, and serve right away, with more cheese to add at the table.

Heirloom Tomatoes with Lobster, Fresh Chiles, Summer Herbs, and Brown-Butter Butter

Think of this dish as a lobster roll in pasta form. The ingredients aren't quite the same, but the concept is: fresh, summery, and luxurious. (If you don't have time to make a batch of Brown-Butter Butter, you can brown some butter in a small saucepan; see page 30.)

Whole live lobsters aren't always available, but you can usually find lobster tails. Just be sure you're using cold-water lobsters, which will come from New England or Canada, rather than a warm-water type, often called a spiny lobster. Nothing wrong with those varieties, but I prefer the sweet, flavorful meat of the cold-water denizens.

As for tomatoes, use whatever gloriously ripe and interesting variety you can find. Beware of

tomatoes in the grocery store that are labeled "heirloom." Often they are bland and mealy, even though they look like a garden-fresh specimen.

To cook your lobster, steam it over boiling water for about 10 minutes per pound. The shell should turn red, but the best test is to crack open the lobster between the body and the tail to check that the meat looks fully opaque and white, not translucent.

As for whether you cook the lobster live or "dispatch" it before adding it to the steamer, I'll leave that to you.

Serves 2 or 3

Kosher salt (preferably Diamond Crystal; see page 17)

Extra-virgin olive oil

3 or 4 garlic cloves, smashed

1 small bunch scallions, trimmed and thinly sliced crosswise

1 or 2 fresh medium chiles, such as habaneros or jalapeños, cut into rings, core and seeds removed

8 ounces (225 g) linguine, bucatini, or spaghetti

3 tablespoons Brown-Butter Butter (page 30)

1 whole lobster or 2 lobster tails, steamed and cooled, meat removed and cut into large chunks

12 ounces (340 g) ripe tomatoes, preferably various colors and varieties, cored and cut into chunks (save the juices)

Small handful of fresh basil leaves

Small handful of fresh mint leaves

Big pinch of fresh tarragon leaves (optional)

1 medium lemon, halved

Fill a large pot (at least 6 quarts/L) with 1 gallon (4 L) of water; add 4 tablespoons (40 g) kosher salt, cover the pot, and bring the water to a boil while you make your sauce. If the water begins to boil before your sauce is ready, turn down the heat, but don't let the volume of the pasta water reduce by boiling off.

Heat a generous glug of olive oil in a large skillet over medium heat. When the oil is hot, add the garlic and cook gently, breaking it up a bit with your spatula, until it is lightly toasted and fragrant but not at all brown, 3 to 4 minutes. Add the scallions and chiles, then add a big splash of water from the pasta pot; slide the skillet off the heat.

Bring the pasta water (back) to a boil, add the noodles, and set your timer for 2 minutes less than the shortest suggested cooking time on the package of pasta; this will ideally be 2 minutes before the pasta is al dente. Stir the noodles several times during the first 2 minutes of cooking to prevent them from sticking to the bottom of the pot or otherwise clumping together.

When the timer goes off, start tasting the noodles. When they seem like they are 1½ to 2 minutes away from a perfect al dente (see page 22), drain and transfer them to the sauce in the skillet using your preferred method (see page 21), making sure to reserve at least 1 cup (240 ml) of the pasta water.

Add the brown butter to the skillet, then slide the skillet back onto medium heat and finish cooking the noodles, tossing and adding plenty of splashes of pasta water to emulsify the butter into the pasta water and bring the noodles to perfect al dente.

Add the lobster meat and toss to coat in the sauce and warm it. Add the tomatoes and the basil and mint leaves, tearing them into a few pieces. Tear up and add the tarragon, too, if using.

Squeeze the juice from one lemon half into the dish. Toss everything together into a glorious tangle; taste and add more salt or lemon juice if you like. If you don't want to eat the hot chiles, pick them out now.

Divide the pasta between two or three warm bowls and serve right away.

MORE WAYS

Use shrimp in place of lobster. Choose wild-caught shrimp, if possible, of any size. Peel, devein, and steam just until opaque, then cut into large chunks.

Fall

Pasta Fagiole Number One: The Classic

Do you have a big group to feed? This is the recipe for you; it's part pasta dish, part soup, and full of hearty, healthful ingredients. The kale isn't classically Italian, but let's make it a new tradition.

You'll need to plan ahead, as I recommend cooking your beans from scratch because the flavorful bean cooking liquid is key (see How to Cook the Best Fresh or Dried Shell Beans, page 326). You could substitute chicken broth or vegetable broth, but those won't give you the depth of flavor that makes this dish so tasty. I use a mix of beans, which makes the dish more complex and interesting to eat.

Serves 8

¼ cup (60 ml) extra-virgin olive oil, plus more for serving

About 20 garlic cloves, smashed

⅔ cup (80 g) finely chopped carrot

⅔ cup (80 g) finely chopped celery

⅔ cup (80 g) finely chopped fennel

⅔ cup (80 g) finely chopped onion

Kosher salt (preferably Diamond Crystal; see page 17)

2 teaspoons dried oregano

1 teaspoon dried chile flakes, plus more to taste

Four 5-inch (12.5 cm) sprigs fresh rosemary

4 cups (170 g) lightly packed 1-inch (2.5 cm) ribbons Tuscan kale

⅓ cup (100 g) tomato paste

2 cups (480 ml) bean cooking liquid (see page 326)

One 28-ounce (794 g) can whole peeled tomatoes, crushed by hand (see page 44), with their juices

Parmigiano rind (optional)

5 to 6 cups (900 g to 1 kg) cooked beans (use a mix of varieties if possible)

8 ounces (225 g) trecce, gemelli, or busiate

50/50 cheese (half Parmigiano-Reggiano, half Pecorino Romano, grated in a food processor; see page 39), for serving

Basil Pesto (page 33; optional)

Fresh basil leaves (optional)

Fresh flat-leaf parsley leaves (optional)

Heat the olive oil in a large Dutch oven or other large, deeper-than-a-skillet pot over medium heat. When the oil is hot, add the garlic and cook gently until it's soft and fragrant and starting to toast (but don't let it actually get brown), 4 to 5 minutes.

Add the carrot, celery, fennel, and onion, season lightly with salt, and cook, stirring frequently, just until the vegetables begin to soften, 4 to 5 minutes. Add the oregano, chile flakes, and rosemary, then add the kale and cook, stirring, until the kale has wilted a bit, 4 to 5 minutes.

Add the tomato paste and cook, smearing it into a thin layer on the surface of the pot, until slightly toasted, 1 to 2 minutes. Pour in the bean cooking liquid and stir to dissolve the tomato paste and blend the ingredients. Simmer until slightly reduced, 4 to 5 minutes.

Add the crushed tomatoes and their juices and the Parmigiano rind, if using, and simmer until the liquid has slightly reduced and thickened, 5 to 6 minutes. Add the cooked beans and stir to distribute them.

Simmer the soup so all the flavors can marry and become more concentrated, 15 to 20 minutes. Taste the liquid and adjust with more chile flakes or salt, remembering that any cheese added later will add some salt. Then slide the pot off the heat.

Meanwhile, fill a large pot (at least 6 quarts/L) with 1 gallon (4 L) of water, add 4 tablespoons (40 g) kosher salt, cover the pot, and bring the water to a boil. If the water begins to boil before your soup is ready, turn down the heat, but don't let the volume of the pasta water reduce by boiling off.

When the soup is ready, add the noodles to the boiling pasta water and set your timer for 2 minutes less than the shortest suggested cooking time on the package of pasta; this will ideally be 2 minutes before the pasta is al dente. Stir the noodles several times during the first 2 minutes of cooking to prevent them from

sticking to the bottom of the pot or otherwise clumping together.

When the timer goes off, start tasting the noodles. When they seem like they are 1½ to 2 minutes away from a perfect al dente (see page 22), drain and transfer them to the soup using your preferred method (see page 21), making sure to reserve at least 1 cup (240 ml) of the pasta water.

Slide the pot of soup back onto medium heat and finish cooking the noodles to al dente in the simmering soup. Add a bit of the pasta water if things are looking too thick, bearing in mind that any cheese added later will thicken the soup.

Retrieve and discard the rosemary sprigs and the Parmigiano rind, if you used one. Taste and adjust the final seasoning.

Serve the pasta fagiole in wide bowls and have the diners garnish as they like with grated cheese, a big spoonful of pesto, fresh basil and parsley leaves (tear them up a bit first), and/or a generous drizzle of good olive oil.

Pasta Fagiole Number Two: The Creamy Bean Version

This may be my favorite recipe, but that's perhaps because I am a bean freak. By no means a traditional pasta fagiole, this version is a terrific expression of the creamy texture of a well-cooked bean and especially of the deep umami flavors that good beans reveal.

It's totally worth your time to cook the beans from scratch (see How to Cook the Best Fresh or Dried Shell Beans, page 326); cooked beans freeze well, so you can cook up a pound or so, use some for this recipe, and freeze the rest for another dish later. Rancho Gordo is an excellent bean producer with an array of heirloom varieties available in many stores and online (see Resources, page 380); I recommend them. If from-scratch beans aren't possible, however, use good-quality canned beans; I like Eden Organic. Rinse canned beans well and use broth as a substitute for the bean cooking liquid.

Use a sturdy pasta noodle—rigatoni is a natural, but penne is also good—and do use the Parmigiano rind if you have one . . . which you probably do if you're using real Parmigiano in your pasta recipes. And as you can tell by reading it, this recipe makes a lot and the dish is filling. Unlike most pastas, it keeps well for a couple of days in the refrigerator, so if you end up with leftovers, all the better.

Serves 4 to 6

2 cups (360 g) cooked cranberry (also called borlotti) beans

1 cup (240 ml) bean cooking liquid (see page 326) or homemade (page 143) or low-sodium store-bought chicken broth

8 ounces (225 g) bulk Italian sausage, sweet or hot

Extra-virgin olive oil

8 to 10 garlic cloves, smashed

⅓ cup (40 g) finely chopped carrot

⅓ cup (40 g) finely chopped celery

⅓ cup (40 g) finely chopped fennel

⅓ cup (50 g) finely chopped onion

3 ounces (85 g) pancetta, chopped

2 teaspoons finely chopped fresh rosemary

1 teaspoon dried chile flakes

3 bay leaves

Parmigiano rind (optional)

Kosher salt (preferably Diamond Crystal; see page 17)

8 ounces (225 g) calamarata, paccheri, or rigatoni

⅓ cup (40 g) 50/50 cheese (half Parmigiano-Reggiano, half Pecorino Romano, grated in a food processor; see page 39), plus more for serving

Put the cooked beans and the bean cooking liquid in a blender and blend until totally creamy, scraping down the sides of the blender jar as necessary. The puree should have the consistency of pancake batter; add a bit of water or broth if needed to thin it out. Set aside.

Shape the sausage into 2 patties. Heat a generous glug of olive oil in a large Dutch oven or other large, deeper-than-a-skillet pot over medium heat. When the oil is hot, add the sausage and sear, smashing the patties down from time to time with your spatula to create a nicely browned crust on the bottom, about 5 minutes.

Flip the patties, add the garlic, and continue cooking until the sausage has browned and the garlic is nicely toasted and softened (but not too dark), another 4 to 5 minutes.

recipe continues →

Add the carrot, celery, fennel, and onion and cook, stirring frequently, just until the vegetables begin to soften, 1 to 2 minutes. Add the pancetta and cook, breaking up the sausage and garlic into small bits with your spatula, until the pancetta has started to render some fat but isn't yet crisp, 3 to 4 minutes.

Add the rosemary, chile flakes, and bay leaves. Add the bean puree and the Parmigiano rind, if using. Adjust the heat so the puree simmers gently. Simmer until the puree has reduced by about one-quarter and the other ingredients are nicely integrated, 15 to 20 minutes. Scrape the sides and bottom of the pot frequently to be sure the puree isn't sticking anywhere.

Taste the puree; if it tastes flat (which it will if you've used canned beans), add a bit of salt, bearing in mind that you will be adding more salty ingredients when you finish the dish with salted pasta water and grated cheese. Then slide the pot off the heat.

Meanwhile, fill another large pot (at least 6 quarts/L) with 1 gallon (4 L) of water, add 4 tablespoons (40 g) kosher salt, cover the pot, and bring the water to a boil. If the water begins to boil before the bean puree is ready, turn down the heat, but don't let the volume of the pasta water reduce by boiling off.

When the puree is ready, bring the pasta water (back) to a boil, add the noodles, and set your timer for 2 minutes less than the shortest suggested cooking time on the package of pasta; this will ideally be 2 minutes before the pasta is al dente. Stir the noodles several times during the first 2 minutes of cooking to prevent them from sticking to the bottom of the pot or otherwise clumping together.

When the timer goes off, start tasting the noodles. When they seem like they are 1½ to 2 minutes away from a perfect al dente (see page 22), drain and transfer them to the bean pot using your preferred method (see page 21), making sure to reserve at least 1 cup (240 ml) of the pasta water.

Slide the bean pot back onto medium heat and finish cooking the noodles, tossing and adding plenty of splashes of pasta water until the noodles are perfectly al dente and the consistency of the sauce is creamy but not thick. If the sauce is too thick, add a little pasta water; if it seems watery, simmer for another few seconds to tighten it up, bearing in mind that the cheese will thicken it.

Reduce the heat to very low. Add the grated cheese and toss to emulsify it with the other sauce ingredients, adding splashes of pasta water (or plain hot water, if things are getting too salty) if needed to keep the consistency creamy and prevent the cheese from clumping. Given that the sauce is quite liquidy, you may not need to add any pasta water to encourage the cheese to melt.

Divide the pasta among warm bowls and serve right away, with more cheese to add at the table.

Pasta Fagiole Number Three: The New Classic

While it's always better with from-scratch beans, using canned beans in this dish is totally acceptable. I often fold in leafy greens such as chard or kale, or even broccoli rabe, which takes longer to cook than the leafy greens and so should be steamed or boiled ahead of time until almost tender.

Serves 2 or 3

- Kosher salt (preferably Diamond Crystal; see page 17)
- 6 ounces (180 g) bulk Italian sausage, sweet or hot
- Extra-virgin olive oil
- 3 garlic cloves, smashed
- ¼ teaspoon dried chile flakes, plus more to taste
- 2 tablespoons tomato paste
- 1 cup (250 g) canned whole peeled tomatoes, crushed by hand (see page 44), with their juices
- 1 teaspoon finely chopped fresh rosemary
- 1½ cups (265 g) cooked borlotti or pinto beans (or one 14-ounce/411 g can beans, drained and rinsed)
- 8 ounces (225 g) orecchiette, ziti, or rotelle
- ⅓ cup (40 g) 50/50 cheese (half Parmigiano-Reggiano, half Pecorino Romano, grated in a food processor; see page 39), plus more for serving
- 2 tablespoons Dried Breadcrumbs (page 36; optional)
- Finishing-quality extra-virgin olive oil, for serving

Fill a large pot (at least 6 quarts/L) with 1 gallon (4 L) of water; add 4 tablespoons (40 g) kosher salt, cover the pot, and bring the water to a boil while you make your sauce. If the water begins to boil before your sauce is ready, turn down the heat, but don't let the volume of the pasta water reduce by boiling off.

Shape the sausage into 2 patties. Heat a glug of olive oil in a large skillet over medium-high heat. When the oil is hot, add the sausage and sear, smashing the patties down to create a nicely browned crust on the bottom, about 5 minutes. Flip the patties, add the garlic and chile flakes, and cook until the sausage has browned and the garlic is toasted and soft (but not too dark), another 3 to 4 minutes.

Add the tomato paste and cook, smearing it onto the surface of the pan, until it has darkened slightly, another minute. Add the crushed tomatoes and their juices, the rosemary, a splash of water from the pasta pot, and the beans, then simmer, breaking up the sausage and garlic into smaller bits with the spatula, until thickened, another 3 to 4 minutes. Move the skillet off the heat.

Bring the pasta water (back) to a boil, add the noodles, and set your timer for 2 minutes less than the shortest suggested cooking time on the package of pasta; this will ideally be 2 minutes before the pasta is al dente. Stir the noodles several times during the first 2 minutes of cooking to prevent them from sticking to the pot.

When the timer goes off, start tasting the noodles. When they seem like they are 1½ to 2 minutes away from a perfect al dente (see page 22), drain and transfer them to the sauce using your preferred method (see page 21), reserving at least 1 cup (240 ml) of the pasta water.

Slide the skillet back onto medium heat and finish cooking the noodles, tossing and adding plenty of splashes of pasta water (or plain hot water, if things are getting salty) until the noodles are perfectly al dente and the sauce is nicely juicy. If the sauce seems watery, simmer for another few seconds to tighten it up, bearing in mind that the cheese will thicken it.

Reduce the heat to very low. Add the grated cheese and toss to emulsify it with the other sauce ingredients, adding splashes of pasta water if needed to keep the consistency creamy and prevent the cheese from clumping. Taste and add more salt or chile flakes if you like.

Divide the pasta between two or three warm bowls, top with the breadcrumbs, if using, drizzle with a bit of good olive oil, and sprinkle with a bit more cheese. Serve right away.

How to Cook the Best Fresh or Dried Shell Beans

Each batch of beans has its own personality. Fresh beans cook much faster than dried ones, but even different batches of the same type of bean can have different cooking times, so this is more guideline than recipe. If you're working with fresh beans, you'll need about 3 pounds (1.3 kg) of fresh beans in their pods to yield 4 cups (675 g) shelled beans.

The key to success is to obsessively watch the beans as they cook and to always keep the heat low. You want to cook the beans until they are just a whisper shy of fully tender and then allow carryover cooking to bring them to the exact doneness as they cool.

Makes 5 cups (900 g) cooked beans and liquor

4 cups (675 g) shelled fresh beans, or 2 cups (190 g) dried beans, picked over to remove any stones or debris

1 bay leaf

1 whole small dried red chile

1 garlic clove, smashed

Big sprig of fresh rosemary

Kosher salt (preferably Diamond Crystal; see page 17)

Extra-virgin olive oil

If you're using dried beans, put them in a bowl or pot and add cool water to cover them by a couple of inches. Soak them overnight at room temperature, then drain and rinse; they should have approximately doubled in volume.

Put the soaked dried beans or shelled fresh beans in a large pot and add the bay leaf, chile, garlic, rosemary, and 1½ teaspoons kosher salt. The pot needs to be big enough to allow the beans to expand, so make sure there's plenty of room. For fresh beans, add about 8 cups (2 L) water; for dried, add about 10 cups (2.5 L). In either case, the water should cover the beans by about 1 inch (2.5 cm), so if it doesn't, add more water.

Bring the water just barely to a boil over high heat, then immediately reduce the heat so that the beans are simmering merrily but not actually boiling hard at all.

Cook, uncovered, until the beans are about halfway soft. You can check by biting into a few—they will be soft enough for you to easily bite them with no crunch, but they'll still be quite dry and crumbly inside. This could take as little as 30 minutes for fresh or 1 hour for dried.

At this point, add another heaping teaspoon of salt and 2 to 3 tablespoons olive oil to the pot. Keep cooking at a gentle simmer and check frequently—the closer you get to doneness, the more frequently you should check. You want to stop cooking the beans when they are very creamy and tender all the way through but not yet mushy or broken up (though a few will split).

When you are just about at that perfect point, slide the pot off the heat and let the beans cool in the cooking liquid. They'll finish softening the last few degrees as they cool.

If you worry that you've gone a bit too far and the beans are at risk of getting mushy, as soon as you take them from the heat, transfer them from the pot to a bowl set over a separate bowl of ice water and stir gently to cool things down quickly.

Once the beans are starting to cool, taste and add more salt, if needed, and another nice glug of olive oil.

Serve the beans on their own, or use them in recipes as directed. Be sure to keep the bean cooking liquid, because you'll use it in several recipes in this book. Store the beans in their liquid in an airtight container in the fridge for up to 1 week, or divide the beans and cooking liquid into smaller portions and freeze for up to 6 months.

Brussels Sprouts with Sun-Dried Tomato and Almond Pesto

Something about the sun-dried-tomato flavor of the pesto brings out the sweetness in Brussels sprouts. Be sure to cook them until they are tender throughout but no more than that; once you head into mushy territory, the flavor of your sprouts can get a bit cruciferous, if you know what I mean.

Serves 2

Kosher salt (preferably Diamond Crystal; see page 17)

Extra-virgin olive oil

⅓ cup (55 g) diced pancetta

3 or 4 garlic cloves, smashed

3 cups (300 g) trimmed and halved Brussels sprouts (quarter any really large ones)

¾ cup (180 g) Sun-Dried Tomato and Almond Pesto (page 33)

8 ounces (225 g) tagliatelle, linguine, or trenette

⅓ cup (40 g) 50/50 cheese (half Parmigiano-Reggiano, half Pecorino Romano, grated in a food processor; see page 39), plus more for serving

Fill a large pot (at least 6 quarts/L) with 1 gallon (4 L) of water; add 4 tablespoons (40 g) kosher salt, cover the pot, and bring the water to a boil while you make your sauce. If the water begins to boil before your sauce is ready, turn down the heat, but don't let the volume of the pasta water reduce by boiling off.

Heat a glug of olive oil in a large skillet over medium heat. When the oil is hot, add the pancetta and garlic and cook, breaking up the garlic a bit with your spatula as it cooks, until the pancetta renders most of its fat and is starting to crisp and the garlic is soft and lightly toasted but not browned, 3 to 4 minutes.

Add the Brussels sprouts (add a bit more oil if the pan looks dryish) and encourage the sprouts to land cut side down. Cook, stirring the pancetta and garlic so they don't burn, until the sprouts are nicely browned on the bottom, then flip them and continue cooking until they are lightly browned on most sides and mostly tender (they'll cook for a few more minutes with the noodles), 12 to 15 minutes total.

Add a splash of water from the pasta pot and the sun-dried tomato pesto to the pan, stir to incorporate all the ingredients and emulsify the pesto, and slide the skillet off the heat.

Bring the pasta water (back) to a boil, add the noodles, and set your timer for 2 minutes less than the shortest suggested cooking time on the package of pasta; this will ideally be 2 minutes before the pasta is al dente. Stir the noodles several times during the first 2 minutes of cooking to prevent them from sticking to the pot or otherwise clumping together.

When the timer goes off, start tasting the noodles. When they seem like they are 1½ to 2 minutes away from a perfect al dente (see page 22), drain and transfer them to the sauce in the skillet using your preferred method (see page 21), making sure to reserve at least 1 cup (240 ml) of the pasta water.

Slide the skillet back onto medium heat and finish cooking the noodles, tossing and adding plenty of splashes of pasta water until the noodles are perfectly al dente, the Brussels sprouts are tender, and the sauce is nicely juicy. If the sauce seems watery, simmer for another few seconds to tighten it up, bearing in mind that the cheese will thicken it.

Reduce the heat to very low. Add the grated cheese and toss to emulsify it with the other sauce ingredients, adding splashes of pasta water (or plain hot water, if things are getting too salty) if needed to keep the consistency creamy and prevent the cheese from clumping. Taste and add more salt if you like.

Divide the pasta between two warm bowls and serve right away, with more cheese on the table.

Chard with Sausage and Whipped Ricotta

A bunch of chard can be maddeningly inconsistent in size, sometimes weighing only 6 ounces (170 g) and other times clocking in closer to 10 ounces (280 g), even when it comes from the same producer. Just one more challenge for the savvy cook, who knows that cooking actually begins with shopping for ingredients. Eight ounces (225 g) is a good amount for this recipe, but a little more or less won't be a deal-breaker.

Serves 2 or 3

1 bunch Swiss chard (about 8 ounces/225 g)

Kosher salt (preferably Diamond Crystal; see page 17)

8 ounces (225 g) bulk Italian sausage, sweet or hot

Extra-virgin olive oil

2 or 3 garlic cloves, smashed

½ teaspoon coarsely ground black pepper, plus more to taste

8 ounces (225 g) rigatoni, penne, or orecchiette

¼ cup (30 g) 50/50 cheese (half Parmigiano-Reggiano, half Pecorino Romano, grated in a food processor; see page 39), plus more for serving

¾ cup (180 g) Whipped Plain Ricotta (page 34)

Cut the thick rib out of each chard leaf, rinse the ribs, then slice them crosswise into ¼-inch (6 mm) pieces. Stack the leaves, roll them into a loose cylinder, and slice crosswise into 1-inch-wide (2.5 cm) ribbons. Rinse and drain the ribbons.

Fill a large pot (at least 6 quarts/L) with 1 gallon (4 L) of water; add 4 tablespoons (40 g) kosher salt, cover the pot, and bring the water to a boil while you make your sauce. If the water begins to boil before your sauce is ready, turn down the heat, but don't let the volume of the pasta water reduce by boiling off.

Shape the sausage into 2 patties; set aside.

Heat a generous glug of olive oil in a large skillet over medium heat. When the oil is hot, add the chard stems, garlic, and black pepper and cook gently, breaking up the garlic a bit with your spatula, until the garlic is lightly toasted and fragrant but not at all brown and the chard stems are beginning to soften, about 4 minutes.

Scoot the chard stems and garlic to the edges of the skillet, add the sausage patties, and sear, smashing them down from time to time with your spatula to create a nicely browned crust on the bottom, about 5 minutes. Keep stirring the chard stems and garlic to continue cooking them gently.

Flip the sausage patties. Add the chard leaves and cook, stirring frequently while breaking the sausage into smaller pieces with your spatula. Splash in a couple of ladlefuls of pasta water and simmer until the chard leaves are slightly tender, 2 to 3 minutes. Slide the skillet off the heat.

Bring the pasta water (back) to a boil, add the noodles, and set your timer for 2 minutes less than the shortest suggested cooking time on the package of pasta; this will ideally be 2 minutes before the pasta is al dente. Stir the noodles several times during the first 2 minutes of cooking to prevent them from sticking to the bottom of the pot or otherwise clumping together.

When the timer goes off, start tasting the noodles. When they seem like they are 1½ to 2 minutes away from a perfect al dente (see page 22), drain and transfer them to the sauce in the skillet using your preferred method (see page 21), making sure to reserve at least 1 cup (240 ml) of the pasta water.

Slide the skillet back onto medium heat and finish cooking the noodles, tossing and adding plenty of splashes of pasta water until the noodles are perfectly al dente, the chard is tender, and the sauce is nicely juicy. If the sauce seems watery, simmer for another few seconds to tighten it up, bearing in mind that the 50/50 cheese will thicken it and the whipped ricotta will loosen it further.

Reduce the heat to very low. Add the 50/50 cheese and toss to emulsify it with the other sauce ingredients, adding splashes of pasta water (or plain hot water, if things are getting too salty) if needed to keep the consistency creamy and prevent the cheese from clumping.

Fold in the whipped ricotta; don't let the sauce boil. Taste and add more salt or black pepper if you like.

Divide the pasta between two or three warm bowls and serve right away, with more 50/50 cheese to add at the table.

Chard with Anchovies, Olives, and Tomato

Anchovy lovers, this one's for you. I'm calling for half a tin here, but you can load up this simple, rustic pasta with even more of this umami-rich ingredient if you like, as the earthy flavor of the chard is a perfect foil for salty anchovies.

The addition of butter rounds out the flavors in this dish, and if you have a finishing-quality extra-virgin olive oil, this would be a great showcase for it. Just a drizzle on the finished pasta will do the trick.

Serves 2

Kosher salt (preferably Diamond Crystal; see page 17)

1 bunch Swiss chard (about 8 ounces/225 g)

Extra-virgin olive oil

5 or 6 garlic cloves, smashed

¼ cup (30 g) sliced jalapeño, cut into rings, core and seeds removed (optional)

About 1 ounce (30 g) oil-packed anchovies (half a can), drained, plus more if you love them

¼ teaspoon dried chile flakes, plus more to taste

One 15-ounce (425 g) can whole peeled tomatoes, crushed by hand (see page 44), with their juices

½ cup (60 g) roughly chopped pitted green or mild black olives

8 ounces (225 g) trecce, gemelli, or busiate

1 tablespoon unsalted butter

⅓ cup (40 g) 50/50 cheese (half Parmigiano-Reggiano, half Pecorino Romano, grated in a food processor; see page 39), plus more for serving

Finishing-quality extra-virgin olive oil, for serving (optional)

Fill a large pot (at least 6 quarts/L) with 1 gallon (4 L) of water; add 4 tablespoons (40 g) kosher salt, cover the pot, and bring the water to a boil while you make your sauce. If the water begins to boil before your sauce is ready, turn down the heat, but don't let the volume of the pasta water reduce by boiling off.

Cut the thick rib out of each chard leaf, rinse the ribs, then slice them crosswise into ¼-inch (6 mm) pieces. Stack the leaves, roll them into a loose cylinder, and slice across into 1-inch (2.5 cm) ribbons. Rinse and drain the ribbons.

Heat a generous glug of olive oil in a large skillet over medium heat. When the oil is hot, add the garlic, chard stems, and jalapeño rings, if using, and cook them all gently until the garlic is nicely toasted and fragrant but not too brown, breaking it up a bit with your spatula, and the chard stems and jalapeño are starting to get soft, 4 to 5 minutes.

Add the anchovies and chile flakes and keep cooking until the anchovies have melted into the oil.

Add the crushed tomatoes and their juices and the chard leaves. Adjust the heat to maintain a lively simmer and cook until the chard is just barely tender and the tomatoes have thickened a bit, about 10 minutes. Add the olives and slide the skillet off the heat.

Bring the pasta water (back) to a boil, add the noodles, and set your timer for 2 minutes less than the shortest suggested cooking time on the package of pasta; this will ideally be 2 minutes before the pasta is al dente. Stir the noodles several times during the first 2 minutes of cooking to prevent them from sticking to the pot or otherwise clumping together.

When the timer goes off, start tasting the noodles. When they seem like they are 1½ to 2 minutes away from a perfect al dente (see page 22), drain and transfer them to the sauce

in the skillet using your preferred method (see page 21), making sure to reserve at least 1 cup (240 ml) of the pasta water.

Slide the skillet back onto medium heat and finish cooking the noodles, tossing and adding plenty of splashes of pasta water until the noodles are perfectly al dente, the chard is tender, and the sauce is nicely juicy. If the sauce seems watery, simmer for another few seconds to tighten it up, bearing in mind that the cheese will thicken it.

Reduce the heat to very low. Add the butter and grated cheese and toss to emulsify them with the other sauce ingredients, adding splashes of pasta water (or plain hot water, if things are getting too salty) if needed to keep the consistency creamy and prevent the cheese from clumping. Taste and add more salt or chile flakes if you like.

Divide the pasta between two warm bowls, drizzle with finishing-quality olive oil, if using, and serve right away, with more cheese to add at the table.

Kale and Chicken "Piccata"

The key components of chicken piccata are at play here—tender chicken, capers, lemon, butter . . . what more do you need? I think you need some kale (it's like the side dish to your piccata), but this dish would work well with any leafy green, such as spinach or chard.

Cooking times among greens will vary, and indeed, kale's cooking time varies from bunch to bunch, so you'll need to use your judgment. The skinnier you cut your ribbons, and the fewer ribs you leave in, the quicker the cooking time. I like a bit of bite to my kale, so I find a ⅜-inch-wide (9 mm) ribbon to be the ideal size.

Serves 2 or 3

Kosher salt (preferably Diamond Crystal; see page 17)

8 ounces (225 g) boneless, skinless chicken breast

Freshly ground black pepper

All-purpose flour

Extra-virgin olive oil

3 tablespoons unsalted butter

½ cup (65 g) finely chopped red onion

4 or 5 garlic cloves, finely chopped

¼ cup (40 g) drained brined capers

¼ teaspoon dried chile flakes, plus more to taste

8 ounces (225 g) Tuscan kale (1 medium bunch), cut crosswise into ⅜-inch-wide (9 mm) ribbons

1 cup (240 ml) homemade (page 143) or low-sodium store-bought chicken broth or water

1 tablespoon finely grated lemon zest

8 ounces (225 g) trecce, gemelli, or busiate

⅓ cup (40 g) 50/50 cheese (half Parmigiano-Reggiano, half Pecorino Romano, grated in a food processor; see page 39), plus more for serving

3 tablespoons fresh lemon juice, plus more to taste

Fill a large pot (at least 6 quarts/L) with 1 gallon (4 L) of water; add 4 tablespoons (40 g) kosher salt, cover the pot, and bring the water to a boil while you make your sauce. If the water begins to boil before your sauce is ready, turn down the heat, but don't let the volume of the pasta water reduce by boiling off.

Cut the chicken breast into pieces about 2 inches (5 cm) long and 1 inch (2.5 cm) wide. The exact size doesn't matter, but you want all the pieces to be about the same size so they'll cook at the same rate and are small enough to integrate into the noodles. Season generously with salt and pepper.

Put a pile of flour in a bowl, add the chicken, and toss so all the pieces are evenly coated. Shake off any excess flour and set the chicken aside.

Heat a small glug of olive oil in a large skillet over medium heat. When the oil is hot, add about half the butter, and when the butter has melted and stopped bubbling, add the chicken. Cook until golden brown on all sides, 3 to 4 minutes total, adjusting the heat so you don't burn the butter. Transfer the chicken to a plate and set aside. (The chicken will be cooked further in another step, so don't worry if the pieces aren't fully cooked yet.)

Add another small glug of oil to the skillet, then add the onion, garlic, capers, and chile flakes. Cook until the onion has softened slightly and the garlic is fragrant, about 3 minutes.

Add the kale, broth, and lemon zest. Increase the heat so the broth is simmering rapidly. Simmer, tossing frequently and adding a touch of pasta water if needed, until the kale is mostly tender, with just a little bite, and the broth has mostly reduced, 12 to 20 minutes, depending on your kale. You want the mixture to be juicy but not swimming in liquid. Slide the skillet off the heat.

Bring the pasta water (back) to a boil, add the noodles, and set your timer for 2 minutes less

than the shortest suggested cooking time on the package of pasta; this will ideally be 2 minutes before the pasta is al dente. Stir the noodles several times during the first 2 minutes of cooking to prevent them from sticking to the bottom of the pot or otherwise clumping together.

When the timer goes off, start tasting the noodles. When they seem like they are 1½ to 2 minutes away from a perfect al dente (see page 22), drain and transfer them to the sauce in the skillet using your preferred method (see page 21), making sure to reserve at least 1 cup (240 ml) of the pasta water.

Slide the skillet back onto medium heat and finish cooking the noodles, tossing and adding plenty of splashes of pasta water until the noodles are perfectly al dente, the kale is tender, and the sauce is nicely juicy. If the sauce seems watery, simmer for another few seconds to tighten it up, bearing in mind that the cheese will thicken it.

Return the chicken and any accumulated juices to the skillet and cook until the chicken is fully cooked. Add the remaining 1½ tablespoons or so of butter.

Reduce the heat to very low. Add the grated cheese and toss to emulsify it with the other sauce ingredients, adding splashes of pasta water if needed to keep the consistency creamy and prevent the cheese from clumping. Add the lemon juice and toss to incorporate. Taste and add more salt, chile flakes, or lemon juice if you like.

Divide the pasta between two or three warm bowls and serve right away, with more cheese to add at the table.

Kale with Spicy Sausage, Cream, and Lemon

The dynamic between the flavors in this dish—spicy, creamy, lemony—is compelling, and the dish feels both rich and light at the same time. I generally use Tuscan kale (also called lacinato kale or cavolo nero), because of its nutty flavor and relatively tender texture, but any kale could work. For tougher varieties, such as Red Russian, cut or tear your pieces a bit smaller.

Serves 2 or 3

- **Kosher salt (preferably Diamond Crystal; see page 17)**
- **5 ounces (140 g) Calabrian or other spicy Italian-style bulk sausage**
- **Extra-virgin olive oil**
- **4 large garlic cloves, smashed**
- **Pinch of dried chile flakes, plus more to taste**
- **¼ teaspoon freshly ground black pepper**
- **⅔ cup (160 ml) heavy or whipping cream**
- **2 cups (80 g) lightly packed torn-up Tuscan kale (remove the stems; tear the leaves into 2-inch/5 cm pieces)**
- **8 ounces (225 g) strozzapreti, rotini, or gemelli**
- **⅓ cup (40 g) 50/50 cheese (half Parmigiano-Reggiano, half Pecorino Romano, grated in a food processor; see page 39), plus more for serving**
- **1½ teaspoons finely grated lemon zest**
- **1 tablespoon fresh lemon juice, plus more to taste**
- **2 tablespoons Dried Breadcrumbs (page 36; optional)**

Fill a large pot (at least 6 quarts/L) with 1 gallon (4 L) of water; add 4 tablespoons (40 g) kosher salt, cover the pot, and bring the water to a boil while you make your sauce. If the water begins to boil before your sauce is ready, turn down the heat, but don't let the volume of the pasta water reduce by boiling off.

Shape the sausage into a patty. Heat a glug of olive oil in a large skillet over medium heat. When the oil is hot, add the sausage and sear, smashing the patty down from time to time; don't move it until a nice crust forms on the bottom, about 5 minutes.

Flip the sausage and add the garlic. Cook until the garlic is browning nicely—but not burning—and the sausage is almost cooked through, another 3 to 4 minutes. With the back of a spoon, smash the garlic and sausage patty into smaller bits.

Add the chile flakes and black pepper to the pan and cook for a few seconds to infuse the oil with the spices.

Add about ½ cup (120 ml) of the pasta water to the pan. Simmer, scraping to dissolve any browned bits from the bottom of the pan, until the sausage is fully cooked and the water has reduced by half, 2 to 3 minutes. Slide the pan off the heat and add the cream.

Bring the pasta water (back) to a boil, add the kale, and boil until the kale is tender, 5 to 7 minutes. Scoop out the kale, shake off any excess water, and transfer to the sauce in the skillet.

Add the noodles to the boiling water and set your timer for 2 minutes less than the shortest suggested cooking time on the package of pasta; this will ideally be 2 minutes before the pasta is al dente. Stir the noodles several times during the first 2 minutes of cooking to prevent them from sticking to the bottom of the pot or otherwise clumping together.

When the timer goes off, start tasting the noodles. When they seem like they are 1½ to 2 minutes away from a perfect al dente (see page 22), drain and transfer them to the sauce in the skillet using your preferred method (see page 21), making sure to reserve at least 1 cup (240 ml) of the pasta water.

recipe continues →

Slide the skillet back onto medium heat and finish cooking the noodles, tossing and adding plenty of splashes of pasta water until the noodles are perfectly al dente, the kale is tender, and the sauce is creamy. If the sauce seems watery, simmer for another few seconds to tighten it up, bearing in mind that the cheese will thicken it.

Reduce the heat to very low. Add the grated cheese and toss to emulsify it with the other sauce ingredients, adding splashes of pasta water (or plain hot water, if things are getting too salty) if needed to keep the consistency creamy and prevent the cheese from clumping.

Add the lemon zest and lemon juice. Taste and add more salt, chile flakes, black pepper, or lemon juice if you like.

Divide the pasta between two or three warm bowls. Top with the breadcrumbs, if using, and serve right away, with more cheese to add at the table.

MORE WAYS

Use chard instead of kale. Cut the chard stems into small dice and cook them along with the sausage and garlic. Treat the chard leaves as you would the kale, but note that they will probably cook faster than kale.

Kale Sauce (Round Three)

I developed this sauce when I wrote my first cookbook, *Six Seasons: A New Way with Vegetables*. I frequently make the sauce for myself, and it quickly became one of the most popular recipes from the book, so I included an updated version in my next book, *Grains for Every Season*. And because I seem to have started a tradition, here is my latest update to the kale sauce, with new variations. The sauce is so versatile that I like to think of it as the new tomato sauce . . . a green one!

Serves 2

Kosher salt (preferably Diamond Crystal; see page 17)

2 or 3 garlic cloves, smashed

Extra-virgin olive oil

12 ounces (340 g) kale (any variety, though Tuscan, aka lacinato, is wonderful), thick ribs cut out

Freshly ground black pepper

8 ounces (225 g) mezzi rigatoni, lumache, or ziti

½ cup (60 g) 50/50 cheese (half Parmigiano-Reggiano, half Pecorino Romano, grated in a food processor; see page 39), plus more for serving

Fill a large pot (at least 6 quarts/L) with 1 gallon (4 L) of water; add 4 tablespoons (40 g) kosher salt, cover the pot, and bring the water to a boil while you make your sauce. If the water begins to boil before your sauce is ready, turn down the heat, but don't let the volume of the pasta water reduce by boiling off.

Combine the garlic and ¼ cup (60 ml) olive oil in a small heavy pot or skillet over medium heat and cook until the garlic begins to sizzle. Reduce the heat to low and gently cook until the garlic is light golden, soft, and fragrant, 5 to 7 minutes. Pour the oil and garlic into a bowl so they can cool quickly.

Bring the water (back) to a boil, add the kale leaves, and boil until they are tender but not mushy or overcooked, about 5 minutes. Scoop out about a mugful of the cooking water, then pull out the kale with tongs or a slotted spoon and transfer them to a blender. It's fine if they are still slightly wet. (Keep the pot of water warm on the stove; you'll use it for the pasta.)

Add the oil and garlic to the blender with the kale and puree, adding just a bit of the reserved cooking water to help the process along and make a nice thick puree. Taste and season with salt and pepper. Measure out 1 cup (240 ml) of the kale puree; if you have more puree than you need, you can freeze the excess for up to 3 months.

Heat a glug of olive oil in a large skillet over medium heat. Splash in a bit of water from the pasta pot and add the kale puree. Bring everything to a simmer, then slide the skillet off the heat.

Bring the pasta water (back) to a boil, add the noodles, and set your timer for 2 minutes less than the shortest suggested cooking time on the package of pasta; this will ideally be 2 minutes before the pasta is al dente. Stir the noodles several times during the first 2 minutes of cooking to prevent them from sticking to the bottom of the pot or otherwise clumping together.

When the timer goes off, start tasting the noodles. When they seem like they are 1½ to 2 minutes away from a perfect al dente (see page 22), drain and transfer them to the sauce in the skillet using your preferred method (see page 21), making sure to reserve at least 1 cup (240 ml) of the pasta water.

Slide the skillet back onto medium heat and finish cooking the noodles, tossing and adding plenty of splashes of pasta water until the noodles are perfectly al dente and the sauce is nicely juicy. If the sauce seems watery, simmer

for another few seconds to tighten it up, bearing in mind that the cheese will thicken it.

Reduce the heat to very low. Add the grated cheese and toss to emulsify it with the other sauce ingredients, adding splashes of pasta water if needed to keep the consistency creamy and prevent the cheese from clumping.

Divide the pasta between two warm bowls. Serve right away, with more cheese to add at the table.

MORE WAYS

Kale Sauce with Tuna: After adding the noodles to the sauce, fold in one 5- or 6-ounce (142 or 170 g) can of tuna (packed in olive oil or water, but drained beforehand) and ¼ cup (60 g) sliced or chopped pickled chiles, such as peperoncini. Continue with the recipe.

Kale Sauce with Walnuts and Basil: Right before you add the cheese, fold in ½ cup (60 g) roughly chopped walnuts and a small handful of fresh basil leaves, torn into a few pieces. Continue with the recipe.

Kale Sauce with Beans: After adding the noodles to the sauce, fold in 1 cup (180 g) cooked beans, such as borlotti or cannellini, preferably cooked from scratch (see page 326). Continue with the recipe; finish by topping each bowl of pasta with a spoonful of Chile Crisp (page 37).

Mushrooms with Sausage, Spicy Chiles, and Burrata

This may be my favorite type of pasta—one that has all the hearty and familiar flavors of a sausage-and-mushroom pizza. I'm leveling up with the addition of a ball of burrata, a form of fresh mozzarella that has a super-creamy center. Cutting a ball of burrata into two portions risks the filling spilling out, so place the burrata in a big serving bowl or on a platter, pile the hot pasta on top, and then let diners scoop out their own portions, including a few spoonfuls of the gooey cheese. (If you can't find burrata, use fresh mozzarella torn into large shreds.)

Serves 2 or 3

Kosher salt (preferably Diamond Crystal; see page 17)

4 ounces (115 g) bulk Italian sausage, sweet or hot

Extra-virgin olive oil

3 or 4 garlic cloves, smashed

3 cups (180 g) thinly sliced cremini mushrooms

1 tablespoon tomato paste

Pinch of dried chile flakes

One 15-ounce (425 g) can whole peeled tomatoes, crushed by hand (see page 44), with their juices

½ cup (60 g) pickled hot chiles, plus a splash of pickling liquid from the jar

8 ounces (225 g) mafaldine, pappardelle, or fettucine

⅓ cup (40 g) 50/50 cheese (half Parmigiano-Reggiano, half Pecorino Romano, grated in a food processor; see page 39)

1 ball burrata

Fill a large pot (at least 6 quarts/L) with 1 gallon (4 L) of water; add 4 tablespoons (40 g) kosher salt, cover the pot, and bring the water to a boil while you make your sauce. If the water begins to boil before your sauce is ready, turn down the heat, but don't let the volume of the pasta water reduce by boiling off.

Shape the sausage into a patty; set it aside.

Heat a generous glug of olive oil in a large skillet over medium heat. When the oil is hot, add the garlic and cook gently, breaking it up a bit with your spatula, until it is lightly toasted and fragrant but not at all brown, about 2 minutes.

Add the sausage patty to the skillet and sear, smashing the patty down from time to time with your spatula to create a nicely browned crust on the bottom, about 5 minutes.

Flip the sausage patty. Add the mushrooms, scooting them around the sausage. Cook, stirring frequently and breaking the sausage into smaller pieces with your spatula, until the liquid released by the mushrooms has evaporated and the mushrooms are tender and slightly browned around the edges, 10 to 14 minutes. The sausage will probably be fully cooked, but it will cook more later, so no worries about doneness.

Clear a little space in the skillet, add the tomato paste, and cook, spreading it thinly on the surface of the pan until it toasts a bit, about 30 seconds.

Add the chile flakes, then add the crushed tomatoes and their juices, along with the pickled chiles and a splash of their pickling liquid. Increase the heat to medium-high, give everything a big stir, and simmer until the sauce has thickened and concentrated, another 4 to 6 minutes. Slide the skillet off the heat.

Bring the pasta water (back) to a boil, add the noodles, and set your timer for 2 minutes less than the shortest suggested cooking time

on the package of pasta; this will ideally be 2 minutes before the pasta is al dente. Stir the noodles several times during the first 2 minutes of cooking to prevent them from sticking to the bottom of the pot or otherwise clumping together.

When the timer goes off, start tasting the noodles. When they seem like they are 1½ to 2 minutes away from a perfect al dente (see page 22), drain and transfer them to the sauce in the skillet using your preferred method (see page 21), making sure to reserve at least 1 cup (240 ml) of the pasta water.

Slide the skillet back onto medium heat and finish cooking the noodles, tossing and adding plenty of splashes of pasta water until the noodles are perfectly al dente and the sauce is nicely juicy. If the sauce seems watery, simmer for another few seconds to tighten it up, bearing in mind that the cheese will thicken it.

Reduce the heat to very low. Add the 50/50 cheese and toss to emulsify it with the other sauce ingredients, adding splashes of pasta water (or plain hot water, if things are getting too salty) if needed to keep the consistency creamy and prevent the cheese from clumping.

Arrange the burrata in the center of a large serving bowl or platter and give each diner an individual plate or pasta bowl. Pile the pasta into the serving bowl on top of the burrata, let it sit for 30 seconds to start melting the cheese, and then serve right away, making sure the diners scoop out plenty of creamy burrata with their portion.

Mushrooms with Onion, Pancetta, and Cream

If you can find good-looking seasonal wild mushrooms, this dish is an excellent showcase for them. Even a small amount mixed in with the creminis can add a nice bit of "forest," but I also love the dish when made with straight creminis or white button mushrooms. Somehow the cream intensifies the umami character of the mushrooms.

Serves 2

Kosher salt (preferably Diamond Crystal; see page 17)

Extra-virgin olive oil

2 ounces (60 g) pancetta, diced

½ cup (70 g) sliced red onion (sliced about ¼ inch/6 mm thick)

3 cups (200 g) sliced cremini mushrooms

1 or 2 garlic cloves, finely chopped

Freshly ground black pepper

1 cup (240 ml) heavy or whipping cream

8 ounces (225 g) papiri, strozzapreti, or garganelli

¼ cup (30 g) 50/50 cheese (half Parmigiano-Reggiano, half Pecorino Romano, grated in a food processor; see page 39), plus more for serving

Big handful of arugula (optional)

Chile Crisp (page 37), for serving (optional)

Fill a large pot (at least 6 quarts/L) with 1 gallon (4 L) of water; add 4 tablespoons (40 g) kosher salt, cover the pot, and bring the water to a boil while you make your sauce. If the water begins to boil before your sauce is ready, turn down the heat, but don't let the volume of the pasta water reduce by boiling off.

Heat a generous glug of olive oil in a large skillet over medium heat. When the oil is hot, add the pancetta and cook just until the fat starts to render, 1 to 2 minutes. Add the onion and continue cooking fairly gently until the pancetta is slightly crisp and the onion is soft and fragrant, another 4 to 5 minutes.

Add the mushrooms and cook, stirring frequently, until the liquid they release has evaporated and the mushrooms are tender and slightly browned around the edges, 10 to 14 minutes. Add the garlic and cook until soft and fragrant but not browned, 1 to 2 minutes.

Season the mushrooms generously with pepper, then add the cream. Adjust the heat so the cream simmers gently. Cook until the cream has thickened slightly and the mushroom flavor has infused the cream, 4 to 5 minutes. Taste and add more pepper as needed to make the sauce nicely peppery. The sauce will get saltier from the pasta water and cheese, so you probably won't need to add salt. Slide the skillet off the heat.

Bring the pasta water (back) to a boil, add the noodles, and set your timer for 2 minutes less than the shortest suggested cooking time on the package of pasta; this will ideally be 2 minutes before the pasta is al dente. Stir the noodles several times during the first 2 minutes of cooking to prevent them from sticking to the bottom of the pot or otherwise clumping together.

When the timer goes off, start tasting the noodles. When they seem like they are 30 seconds away from a perfect al dente (see page 22), drain and transfer them to the sauce in the skillet using your preferred method (see page 21), making sure to reserve at least 1 cup (240 ml) of the pasta water.

Slide the skillet back onto medium heat and finish cooking the noodles, tossing and adding plenty of splashes of pasta water until the noodles are perfectly al dente and the sauce is nicely creamy. (This shouldn't take long because you've almost fully cooked the noodles already.) If the sauce seems watery, simmer for another few seconds to tighten it up, bearing in mind that the cheese will thicken it.

recipe continues →

Reduce the heat to very low. Add the grated cheese and toss to emulsify it with the other sauce ingredients, adding splashes of pasta water (or plain hot water, if things are getting too salty) if needed to keep the consistency creamy and prevent the cheese from clumping. Taste and add more salt or pepper if you like.

Add the arugula, if using, and toss a couple of times to integrate it, but not so much that it wilts.

Divide the pasta between two warm bowls, top with the chile crisp, if using, and serve right away, with more cheese to add at the table.

Baked Mushroom and Chicken Ragu Bianco "Potpie"

A perfect showcase for a batch of Chicken Ragu Bianco, this baked pasta dish was inspired by the chicken potpies of my childhood, but it's a whole lot more interesting. Cremini mushrooms have good flavor, but if you have wild mushrooms available, use a mix of wild and "domesticated."

Serves 4 to 6

- Kosher salt (preferably Diamond Crystal; see page 17)
- 8 ounces (225 g) sagne a pezzi, campanelle, or lumache
- Extra-virgin olive oil
- 1 pound (450 g) cremini or wild mushrooms (or a mix), trimmed and cut into chunks
- 2 tablespoons unsalted butter, plus more for the baking dish and (if you like) the breadcrumb topping
- 1 cup (150 g) small-diced sweet onion, such as Vidalia or Walla Walla
- 3 or 4 garlic cloves, finely chopped
- 3 tablespoons all-purpose flour
- 2 cups (500 g) Chicken Ragu Bianco (page 72)
- 1 cup (140 g) peas (frozen is fine)
- ½ cup (15 g) roughly chopped fresh flat-leaf parsley leaves and tender stems
- 1 teaspoon chopped fresh rosemary
- 1 teaspoon chopped fresh thyme
- ¼ teaspoon freshly ground black pepper, plus more to taste
- 2 cups (500 g) whole-milk ricotta (I like Calabro)
- 1 cup (120 g) grated Fontina
- ½ cup (25 g) Dried Breadcrumbs (page 36) or panko-style breadcrumbs
- ½ cup (60 g) 50/50 cheese (half Parmigiano-Reggiano, half Pecorino Romano, grated in a food processor; see page 39)

Fill a large pot (at least 6 quarts/L) with 1 gallon (4 L) of water; add 4 tablespoons (40 g) kosher salt, cover the pot, and bring the water to a boil. Add the noodles and set your timer for 2 minutes less than the shortest suggested cooking time on the package of pasta; this will ideally be 2 minutes before the pasta is al dente. Stir the noodles several times during the first 2 minutes of cooking to prevent them from sticking to the bottom of the pot or otherwise clumping together.

When the timer goes off, start tasting the noodles. When they seem like they are close to but not quite al dente (see page 22), drain well using your preferred method (see page 21), reserving about 2 cups (480 ml) of the pasta water, and transfer them to a large bowl (with enough room to toss the pasta with all the other ingredients).

Heat a glug of olive oil in a large skillet or Dutch oven over medium heat. When the oil is hot, add the mushrooms, spreading them in an even single layer if possible (if they'll be super crowded, cook them in two batches); season lightly with salt. Cook, undisturbed, until they are nicely browned on the bottom, 6 to 8 minutes. Flip, add the butter and onion, and cook, stirring and flipping the mushrooms and onion, until the mushrooms are browned on a few more sides and the onion is soft and fragrant, another 8 to 12 minutes; don't let the onion get too brown. Add the garlic and cook for another 1 to 2 minutes to soften it; don't let it burn.

Sprinkle the flour over the vegetables. Cook, stirring and scraping the bottom of the pan, for another minute.

Add about 1 cup (240 ml) of the pasta water and stir until it thickens. Then add the chicken ragu. Bring to a simmer and cook until the liquid has the consistency of a light gravy and the ragu is hot, 4 to 5 minutes; if the mixture seems dry, add more pasta water.

recipe continues →

Add the peas, parsley, rosemary, thyme, and black pepper. Taste and add more salt or pepper if you like. Set aside.

Heat the oven to 375°F (190°C). Butter a 9 by 13-inch (22.5 by 32.5 cm) baking dish (or something with an equivalent volume, about 3 quarts/L).

Evaluate the consistency of the chicken-and-mushroom sauce. You want it to be fairly loose and saucy, because the noodles and the other ingredients will drink up some of the liquid as the dish bakes, so add another ½ cup (120 ml) or so of pasta water if needed and fold to blend well.

Add the chicken-and-mushroom sauce to the noodles. Add the ricotta and Fontina and fold everything together. Taste and adjust with more salt or pepper or even more pasta water if needed. Pour the mixture into the prepared baking dish.

Put the breadcrumbs and grated cheese in a small bowl and stir to mix. Add about 2 tablespoons olive oil or melted butter and stir again; the crumb-cheese mixture should be sort of clumpy but not an actual paste.

Distribute the crumb mixture evenly over the surface of the chicken mixture, patting it into place.

Loosely cover the baking dish with foil. Bake for 15 minutes, then uncover and bake until the chicken and noodles are very hot, the crumb topping is browned, and the juices are bubbling around the edges, another 20 to 30 minutes.

Let the potpie rest for 10 minutes, then dig in.

MORE WAYS

Fold about 1 cup (225 g) celery root puree (see page 367) into the chicken ragu when you add the peas and herbs.

Boost the woodsy mushroom flavor by adding a big pinch of porcini powder to the chicken ragu.

Winter

Baked Ziti with Broccoli Rabe

Most baked ziti recipes use a meat sauce, but this vegetarian version gets plenty of "meaty" texture from broccoli rabe (of course, you can add meat to the Marinara Sauce if you'd like).

Broccoli rabe, also called rapini, is a sturdy green that looks a bit like scraggly broccoli—thinner stalks, more leaves, and less uniform florets. The flavor is assertive, and a bit bitter, but plenty of cheese will balance the flavor. (Note that broccolini looks slightly similar, and while it's delicious, it's not a great substitute in this dish.)

Serves 6 to 8

Kosher salt (preferably Diamond Crystal; see page 17)

1 bunch broccoli rabe (about 12 ounces/340 g), ends trimmed

1 pound (450 g) ziti, penne, or rigatoni

1 recipe Marinara Sauce (page 67)

1 pound (450 g) whole-milk ricotta (I like Calabro)

1 pound (450 g) whole-milk low-moisture mozzarella, shredded (don't use preshredded)

¾ cup (90 g) 50/50 cheese (half Parmigiano-Reggiano, half Pecorino Romano, grated in a food processor; see page 39)

Extra-virgin olive oil or unsalted butter, for finishing

Fill a large pot (at least 6 quarts/L) with 1 gallon (4 L) of water; add 4 tablespoons (40 g) kosher salt, cover the pot, and bring the water to a boil. Add the broccoli rabe and cook for 3 to 4 minutes (it will only be partially cooked at this point). Retrieve the broccoli rabe from the water with tongs or a slotted spoon, drain, and cool slightly. Keep the water hot but don't let it boil off.

Cut the broccoli rabe stems into 1-inch (2.5 cm) pieces and the leafy parts and florets a bit bigger. Put the chopped broccoli rabe in a large bowl (one that will accommodate the noodles and sauce as well).

Bring the pasta water (back) to a boil, add the noodles, and set your timer for 2 minutes less than the shortest suggested cooking time on the package of pasta; this will ideally be 2 minutes before the pasta is al dente. Stir the noodles several times during the first 2 minutes of cooking to prevent them from sticking to the bottom of the pot or otherwise clumping together.

When the timer goes off, start tasting the noodles. When they seem like they are 1½ to 2 minutes away from a perfect al dente (see page 22), transfer them to the bowl with the broccoli rabe using your preferred method (see page 21), making sure to reserve at least 1 cup (240 ml) of the pasta water.

Pour in the marinara sauce, add the reserved pasta water, and stir to thoroughly incorporate the noodles and sauce, making sure the sauce makes its way into the ziti interiors.

Heat the oven to 375°F (190°C).

Spread about one-third of the ziti mixture in the bottom of a 9 by 13-inch (22.5 by 32.5 cm) baking dish. Dollop half the ricotta over the ziti, spreading it into as even a layer as you can get without disturbing the ziti layer.

Top with half the mozzarella in an even layer. Repeat with another third of the ziti and the remaining ricotta and mozzarella.

Finish with the remaining ziti and then sprinkle the 50/50 cheese evenly over the top. Drizzle with a little olive oil or dot with butter.

Bake until the cheese is browned and the juices at the edges of the baking dish are browned and bubbling, 35 to 40 minutes. For an extra-crisp top, increase the oven temperature to 475°F (245°C) for the last 5 minutes of cooking.

Let the casserole rest for 10 to 15 minutes before serving.

MORE WAYS

Make the dish heartier by using 6 cups (1.5 kg) Beef and Pork Ragu (page 81) or a double recipe of Sausage Ragu (page 89) instead of the marinara.

How to Invent Your Own Baked Pasta

A baked pasta—bubbling around the edges, loaded with tender (but not overcooked!) noodles, and shot through with melted cheese—is a wonderful thing. The appeal of the flavors and textures is obvious, but baked pasta dishes have other virtues, too, especially the fact that you make them ahead of time, meaning they are excellent for bringing to potlucks, serving at parties, taking on ski trips, or just having in the freezer for those nights when you wish you were on a ski trip but in reality you worked late and you're tired and hungry.

Another winning characteristic of a baked pasta is its flexibility. Not quite an anything-but-the-kitchen-sink dish, a baked pasta can be made from a wide range of ingredients, provided you follow a few guidelines.

Choose a short noodle. Or a long one. Short noodles work best because they tend to be more robust and their interior spaces allow the sauce and cheese to integrate well—think rigatoni or ziti. But you can definitely bake up long noodles; they tend to form a large block of noodle, but you'll deal with that when you scoop or cut your portions.

Baked pasta is a good destination for all your little leftover noodle odds and ends—the pasta mista, or "mixed pasta."

Here are shapes that do well in a casserole dish:

- **Conchiglie** is a pasta whose shell shape is excellent at inviting sauce and cheese inside.
- **Penne rigate** is another great choice. Its ridges help hold on to sauce, and it maintains its shape and texture after baking.
- **Pipe rigate** (shaped sort of like a snail) not only is easy to fork but has a curved tubular shape that helps hold sauce within its opening.
- **Rigatoni** is also ridged and tubular, similar to penne but larger, making it an ideal candidate.
- **Rotelle** (wagon wheel) may seem like a for-kids shape, but it should be taken seriously for baked pasta, which might just be the best use for this noodle.
- **Ziti** is tubular and sturdy, so it captures sauce and cheese well and maintains its integrity after baking.

Make cheese your friend (you'll need more than you think). Soft cheese, hard cheese, semisoft cheese, fresh cheese . . . all the cheese. Grate it, rip it, layer it, fold it in. Melted cheese is like the connective tissue of a baked pasta, and using different styles of cheese adds a lot of texture and intrigue. Also, have more cheese on hand for serving—whipped ricotta, grated hard cheese, anything that ensures more cheese!

If you're looking for a cheese that will melt in your baked pasta, try Fontina, a young Asiago, Taleggio, or provolone. As for the ubiquitous mozzarella, if you want it to melt in your casserole, choose a whole-milk, low-moisture, not-very-artisanal mozz (the kind you can slice); don't use preshredded, though, because of the anticlumping stuff they toss it in.

Be generous with the sauce. You need an actual sauce or ragu (or both); if you simply toss chopped tomato with the noodles, you won't get the luscious consistency you want. Any type of sauce that's fluid enough to coat the noodles and other ingredients will be great—tomato-based sauces, creamy sauces (such as béchamel), ragus, vegetable purees. I sometimes like to use a couple of different sauces and layer them.

Mix things up in a bowl first, like a pasta salad, and then add to the baking dish. Tossing the sauce, cheese, and other add-ins together with the noodles ensures that everything gets coated and evenly distributed. Now that I've said that, sometimes you don't want to toss, you want to layer it up—like nachos!

Choose a wide dish. A gratin dish or a basic 9 by 13-inch (22.5 by 32.5 cm) Pyrex baking dish is perfect. The shallow depth and wide surface of these baking dishes means you'll have all that surface terrain to get browned and bubbly. And if you've frozen your baked pasta, it will thaw and heat through quickly. I like to butter my dish before adding the pasta because, well, butter.

Think future meals. Making the components and assembling the casserole can be a lot of prep, so every time I make a baked pasta, I make at least a double batch, and I freeze the extra one whole and unbaked; I use a metal baking dish so I can go from freezer to oven. First wrap it in foil, then wrap it in plastic or put it in a plastic freezer bag. Label the dish clearly (I'm not kidding about this), and when it's time for dinner, pull it out of the freezer, let it sit for about an hour before baking, then let it rip! (Or let the casserole thaw overnight in the fridge.)

Use pizza as your inspiration. Think classic combos—tomatoes, mozzarella, sausage—but don't stop there. You can translate all your favorite pizza toppings into a baked pasta. And baked pastas are the perfect opportunity to clear those still-fresh odds and ends from the fridge—pickled chiles, the last few olives, two lonely slices of bacon, a handful of basil leaves. Adding a touch of creaminess will elevate even ordinary combinations, so think about spreading a layer of béchamel sauce (see page 135) or whipped ricotta (pages 34–35) over the bottom of the baking dish.

Bake at two temperatures. Start with a moderate oven temperature (350° to 375°F/ 175° to 190°C) with your dish covered with foil until the ingredients are heated through (they should all be already-cooked or will cook easily, such as small pieces of chicken or shrimp). Once you can tell that things are hot from top to bottom (stick a paring knife into the dish and feel whether it comes out hot), take off the foil, crank the heat to 475°F (245°C), and blast it for a few minutes, until the cheese on top is browned and the juices are bubbling. But keep your eye on it; the line between crisp and dried out is a thin one!

And finally, step away from the baking dish . . . for at least 10 to 15 minutes after you pull it from the oven. During this rest, the sauce and cheese will settle down and thicken up, and all the ingredients will come to relate in a more harmonious manner.

Cabbage with Whipped Lemon Ricotta and Chile Crisp

Cabbage can sometimes feel a bit stodgy, but a lovely cloak of whipped lemony ricotta and a finishing spoonful of spicy chile crisp transform this staple of the winter kitchen into something elevated.

Serves 2

1 pound (450 g) green or savoy cabbage (about ½ small head)

Extra-virgin olive oil

Kosher salt (preferably Diamond Crystal; see page 17)

Freshly ground black pepper

2 tablespoons unsalted butter, cut into small bits

2 or 3 garlic cloves, smashed

1 teaspoon roughly chopped fresh thyme (use lemon thyme, if you have it)

¼ teaspoon dried chile flakes, plus more to taste

¾ cup (180 g) Whipped Lemon Ricotta (page 35)

8 ounces (225 g) fettucine, tagliatelle, or pappardelle

⅓ cup (40 g) 50/50 cheese (half Parmigiano-Reggiano, half Pecorino Romano, grated in a food processor; see page 39), plus more for serving

2 spoonfuls Chile Crisp (page 37)

2 tablespoons roughly chopped toasted pine nuts (optional)

Heat the oven to 425°F (220°C).

Cut the cabbage into large wedges, about 3 inches (7.5 cm) wide, then cut off most of the dense core, preserving enough so the leaves stay mostly intact. Coat the wedges in olive oil and season generously with salt and pepper. Arrange the wedges on a sheet pan and then tuck the butter bits between the leaves.

Roast until the wedges are nicely browned around the edges and mostly tender, 20 to 30 minutes. Cool the cabbage until you can comfortably handle it, then cut it into pieces about the size and shape of the noodle you're using.

Fill a large pot (at least 6 quarts/L) with 1 gallon (4 L) of water; add 4 tablespoons (40 g) kosher salt, cover the pot, and bring the water to a boil while you make your sauce. If the water begins to boil before your sauce is ready, turn down the heat, but don't let the volume of the pasta water reduce by boiling off.

Heat a glug of olive oil in a large skillet over medium heat. When the oil is hot, add the garlic and cook gently, breaking it up a bit with your spatula, until it is lightly toasted and fragrant but not at all brown, 3 to 4 minutes.

Add the thyme and chile flakes, cook for a few seconds, then add the cabbage and a splash of water from the pasta pot. Add the whipped ricotta and slide the skillet off the heat.

Bring the pasta water (back) to a boil, add the noodles, and set your timer for 2 minutes less than the shortest suggested cooking time on the package of pasta; this will ideally be 2 minutes before the pasta is al dente. Stir the noodles several times during the first 2 minutes of cooking to prevent them from sticking to the bottom of the pot or otherwise clumping together.

When the timer goes off, start tasting the noodles. When they seem like they are almost a perfect al dente (see page 22), drain and transfer them to the sauce in the skillet using your preferred method (see page 21), making sure to reserve at least 1 cup (240 ml) of the pasta water.

Slide the skillet back onto medium heat and finish cooking the noodles, tossing and adding splashes of pasta water until the noodles are perfectly al dente, the cabbage is tender, and the sauce is nicely juicy. If the sauce seems watery, simmer for another few seconds to tighten it up, bearing in mind that the cheese will thicken it.

Reduce the heat to very low. Add the 50/50 cheese and toss to emulsify it with the other sauce ingredients, adding splashes of pasta water if needed to keep the consistency creamy and prevent the cheese from clumping. Taste and add more salt or chile flakes if you like, bearing in mind that the chile crisp will add more heat.

Divide the pasta between two warm bowls, top with the chile crisp and pine nuts, if using, and serve right away, with more 50/50 cheese to add at the table.

Cabbage with Pancetta and Calabrian Chile

Cabbage is the unsung hero of the winter kitchen—available anywhere, long-lasting in the fridge, and super-affordable. It is also an excellent partner for pasta. Caramelizing the cabbage in butter creates a deep sweetness and silky texture, with the denser portions of the leaves retaining a bit of juicy crunch.

Here spicy Calabrian chiles add a contrasting kick of heat; look for them in a jar in the condiment section of the grocery store. Add them late in the cooking process so their flavor doesn't fully permeate the whole dish but rather creates little pops of heat and acidity in each bite. The recipe calls for 1 teaspoon, which is a moderate amount; if you're a hothead, increase that amount.

Serves 2

Kosher salt (preferably Diamond Crystal; see page 17)

Extra-virgin olive oil

2 ounces (60 g) pancetta, diced or cut into strips

1½ tablespoons unsalted butter

4 cups (8 ounces/225 g) thinly sliced green, white, or savoy cabbage

1 teaspoon thinly sliced oil-packed Calabrian chiles (from a jar; remove their seeds before slicing), plus more to taste

8 ounces (225 g) spaghetti, tagliatelle, or pappardelle

½ cup (60 g) 50/50 cheese (half Parmigiano-Reggiano, half Pecorino Romano, grated in a food processor; see page 39), plus more for serving

2 lemon wedges (optional)

Fill a large pot (at least 6 quarts/L) with 1 gallon (4 L) of water; add 4 tablespoons (40 g) kosher salt, cover the pot, and bring the water to a boil while you make your sauce. If the water begins to boil before your sauce is ready, turn down the heat, but don't let the volume of the pasta water reduce by boiling off.

Heat a glug of olive oil in a large skillet over medium heat. When the oil is hot, add the pancetta and cook gently until it turns brown and crisp, 4 to 5 minutes. Take the pancetta out of the pan and set it aside, leaving the rendered fat in the pan.

Add half the butter to the pan and let it bubble and start to brown, then add the cabbage. Cook, stirring frequently, until the cabbage is tender and caramelizing a bit, about 10 minutes; you may need to increase the heat, but don't let the bottom of the pan get too dark.

Add the Calabrian chiles and a splash of water from the pasta pot and simmer until the water has evaporated, another 1 to 2 minutes. Slide the skillet off the heat.

Bring the pasta water (back) to a boil, add the noodles, and set your timer for 2 minutes less than the shortest suggested cooking time on the package of pasta; this will ideally be 2 minutes before the pasta is al dente. Stir the noodles several times during the first 2 minutes of cooking to prevent them from sticking to the bottom of the pot or otherwise clumping together.

When the timer goes off, start tasting the noodles. When they seem like they are 1½ to 2 minutes away from a perfect al dente (see page 22), drain and transfer them to the sauce in the skillet using your preferred method (see page 21), making sure to reserve at least 1 cup (240 ml) of the pasta water.

Slide the skillet back onto medium heat and finish cooking the noodles, tossing and adding plenty of splashes of pasta water until the noodles are perfectly al dente, the cabbage is tender, and the sauce is nicely juicy. If the sauce seems watery, simmer for another few seconds to tighten it up, bearing in mind that the cheese will thicken it.

Reduce the heat to very low. Add the pancetta, the grated cheese, and the remaining butter and toss to emulsify the cheese with the other sauce ingredients, adding splashes of pasta water (or plain hot water, if things are getting too salty) if needed to keep the consistency creamy and prevent the cheese from clumping. Taste and add more salt or Calabrian chiles if you like.

Divide the pasta between two warm bowls, tuck a lemon wedge into each bowl, if using, and serve right away, with more cheese to add at the table.

MORE WAYS

Slice up a few peperoncini and add them to the sauce when you add the Calabrian chiles; they'll contribute a nice acidity and a bit of a sauerkraut flavor.

Charred Cabbage with Pork Shoulder Ragu with Lemon

Simple and satisfying, this dish is so easy to whip up if you have the pork ragu in portions in your freezer. Roasting the cabbage at a high temperature develops more complexity to its flavor; the charred edges are almost spicy, while the thicker center pieces become sweet and juicy. Regular green cabbage works beautifully; savoy cabbage would also be delicious but may lose its texture more quickly, so for savoy, cut your slabs a bit thicker. I don't use red cabbage because I don't like the dull color, but the flavor would be fine.

Serves 2

1 pound (450 g) green or savoy cabbage (about ½ small head)

Extra-virgin olive oil

Kosher salt (preferably Diamond Crystal; see page 17)

½ teaspoon whole black peppercorns

1 cup (250 g) Pork Shoulder Ragu with Lemon (page 78)

8 ounces (225 g) paccheri, rigatoni, or fusilli

⅓ cup (40 g) 50/50 cheese (half Parmigiano-Reggiano, half Pecorino Romano, grated in a food processor; see page 39)

Freshly ground black pepper (optional)

Shaved Parmigiano-Reggiano, for serving (optional)

Heat the oven to 450°F (230°C).

Cut out the densest part of the cabbage core, leaving just enough to hold the leaves together. Cut the cabbage into 1-inch-thick (5 cm) slabs or wedges. Drizzle some olive oil on a sheet pan and then arrange the cabbage slabs on the pan, sliding them around so their undersides get lightly coated with oil. Drizzle more oil over the slabs and season lightly with salt. If some leaves come loose, just tuck them into the mix.

Roast the cabbage until the edges are deeply browned and even charred in some places and the thicker centers are mostly tender, 20 to 30 minutes. You're aiming for a range of textures (and flavors), from crisp and almost burnt to succulent and juicy, but don't cook the cabbage so much that it becomes completely wilted.

Transfer the cabbage to a cutting board and chop into large pieces, keeping the texture varied. Set aside.

Fill a large pot (at least 6 quarts/L) with 1 gallon (4 L) of water; add 4 tablespoons (40 g) kosher salt, cover the pot, and bring the water to a boil while you make your sauce. If the water begins to boil before your sauce is ready, turn down the heat, but don't let the volume of the pasta water reduce by boiling off.

Crack the peppercorns following the method on page 43.

Set a large skillet over medium heat. Add the cracked black pepper to the dry pan and toast, stirring, until you smell a lovely black pepper fragrance, 15 to 30 seconds. Don't go too far or the pepper will be bitter. When the pepper is toasted, splash some pasta water into the skillet to stop the cooking.

Add the pork ragu to the skillet and stir to blend. Cook just until the ragu has warmed through, then slide the skillet off the heat.

Bring the pasta water (back) to a boil, add the noodles, and set your timer for 2 minutes less than the shortest suggested cooking time on the package of pasta; this will ideally be 2 minutes before the pasta is al dente. Stir the noodles several times during the first 2 minutes of cooking to prevent them from sticking to the bottom of the pot or otherwise clumping together.

When the timer goes off, start tasting the noodles. When they seem like they are 1½ to 2 minutes away from a perfect al dente (see page 22), drain and transfer them to the sauce in the skillet using your preferred method (see

page 21), making sure to reserve at least 1 cup (240 ml) of the pasta water.

Slide the skillet back onto medium heat and finish cooking the noodles, tossing and adding plenty of splashes of pasta water until the noodles are almost at al dente. Fold in the cabbage and cook for another few seconds, until the cabbage is heated through, the noodles are perfectly al dente, and the sauce is nicely juicy. If the sauce seems watery, simmer for another few seconds to tighten it up, bearing in mind that the cheese will thicken it.

Reduce the heat to very low. Add the 50/50 cheese and toss to emulsify it with the other sauce ingredients, adding splashes of pasta water (or plain hot water, if things are getting too salty) if needed to keep the consistency creamy and prevent the cheese from clumping. Taste and adjust the seasoning with salt or freshly ground black pepper if you like.

Divide the pasta between two warm bowls and top with plentiful shavings of Parmigiano, if using, then serve right away.

Celery Root with Salt Cod, Chickpeas, and Rosemary

With its unique flavor and texture (like flaky fresh cod, but chewier), salt cod isn't for everyone, but if you do like it, you love it. Another common name for salt cod is bacalao. Some salt cod is sold already desalted and then frozen; you can simply thaw it and use it right away. But mostly you find heavily salted dried fish that needs to soak in water for up to 2 days to desalt, so definitely plan ahead.

Serves 2

4 ounces (115 g) dried salt cod, desalted ahead of time (see page 368)

Milk or broth, for poaching the salt cod

1 cup (4 ounces/115 g) cubed peeled celery root (1-inch/2.5 cm cubes)

¾ cup (180 ml) whole milk

1 bay leaf

Kosher salt (preferably Diamond Crystal; see page 17)

Extra-virgin olive oil

3 or 4 garlic cloves, smashed

2 teaspoons finely chopped fresh rosemary

Big pinch of dried chile flakes, plus more to taste

1 cup (165 g) cooked chickpeas (canned is fine; to cook chickpeas from scratch, see page 326)

8 ounces (225 g) anellini, rotelle, or fettucine

2 tablespoons fresh lemon juice, plus more to taste

Lemon Agrumato (lemony extra-virgin olive oil; see page 41; optional)

Put the desalted cod in a medium saucepan with just enough milk or broth to cover it. Bring to a gentle simmer and poach just until tender, 5 to 10 minutes. Drain the fish, blot dry, and set aside.

Put the celery root, whole milk, and bay leaf in a small saucepan over medium-low heat. Gently bring to a simmer and cook, uncovered, until the celery root is thoroughly tender, 15 to 20 minutes. Stir a few times during the cooking time to make sure the celery root cubes are cooking evenly.

Cool slightly, then remove and discard the bay leaf. Transfer the milk and celery root to a blender, and blend until completely smooth. You should have about ⅔ cup (150 g) of celery root puree; a couple tablespoons more or less is fine.

Fill a large pot (at least 6 quarts/L) with 1 gallon (4 L) of water; add 4 tablespoons (40 g) kosher salt, cover the pot, and bring the water to a boil while you make your sauce. If the water begins to boil before your sauce is ready, turn down the heat, but don't let the volume of the pasta water reduce by boiling off.

Add a generous glug of olive oil to a large skillet over medium heat. When the oil is hot, add the garlic, rosemary, and chile flakes and cook gently, breaking up the garlic a bit with your spatula, until the garlic is softened and lightly toasted but not browned and the chile flakes and rosemary have infused into the oil, 3 to 4 minutes.

Add the chickpeas and cook, stirring often, until they are golden brown and slightly crispy, 2 to 3 minutes. Splash a bit of water from the pasta pot into the pan to stop the cooking. Break the salt cod into flakes and add it to the chickpeas along with the celery root puree. Then slide the skillet off the heat.

Bring the pasta water (back) to a boil, add the noodles, and set your timer for 2 minutes less than the shortest suggested cooking time on the package of pasta; this will ideally be 2 minutes before the pasta is al dente. Stir the noodles several times during the first 2 minutes of cooking to prevent them from sticking to the bottom of the pot or otherwise clumping together.

When the timer goes off, start tasting the noodles. When they seem like they are 1½ to 2 minutes away from a perfect al dente (see page 22), drain and transfer them to the sauce in the skillet using your preferred method (see page 21), making sure to reserve at least 1 cup (240 ml) of the pasta water.

Slide the skillet back onto medium heat and finish cooking the noodles, tossing and adding plenty of splashes of pasta water until the noodles are perfectly al dente, the salt cod is tender, and the sauce is nicely juicy. If the sauce seems watery, simmer for another few seconds to tighten it up.

Slide the skillet off the heat and add the lemon juice. Taste and add more salt, chile flakes, or lemon juice if you like.

Divide the pasta between two warm bowls, drizzle with Agrumato, if using, and serve right away.

MORE WAYS

Transform this dish into a baked pasta: Prepare the pasta with its sauce as directed in the recipe. Also prepare a basic béchamel (see page 135). Spoon a layer of the béchamel over the bottom of a baking dish, add the pasta, and top with a mix of breadcrumbs and 50/50 cheese moistened with a little olive oil. Bake at 375°F (190°C) for 25 to 35 minutes (cover the dish with foil for the first 15 minutes).

How to Prepare Salt Cod

If your salt cod is not already desalted, rinse off the surface salt, then place the fish in a bowl, add cool water to cover, and soak for 24 to 48 hours in the refrigerator, depending on how salty and/or thick the pieces of fish are. During this time, you'll need to change the soaking water at least five times. To determine whether you've removed enough salt, taste a small piece—it should still taste salty, but pleasantly so. You can desalt salt cod up to 3 days ahead of using it; keep it in the fridge.

Celery Root Cacio e Pepe

This is an outrageously simple pasta dish that looks a lot like classic cacio e pepe (page 106) but delivers a different fragrance and flavor, plus the nutrition from the root vegetable. Make a larger batch of puree and keep the extra portion in the freezer. This makes even more sense when you consider the softball size of a typical celery root.

Serves 2

1 cup (4 ounces/115 g) cubed peeled celery root (1-inch/2.5 cm cubes)

¾ cup (180 ml) whole milk

1 bay leaf

Kosher salt (preferably Diamond Crystal; see page 17)

1½ teaspoons (4 g) whole black peppercorns

8 ounces (225 g) radiatore, torchietti, or spaghetti

2 tablespoons unsalted butter

⅓ cup (40 g) 50/50 cheese (half Parmigiano-Reggiano, half Pecorino Romano, grated in a food processor; see page 39), plus more for serving

Freshly ground black pepper (optional)

Put the celery root, milk, and bay leaf in a small saucepan over medium-low heat. Gently bring to a simmer and cook, uncovered, until the celery root is tender, 15 to 20 minutes. Stir a few times to make sure the celery root cubes cook evenly.

Cool slightly, then remove and discard the bay leaf. Transfer the milk and celery root to a blender, and blend until completely smooth. You should have about ⅔ cup (150 g) of celery root puree; a couple tablespoons more or less is fine.

Fill a large pot (at least 6 quarts/L) with 1 gallon (4 L) of water; add 4 tablespoons (40 g) kosher salt, cover the pot, and bring the water to a boil while you make your sauce. If the water begins to boil before your sauce is ready, turn down the heat, but don't let the volume of the pasta water reduce by boiling off.

Crack the peppercorns following the method on page 43.

Set a large skillet over medium heat. Add the cracked black pepper to the dry pan and toast, stirring, until you smell a lovely black pepper fragrance, 15 to 30 seconds. Don't go too far or the pepper will be bitter. When the pepper is toasted, splash some pasta water into the skillet to stop the cooking.

Stir in the celery root puree. Bring to a simmer, then slide the skillet off the heat.

Bring the pasta water (back) to a boil, add the noodles, and set your timer for 2 minutes less than the shortest suggested cooking time on the package of pasta; this will ideally be 2 minutes before the pasta is al dente. Stir the noodles several times during the first 2 minutes of cooking to prevent them from sticking to the bottom of the pot or otherwise clumping together.

When the timer goes off, start tasting the noodles. When they seem like they are 1½ to 2 minutes away from a perfect al dente (see page 22), drain and transfer them to the sauce using your preferred method (see page 21), reserving at least 1 cup (240 ml) of the pasta water.

Slide the skillet back onto medium heat and finish cooking the noodles, tossing and adding plenty of splashes of pasta water until the noodles are perfectly al dente and the sauce is nicely juicy. If the sauce seems watery, simmer for another few seconds to tighten it up, bearing in mind that the cheese will thicken it.

Reduce the heat to very low. Add the butter and the grated cheese and toss to emulsify them with the other sauce ingredients, adding splashes of pasta water (or plain hot water, if things are getting too salty) if needed to keep the consistency creamy and prevent the cheese from clumping. Taste and adjust with more salt or freshly ground black pepper if you like.

Divide the pasta between two warm bowls and serve right away, with more cheese to add at the table.

Celery Root and Seafood "Chowder"

A vegetable puree plays the part of actual cream in this creamy dish, creating a lovely texture and adding celery root's intriguing flavor. We should all eat more celery root!

When buying scallops, ask for ones that are "dry-packed." Many scallops are soaked in a solution meant to preserve them but also plump them up so they weigh more; either way, I find this packing method gross and do not like the flavor or texture of soaked, or "wet," scallops.

Serves 2 or 3

- 1 cup (4 ounces/115 g) cubed peeled celery root (1-inch/2.5 cm cubes)
- ¾ cup (180 ml) whole milk
- 1 bay leaf
- 3 ounces (85 g) raw scallops, cut into large dice
- 3 ounces (85 g) raw shrimp, any size, preferably wild, peeled and deveined, cut into large dice
- 3 ounces (85 g) white-fleshed fish, such as halibut or cod, cut into large dice
- Kosher salt (preferably Diamond Crystal; see page 17)
- Extra-virgin olive oil
- 2 ounces (60 g) pancetta, cut into lardons (skinny 1-inch/2.5 cm batons) or chopped
- 3 or 4 garlic cloves, smashed
- Pinch of dried chile flakes, plus more to taste
- 8 ounces (225 g) fettucine, pappardelle, or spaghetti alla chitarra
- 2 tablespoons fresh lemon juice, plus more to taste
- ⅓ cup (20 g) roughly chopped fresh flat-leaf parsley leaves
- Lemon Agrumato (lemony extra-virgin olive oil; see page 41; optional)

Put the celery root, milk, and bay leaf in a small saucepan over medium-low heat. Gently bring to a simmer and cook, uncovered, until the celery root is thoroughly tender, 15 to 20 minutes. Stir a few times during the cooking time to make sure the celery root cubes are cooking evenly.

Cool slightly, then remove and discard the bay leaf. Transfer the milk and celery root to a blender, and blend until completely smooth. You should have about ⅔ cup (150 g) of celery root puree; a couple tablespoons more or less is fine. Set aside.

Pile the scallops, shrimp, and fish on a cutting board and chop through everything a few times with a large chef's knife; the idea is to create a very coarsely chopped mixture. Set aside.

Fill a large pot (at least 6 quarts/L) with 1 gallon (4 L) of water; add 4 tablespoons (40 g) kosher salt, cover the pot, and bring the water to a boil while you make your sauce. If the water begins to boil before your sauce is ready, turn down the heat, but don't let the volume of the pasta water reduce by boiling off.

Heat a glug of olive oil in a large skillet over medium heat. When the oil is hot, add the pancetta and cook until most of the fat has rendered, 2 to 3 minutes. Add the garlic and chile flakes and continue cooking, breaking up the garlic a bit with your spatula, until the garlic is lightly toasted and fragrant but not at all brown and the pancetta is crisp around the edges, 3 to 4 minutes.

Add the chopped scallops, shrimp, and fish in an even layer, increase the heat to medium-high, and cook until the seafood gets a little bit of color on it, about 45 seconds.

Add a hefty splash of water from the pasta pot and the celery root puree. Stir to blend the ingredients and then slide the skillet off the heat.

recipe continues →

Bring the pasta water (back) to a boil, add the noodles, and set your timer for 2 minutes less than the shortest suggested cooking time on the package of pasta; this will ideally be 2 minutes before the pasta is al dente. Stir the noodles several times during the first 2 minutes of cooking to prevent them from sticking to the bottom of the pot or otherwise clumping together.

When the timer goes off, start tasting the noodles. When they seem like they are 1½ to 2 minutes away from a perfect al dente (see page 22), drain and transfer them to the sauce in the skillet using your preferred method (see page 21), making sure to reserve at least 1 cup (240 ml) of the pasta water.

Slide the skillet back onto medium heat and finish cooking the noodles, tossing and adding plenty of splashes of pasta water until the noodles are perfectly al dente, the seafood is fully cooked, and the sauce is nicely juicy. If the sauce seems watery, simmer for another few seconds to tighten it up.

Take the skillet off the heat, add the lemon juice and parsley, and toss to blend. Taste and add more salt, chile flakes, or lemon juice if you like.

Divide the pasta between two or three warm bowls, drizzle with some Agrumato, if using, and serve right away.

MORE WAYS

Go "full Alfredo" and finish the dish with ¼ cup (30 g) or so of grated Parmigiano.

Butternut Squash with Sausage, Sage, and Spicy Chiles

A roasted squash puree gives this dish a rich creaminess without any cream. Make a double batch of the puree and freeze half for the next time you make this dish.

I call for butternut squash here rather than another variety because I like the flavor, it's easy to find, and the shape of the squash is cooperative when it comes to peeling and cooking—no weird crenellations. But the world of winter squash is wide and delicious, so substitute other varieties and see what you like best.

Serves 2 or 3

Kosher salt (preferably Diamond Crystal; see page 17)

6 ounces (170 g) bulk Italian sausage, sweet or hot

Extra-virgin olive oil

3 garlic cloves, smashed

8 to 10 fresh medium sage leaves

1 teaspoon thinly sliced oil-packed Calabrian chiles (from a jar; remove their seeds before slicing), plus more to taste

Freshly ground black pepper

1 cup (225 g) Butternut Squash Puree (recipe follows)

8 ounces (225 g) casarecce, gemelli, or strozzapreti

¼ cup (30 g) 50/50 cheese (half Parmigiano-Reggiano, half Pecorino Romano, grated in a food processor; see page 39), plus more for serving

2 tablespoons unsalted butter

Fill a large pot (at least 6 quarts/L) with 1 gallon (4 L) of water; add 4 tablespoons (40 g) kosher salt, cover the pot, and bring the water to a boil while you make your sauce. If the water begins to boil before your sauce is ready, turn down the heat, but don't let the volume of the pasta water reduce by boiling off.

Shape the sausage into a patty. Heat a generous glug of olive oil in a large skillet over medium-high heat. When the oil is hot, add the sausage and sear, smashing the patty down from time to time; don't move it until a nice crust forms on the bottom, about 5 minutes.

Flip the sausage, add the garlic and sage, and reduce the heat to medium. Remove the sage leaves as soon as they become slightly crisp, 30 seconds to 1 minute; transfer to a paper towel to drain. Cook the garlic and sausage until the garlic is browning nicely and the sausage is almost cooked through, another 2 to 3 minutes. With your spatula or the back of a spoon, smash the garlic into the oil and break up the sausage patty into smaller bits.

Add the Calabrian chiles, season with many twists of black pepper, and cook for a few seconds to infuse the oil with the spices.

Add about ½ cup (120 ml) of water from the pasta pot to the pan and simmer, scraping to dissolve any browned bits on the bottom of the pan, until the sausage is fully cooked and the water has reduced by half, 2 to 3 minutes.

Add the squash puree and cook, stirring, for a few seconds to integrate all the ingredients. Slide the skillet off the heat.

Bring the pasta water (back) to a boil, add the noodles, and set your timer for 2 minutes less than the shortest suggested cooking time on the package of pasta; this will ideally be 2 minutes before the pasta is al dente. Stir the noodles several times during the first 2 minutes of cooking to prevent them from sticking to the bottom of the pot or otherwise clumping together.

When the timer goes off, start tasting the noodles. When they seem like they are 1½ to 2 minutes away from a perfect al dente (see page 22), drain and transfer them to the sauce in the skillet using your preferred method (see page 21), making sure to reserve at least 1 cup (240 ml) of the pasta water.

recipe continues →

Slide the skillet back onto medium heat and finish cooking the noodles, tossing and adding plenty of splashes of pasta water until the noodles are perfectly al dente and the sauce is nicely juicy. If the sauce seems watery, simmer for another few seconds to tighten it up, bearing in mind that the cheese will thicken it.

Reduce the heat to very low. Add the grated cheese and butter and toss to emulsify with the other sauce ingredients, adding splashes of pasta water (or plain hot water, if things are getting too salty) if needed to keep the consistency creamy and prevent the cheese from clumping. Taste and add more salt or black pepper if you like.

Divide the pasta between two or three warm bowls, crumble the fried sage over the top, and serve right away, with more cheese to add at the table.

MORE WAYS

Make a simpler version of the dish by cooking some noodles, finishing them in the squash puree, and topping with a sprinkle of sliced Calabrian chiles and tons of grated Parmigiano—almost-instant pasta.

Butternut Squash Puree

One pound (450 g) of butternut squash will yield approximately 1 cup (225 g) puree, depending on the squash (its shape, the size of its seed cavity, and so on). To make sure you have enough for your recipe, err on the side of too much; you can use leftover puree in other dishes or freeze it for later use.

Butternut squash

Extra-virgin olive oil

Kosher salt
(preferably Diamond Crystal;
see page 17)

Heat the oven to 450°F (230°C).

Line a sheet pan with parchment paper. Cut the squash in half lengthwise, scoop out the seeds, drizzle the cut faces with olive oil, and season lightly with salt. Arrange the squash cut side up on the prepared sheet pan and roast for 20 minutes. Then reduce the oven temperature to 325°F (160°C) and roast until the squash is totally tender when pierced with a paring knife in a few places, another 20 to 40 minutes.

Let the squash cool until you can handle it, then scoop the flesh into a blender or food processor (for small quantities, a food processor will work better); discard the skin. Puree the squash, adding a glug or two of olive oil and a splash of water as needed to create a thickish puree; season lightly with salt.

Use the squash puree right away or freeze for up to 3 months.

Roasted Winter Squash with Nut Ragu

Definitely a cold-weather dish, this heartwarming and belly-filling pasta is also vegetarian. You can roast the squash up to 1 day ahead, so if you have the nut ragu in the freezer and a batch of roasted squash, dinner is on the table in minutes. If you do use made-ahead squash, let it come to room temperature before adding it to the pasta so that it heats up quickly.

Serves 2

3 cups (450 g) diced butternut or other winter squash (1-inch/2.5 cm cubes)

Extra-virgin olive oil

Kosher salt (preferably Diamond Crystal; see page 17)

Freshly ground black pepper

10 to 12 fresh medium sage leaves

1 cup (250 g) Nut Ragu (page 71)

8 ounces (225 g) casarecce, gemelli, or strozzapreti

2 tablespoons unsalted butter

¼ cup (30 g) 50/50 cheese (half Parmigiano-Reggiano, half Pecorino Romano, grated in a food processor; see page 39)

Ricotta salata, for serving

Heat the oven to 400°F (205°C).

Pile the squash cubes onto a sheet pan, drizzle generously with olive oil, and season generously with salt and black pepper. Spread into an even layer and roast until tender but not mushy and nicely browned around the edges, 25 to 30 minutes. Transfer to a plate and set aside.

Meanwhile, heat a generous glug of olive oil in a small skillet over medium-high heat. When the oil is hot, add the sage and fry until crisp, about 45 seconds. Drain on paper towels; set aside.

Fill a large pot (at least 6 quarts/L) with 1 gallon (4 L) of water; add 4 tablespoons (40 g) kosher salt, cover the pot, and bring the water to a boil while you make your sauce. If the water begins to boil before your sauce is ready, turn down the heat, but don't let the volume of the pasta water reduce by boiling off.

Put a splash of pasta water in a large skillet, add the nut ragu, and cook gently over medium heat until the ragu is loosened and heated through; slide the skillet off the heat.

Bring the pasta water (back) to a boil, add the noodles, and set your timer for 2 minutes less than the shortest suggested cooking time on the package of pasta; this will ideally be 2 minutes before the pasta is al dente. Stir the noodles several times during the first 2 minutes of cooking to prevent them from sticking to the pot or otherwise clumping together.

When the timer goes off, start tasting the noodles. When they seem like they are 1½ to 2 minutes away from a perfect al dente (see page 22), drain and transfer them to the sauce in the skillet using your preferred method (see page 21), making sure to reserve at least 1 cup (240 ml) of the pasta water.

Slide the skillet back onto medium heat and finish cooking the noodles, tossing and adding plenty of splashes of pasta water until the noodles are perfectly al dente and the sauce is nicely juicy. If the sauce seems watery, simmer for another few seconds to tighten it up, bearing in mind that you'll be adding the squash and the cheese will thicken the sauce as well.

Fold in the roasted squash and the butter and cook for another few seconds to heat the squash through. Reduce the heat to very low. Add the 50/50 cheese and toss to emulsify it with the other sauce ingredients, adding splashes of pasta water (or plain hot water, if things are getting too salty) if needed to keep the consistency creamy and prevent the cheese from clumping. Taste and add more salt or pepper if you like.

Divide the pasta between two warm bowls, crumble the fried sage over the top, and shave or crumble a nice pile of ricotta salata over everything. Serve right away.

Resources

Here are the producers and products that I like and have mentioned in this book. Most are available from several sources; I listed the primary company website, where applicable, or a major independent retailer.

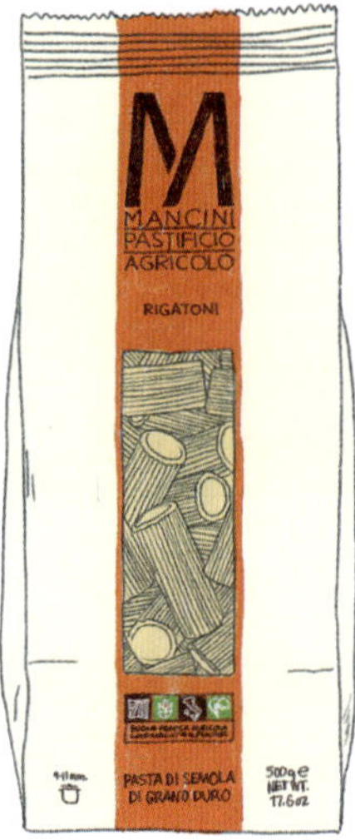

BUTTER

Le Beurre Bordier, available from various retailers including **french.us**

Organic Valley unsalted butter, **organicvalley.coop**

Ploughgate Creamery cultured butter, **ploughgate.com**

Rodolphe Le Meunier Beurre de Baratte salted butter, available from various retailers including Formaggio Kitchen, **formaggiokitchen.com**

COOKWARE AND TABLEWARE

ANK Ceramics, **ankceramics.com**

BKLYN CLAY, **bklynclay.com**

Esh Ceramics, **eshceramics.com**

Fog Linen, **shop-foglinen.com**

Heath Ceramics, **heathceramics.com**

Luvhaus, **luvhaus.com**

M. Crow, **mcrowcompany.com**

Sarah Kersten Studio, **sarahkersten.com**

Williams Sonoma, **williams-sonoma.com**

NOODLES

Della Terra Pasta, **dellaterrapasta.com**

Flour + Water, **flourandwaterfoods .com**

Mancini Pastificio Agricolo, **pastamancini.com**

Martelli, **martellifoods.com**

Molino e Pastificio, available from various retailers including **gourmetfoodworld.com**

Monograno Felicetti, **shopfelicettipasta.com**

Morelli, available from various retailers including **mercatodibellina.com**

Pastificio Faella, available from various retailers including **gustiamo.com**

Pastificio Gentile, available from various retailers including **zingermans.com**

Rustichella d'Abruzzo, available from various retailers including **markethallfoods.com**

Sfoglini, **sfoglini.com**

OIL AND VINEGAR

Agrumato,
available from various retailers including
olio2go.com

Algae Cooking Oil,
algaecookingclub.com

Graza Olive Oil,
graza.co

Katz Farm extra-virgin olive oil and vinegars,
katzfarm.com

Lindera Farms vinegars,
linderafarms.com

OTHER PANTRY

Eden Organic canned beans,
store.edenfoods.com

Freddy Guys hazelnuts,
freddyguys.com

J.P. Graziano Hot Giardiniera,
tasterealchicago.com

New York Shuk Preserved Lemon Paste,
nyshuk.com

Rancho Gordo,
ranchogordo.com

Red Boat fish sauce,
redboatfishsauce.com

Sacred Sea Tuna,
sacredseatuna.com

Underground Meats, cured meats and 'nduja,
undergroundmeats.com

SPICES

Jacobsen Salt Co.,
jacobsensalt.com

Männkitchen Pepper Cannon,
mannkitchen.com

Reluctant Trading Experiment, black peppercorns and other spices,
reluctanttrading.com

Rico Rico, chiles de árbol,
shopricorico.com

TOMATOES

Alta Cucina,
stanislaus.com

Bianco DiNapoli,
biancodinapoli.com

Cento,
cento.com

Muir Glen Organic,
muirglen.com

Acknowledgments

FIRST AND FOREMOST, to my mother, father, and grandmother—thank you for filling my childhood with the simple magic of pasta. Those early bowls weren't just food; they were the foundation of a lifelong passion.

Susie, your gardens and Sun Gold tomatoes sparked a debate with a French chef (which I won) and led me to create my first dish that truly felt like my own: Sun Gold Tomatoes with Basil and Garlic. That moment changed everything.

Martha Holmberg, this would not exist without you—thank you, thank you, and thank you! Judy Pray, Lia Ronnen, Allison McGeehon, Cindy Lee, and everyone at Artisan and Workman Publishing—your patience, belief, and dedication brought this to life. Marie, for eating all the pasta, good or bad, for the last-minute ingredient runs, for the clean-ups—your support was never unnoticed. AJ Meeker, your laughter and brilliant photography captured more than just images; you captured the soul of this journey.

Williams Sonoma, your support has meant the world. Kristin Perrakis, my ever-reliable sound-checker—thank you for listening, adjusting, and always keeping me on track. SMEG, for boiling my pasta water at lightning speed. La Marzocco, for ensuring I stayed caffeinated through the long days (and longer nights).

Mark Ladner, your wisdom, skill, and passion taught me the true craft of cooking and saucing pasta. Burt, the soundtrack to this journey wouldn't be the same without you—keep those new speakers safe, and I'll see you in five years (or less) for those. Matthew Halsall, your music was the heartbeat of every recipe-testing session—always on, always perfect.

Cameron, I'll never forget you jumping up and down with a bowl of Pomodoro. I miss you, and I thank you for you. Ross, JoMarie, Duane, Yasu, Brookes, Wes, Tyler, Kyle, and the entire Ava Gene's team—over the years, you made that space more than a restaurant.

And finally, to the farmers—especially the grain farmers, past, present, and future—who keep good, non-GMO grains alive and thriving. You are the quiet architects of perfect noodles.

—Joshua McFadden

THANK YOU JOSHUA for once again trusting me to do a mind-meld with you and your delicious food. As always, I'm so grateful for my Artisan family—Lia, Judy, Allison, Suet, Zach, Hillary, Jane, Nancy, Donna, and countless others who work to make such wonderful books. Big thanks to my fantastic testers Helen Baldus, Millissa Frost, and Kate Lebo. And to my husband John D'Anna, who has (among his many talents) a marvelous palate and an unflagging enthusiasm for a good bowl of pasta, thank goodness.

—Martha Holmberg

Index

Page numbers in *italic* indicate photos.

Here's the (only) way to reheat leftover pasta: Spread two slices of bread with Garlic Butter (page 27), layer them with cheese (mozzarella, 50/50, or your choice), pile on the leftover pasta, and then fry the whole thing up like a grilled cheese sandwich.

About the Authors

JOSHUA McFADDEN is bringing fresh energy to Berney Farm, a historic fifty-acre farm in Springdale, Oregon. He is building a unique agricultural complex where farming, food, and design come together in creative collaborations. When he is not working on the land, Joshua is a sought-after consultant in the food world—helping to craft packaged and prepared foods, launch brands from the ground up, and rethink what fast casual and fast food can be. His first book, *Six Seasons: A New Way with Vegetables*, also written with Martha Holmberg, won a James Beard Award in 2018. His second book, *Grains for Every Season: Rethinking Our Way with Grains*, was a James Beard Award finalist in 2021. Follow Joshua on Instagram at @jj__mc.

MARTHA HOLMBERG has spent her career either cooking or writing about cooking, beginning with earning the Grand Diplôme from L'Ecole de Cuisine La Varenne in Paris. Martha has been the editor in chief of *Fine Cooking* magazine and the food editor of *The Oregonian* newspaper in Portland. For the past decade, she has immersed herself in cookbooks, coauthoring books with Joshua McFadden, including *Six Seasons*, which won a James Beard Award in 2018, and *Grains for Every Season*. Other recent book projects include *The Noma Guide to Fermentation* and *Noma 2.0*. Martha has written five cookbooks of her own, including *Modern Sauces*, which was nominated for a James Beard Award in 2013, and *Simply Tomato*, published in 2023 by Artisan. She lives in Spokane, Washington, with her husband. Follow Martha on Instagram at @marthaholmberg.